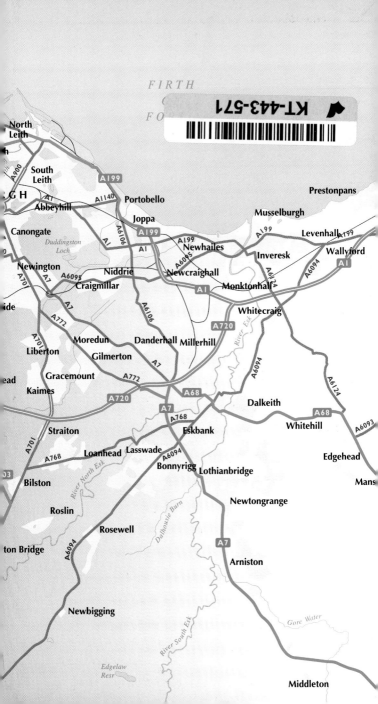

Published by Collins
An imprint of HarperCollins*Publishers*
77-85 Fulham Palace Road, Hammersmith, London W6 8JB

The HarperCollins website address is: www.**fire**and**water**.com

Copyright © HarperCollins*Publishers* Ltd 1999
Mapping © Bartholomew Ltd 1999

Collins® is a registered trade mark of HarperCollins*Publishers* Limited

Bartholomew website address is: www.bartholomewmaps.com

Maps on pages 68 to 105 are based upon the Ordnance Survey Mapping with the permission of
The Controller of Her Majesty's Stationery Office © Crown copyright 399302

Photographs reproduced by kind permission of the following:
Rosemary MacLeod; pages 1,2,7,9,17,18,19,20,22,23,29,30,34,35,39,40,42,45,49,51,58,61
The Image Bank; pages 5,8,13,21,27,31,44,50,56,57,59,60
Yacht Events Ltd; page 6

Design of pages ii to 63 and 132 to 142 by Rebecca Mazonowicz

Printed in Italy   ISBN 0 00 449017 7   MI10317   RNN

e-mail: roadcheck@harpercollins.co.uk

COLLINS
EDINBURGH
2000
VISITORS' GUIDE

CONTENTS

ii	Introduction
1 - 4	Millennium Attractions
5	The Scottish Parliament
6 - 51	Edinburgh Attractions
9 - 16	Edinburgh Castle
31 - 48	Royal Mile
52 - 57	Other Attractions
58 - 63	Edinburgh Festival
64 - 65	Key to Map Pages
66 - 67	Key to Map Symbols
68 - 105	Edinburgh Mapping
106 - 131	Index to Streets
132 - 142	Edinburgh Directory

Introduction

Edinburgh is one of the most attractive and historic cities in Europe. The city has preserved its heritage and embraced the new. It is a vibrant cultural, shopping and business centre with a huge amount to offer the visitor.

The castle, perched high on the dark volcanic Castle Rock, dominates the city skyline while the tall, cramped buildings and narrow closes of the Old Town cluster along the slope stretching to the east of the crag. In striking contrast, and just five minutes walk away, is the Georgian elegance of the 18thC New Town. The broad streets here include Princes Street, the major shopping thoroughfare of the city.

Edinburgh's annual festivals are acclaimed worldwide – the Edinburgh International Festival, the Festival Fringe, the Edinburgh Tattoo, and the International Jazz and Blues, Film and Book Festivals present a wide range of events. Edinburgh's Hogmanay, another of the city's major festivals, will be an even greater draw for visitors to the capital for the start of the year 2000. A special Millennium New Year programme will include concerts, parties and street theatre, a Torchlight Procession, Fire Festival, and massed bands Beating the Retreat from the 20thC.

Edinburgh's profile has been further enhanced by many exciting new visitor attractions. Our Dynamic Earth, a unique geological visitor centre, and the inland waterways Millennium Link project were launched for the Millennium. The new Museum of Scotland opened in 1998, and the former Royal Yacht Britannia opened to the public in the same year. Another focus of interest in the capital is the new Scottish Parliament which was officially opened by the Queen on 1st July 1999.

This guide lists all the main visitor attractions in Edinburgh with informative descriptions, and opening hours where appropriate. Each place of interest is referenced to the full colour map section which is at a scale of 4.2 inches to 1 mile. The listings include all of Edinburgh's new attractions, plus Edinburgh Castle, the Palace of Holyroodhouse and many of the notable buildings along the Royal Mile. Museums and art galleries, Edinburgh Zoo, and the Royal Botanic Garden are also among the entries. The Edinburgh Festival on page 58 tells you what to expect and how to book for all the festivals held in the city. The Edinburgh Directory on page 132 tells you how to get around and where to find post offices, bureaux de change, chemists, cinemas and theatres. The directory also includes useful telephone numbers and practical tourist information to help you get the most out of your stay.

Edinburgh is an immensely rewarding place to visit at any time of the year with a wealth of interest tightly packed into just a few square miles. This guide should prove to be an invaluable companion.

Millennium Attractions

OUR DYNAMIC EARTH

`84 A3`

An adventure that should excite and stimulate visitors of all ages, a unique centre and the first of its kind in the world. This is the story of our planet and how the interaction of the overwhelming forces of nature have changed and shaped the earth over 4500 million years.

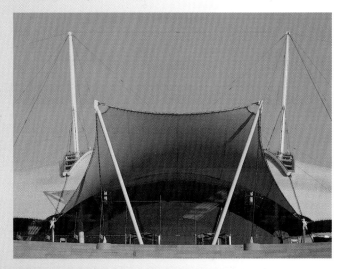

Our Dynamic Earth invites participation. Making full use of the latest modern technology, audiovisual and interactive displays demonstrate how the Earth was made, how it works and how it may evolve in the future. You can see, hear, feel, and even smell the planet. The Tropical Rainforest Gallery is hot and humid but visitors may be splashed in a tropical rainstorm. In an area which demonstrates what goes on inside the planet, the ground shakes as in an earthquake, there is the pungent sulphurous smell and smoke of a volcano, and boiling lava flows slowly towards the onlooker. Creaking ice resounds in the polar region, and there is an enormous ice sculpture designed to be touched.

There are ten Earth Galleries each with a specific theme, and each full of surprises and intriguing facts. The first gallery is named State of the Earth and is very much state of the art, showing how the earth is monitored at the present time. Displays are continually updated, with information supplied by NASA, National Geographic, the BBC and Reuters news agency. Video footage as seen from space shows weather fronts as they approach, and if there is an earthquake or volcanic eruption anywhere in the world, visitors will know about it here.

From the present day, the visitor is taken back through the Time Machine, to witness the Big Bang and the start of the physical Universe. From the bridge of a spaceship, there are close encounters with meteors. This is followed by dramatic displays of all the forces that interact to form and change the landscape and environment of the planet, such as volcanic activity, glaciation, the relationship between the oceans and the atmosphere, and the effect of biological processes. You are led into the principal climatic regions of the world to discover the difference between the Arctic and the Antarctic, and how the great diversity of plant life in the tropical rain forest regions of the world acquire their energy from the sun.

The grand finale to Our Dynamic Earth is a stunning audiovisual presentation in the Showdome of the Earth's most dramatic and powerful natural phenomena – tidal waves, lightening, and earthquakes. Entertaining and fun, the centre also provides the opportunity to acquire a better understanding of the planet. A tour takes one-and-a-half hours.

Our Dynamic Earth is a Millennium Commission project, built with the support of National Lottery funds and opened in 1999. It is one of the largest Millennium projects in Scotland and one of the Commission's five major new Science Centres in Britain. It is situated in the William Younger Centre, designed by internationally renowned architect, Sir Michael Hopkins. The pavilion style building rises to three levels and features a translucent tented roof. In front of the building is a stone amphitheatre which will seat 1000 people. Besides housing Our Dynamic Earth, the William Younger Centre includes The Atmosphere conference and private hire facilities, whilst the amphitheatre is a venue for outdoor events and performances.

Built as part of an urban renewal project, on the site of William Younger's former Holyrood Brewery, Dynamic Earth is close to the Palace of Holyroodhouse, with Salisbury Crags and Arthur's Seat providing a towering backdrop. Opposite is the new Scottish Parliament building and alongside the *Scotsman* newspaper building.

Facilities for the disabled include toilets, tactile interactive displays, taped commentaries, written transcripts and wheelchairs for

Our Dynamic Earth against the backdrop of Salisbury Crags

visitor use. Centre staff will entertain and supervise children in a soft play and activity area while adults have a drink or meal.

William Younger Centre, Holyrood Road. Tel: 0131 550 7800.
Group Booking Hotline Tel: 0131 550 7800.
Open Apr–Oct 10.00–18.00 (Mon–Sun); Nov–Mar 10.00–17.00 (Wed–Sun).
Closed Christmas Eve and Christmas Day.
Admission charge – discount for groups of 12 or more. Licensed restaurant and bar.
Full access for the disabled.
Underground car park.
email: enquiries@dynamicearth.co.uk
Website: www.dynamicearth.co.uk

MILLENNIUM LINK

A waterway link between Edinburgh and Glasgow, to be completed in the spring of 2001 by the restoration and reopening of the 200-year-old Forth & Clyde and Union canals. Construction work started in March 1999, and the waterway will be navigable from the Firth of Clyde to the Firth of Forth by Easter 2001.

The Link will provide not only an attractive navigable waterway, but also a place for local people and visitors to walk and enjoy other recreational pursuits along its 110km (69 miles) length. Moorings, boat trips, rowing boats for hire, pubs and campsites are some of the facilities envisaged. Access to the canal is being improved and areas of dereliction are being reclaimed, restored and landscaped. The towpath in Edinburgh will serve as a pedestrian route into the city centre, the waterway terminating at Lochrin Basin, 1.5km (1 mile) southwest of Waverley Bridge.

The Union Canal, more formally known as the Edinburgh and Glasgow Union canal, was completed in 1822 to bring coal into Edinburgh. It stretched for 51km (31 miles) from the centre of Edinburgh via Linlithgow to Falkirk, where it joined the Forth & Clyde Canal at Lock 16. Unlike the Forth & Clyde canal with 39 locks, the Union Canal followed the natural contours of the land and consequently had no locks until it reached Falkirk. Among its most notable features are the only canal tunnel in Scotland (at Falkirk) and the Avon Aqueduct (250m/810 feet long) near Linlithgow, the second longest in Britain, and the longest and tallest in Scotland.

The Forth & Clyde Canal, between Grangemouth on the Forth Estuary and Bowling on the River Clyde, was 62km (35 miles) long, with a 4.5km (3 mile) long branch into the centre of Glasgow. Built between 1768 and 1790, it was the world's first man-made sea-to-sea ship canal and provided a route to serve trade and industry.

Both canals were closed to navigation in the early 1960s, by which time many locks were derelict, bridges had been built with insufficient headroom, and stretches of the canal were overgrown and even filled in. The original Edinburgh terminus at Port Hopetoun basin had been filled in 1922 – Lothian House in Lothian Road now stands on the site. The civil engineers of the Millennium Link are presented with an enormous challenge, as were the engineers who built the original canals. New cuts have to be excavated through infilled areas and new bridges, aqueducts and locks are required. On completion, the Union Canal will have a navigable depth of 1.07m (3 feet 6 inches), and the Forth & Clyde a depth of 1.83m (6 feet). In the Edinburgh area, the first work to commence was the construction of a new stretch of canal and bridges at Wester Hailes, on the south west outskirts of the city.

The unique feature of the waterway will be the Millennium Wheel, a device to link the Union and Forth & Clyde Canals at Falkirk. The 25m (80 feet) diameter wheel will transfer craft between the canals by means of cradles, with the whole operation taking only 15 minutes. A more conventional approach would have required the building of a flight of ten or more locks to raise and lower boats the 25m (80 feet) difference between the levels of the canals. A spectacular sight, and a great feat of mechanical, electronic and hydraulic engineering, the Millennium Wheel should be well worth a visit.

Crossing Lowland Scotland from east to west, the waterway is an unusual and interesting way to explore the region. As well as the access it gives to the cities of Edinburgh and Glasgow and the historic town of Linlithgow, it passes through long stretches of countryside with lochs, hills, mountains and coastal resorts all within reach. Along the length of the canals there are 31 listed buildings, 30 ancient monuments, and five sites of special scientific interest. The Millennium Wheel is sited near the Roman Antonine Wall and the Forth & Clyde runs close to the route of the wall for much of its length.

Besides preserving Scotland's canal heritage and improving the environment, it is hoped that commercial enterprises will develop along the Millennium Link, stimulating regeneration and providing jobs. Managed by British Waterways together with public, private and voluntary organisations, the project is enormously popular with the people of the region and beyond, and has huge public backing. It is being funded by various organisations including the Millennium Commission, the European Union, Scottish Enterprise, local enterprise companies and local authorities.

Millennium Link Helpline. Tel: 0345 95 2000.
Website: www.millenniumlink.org.uk

The Scottish Parliament

`84 A3`

The Scottish Parliament, which was officially opened on 1 July 1999 by the Queen, comprises 129 members; 73 of these are elected under the *first past the post* system with the constituencies coinciding with those of the current UK Parliamentary constituencies; the remaining 56 are selected on a proportional basis from party lists drawn up for each of the current eight European Parliamentary constituencies.

Each elector is able to cast two votes: one for a constituency MSP (Member of the Scottish Parliament) and one for the party of their choice under the list system.

The permanent home of the Scottish Parliament will be a custom designed building occupying a 1.6ha (4 acre) site on the Royal Mile, adjacent to the Palace of Holyroodhouse and Holyrood Park.

The site, at the end of the Royal Mile, is bounded by Holyrood Road and Canongate.

The architect responsible for the new Parliament Building is Enric Miralles of Barcelona who, in collaboration with RMJM (Scotland) Ltd, secured the contract with a dramatic design based upon a theme of upturned fishing boats. As the new Scottish Parliament building will not be ready for occupation until Autumn of 2001, from May 1999, the Parliament has been operating from various locations within central Edinburgh.

The First Minister, and several other Scottish Ministers have their offices in St Andrews House. In addition, Members of the Scottish Parliament, including the Ministers, have office accommodation in the former City of Edinburgh Council building on George IV Bridge. The Parliament Debating Chamber is housed in the Church of Scotland Assembly Hall in Lawnmarket.

The Church of Scotland Assembly Hall.

Edinburgh Attractions

ARTHUR'S SEAT
84 C5

Rising to a height of 251m (822 feet), Arthur's Seat is the igneous core of an extinct volcano. The area remains surprisingly wild in spite of the city that has spread around it. There were four prehistoric hill forts here, and evidence of cultivation terraces, dating from the Dark Ages, have been found on the eastern slopes of Arthur's Seat. There are two lochs, Dunsapie and St Margaret's; it is by the latter that the remains of St Anthony's Chapel can be seen. Of late medieval date, its origins are not known. Salisbury Crags, of which Arthur's Seat is the highest point, provide a magnificently precipitous backdrop for the Palace of Holyroodhouse: below them were the Wells o'Wearie, where the hapless trudged for water when the city's supply failed.

A path leads from just outside Dynamic Earth along the base of the red cliffs and up to the summit.

BRITANNIA
73 E1

The former Royal Yacht Britannia can be boarded at her final mooring place in Edinburgh's historic docks at Leith. She is proving a popular tourist attraction and pre-booking tickets at weekends and holidays is recommended. Alongside is a purpose built visitor centre.

Former Royal Yacht Britannia moored at Leith Docks

Possibly one of the best-known ships in the world, the Royal Yacht served Her Majesty the Queen and other members of the royal family for over 40 years and sailed over a million miles around the world.

Besides royal honeymoons and family holidays, Britannia was used for 968 royal and official visits until her retirement in 1997. Kings, queens, presidents and prime ministers have all been entertained on board.

Britannia is unique and was designed by naval architect Dr John Brown as a royal yacht, with the possibility to function as a hospital ship. Sir Hugh Casson designed the interior. The Queen and the Duke of Edinburgh were also involved with the design of the yacht, choosing furniture, fabrics and paintings. Built at John Brown's shipyard at Clydebank, she was launched on 16 April 1953, continuing an unbroken tradition of royal yachts that can be traced back to Charles II.

Streamlined and elegant, Britannia is 125m (400 feet) long. She has no rivets and no name on the side, and unusually, her crest is on

the stern. She is painted deep blue, known as Britannia Blue – the colour was chosen by the Queen in preference to the traditional black. The decks are made of Burmese Teak.

Britannia was commanded by an Admiral, and in the last few years was manned by 220 crew and 24 officers. On royal tours there was a 26-strong Royal Marine Band on board, while for full state visits there were up to 45 extra staff, including 25 royal servants. Britannia's maximum speed was 22 knots.

Hands-on exhibits, newsreel and video in the visitor centre give an insight into the history of the yacht and her voyages, as well as a flavour of life on board. Visitors can enter the original wheelhouse which has been reconstructed here, and on view is the Royal Barge, the launch used by the royal family to travel ashore when anchored in harbours around the world. Photographs of the royal family taken on Britannia, many previously unpublished, are on display in the Royal Picture Gallery.

The tour of Britannia itself takes in the four main decks. The fabric of the yacht has undergone extensive restoration and among the highlights of the visit are the elegant state dining and drawing rooms, the Queen's and Duke of Edinburgh's bedrooms, the sun lounge, the bridge, the Admiral's cabin and quarters and the gleaming engine room. Gifts to the Queen from countries all over the world are displayed on the yacht, and prints and paintings from the Royal Collection hang on the walls. Visitors are guided around Britannia with the aid of an audio handset.

Leith Docks. Tel: 0131 555 5566.
Open all year, 10.30–16.30. Telephone for possible extended summer openings, restrictions in winter and for pre-booking to ensure admission and avoid queues.
Admission charge.
Disabled access.
Café.
No dogs except guide dogs.
Dedicated bus services run from Waverley Bridge.

DEAN GALLERY

Opened in 1999 opposite the Scottish National Gallery of Modern Art, the Dean Gallery is also dedicated to 20thC art. It houses a large collection of work by the distinguished Scottish sculptor, Eduardo Paolozzi, and the Dada and Surrealist collections from the Gallery of Modern Art. Temporary exhibitions of modern and contemporary art are a major feature of this new centre.

The neoclassical building of 1833 by Thomas Hamilton was once the Dean Orphan Hospital.

Belford Road. General enquiries tel: 0131 624 6200. Recorded information tel: 0131 332 2266.
Open all year (except Christmas Day and Boxing Day) Mon–Sat 10.00–17.00, Sun 14.00–17.00. Extended hours during the Edinburgh Festival.
Admission free but charges may be made for special loan exhibitions.
Disabled access.
Café.

The Dean Gallery, built in 1833 by Thomas Hamilton

EDINBURGH CASTLE

In a theatrical position on top of a rocky crag, Edinburgh Castle dominates the city which has grown up around it. The crag was left exposed by an Ice Age glacier which carved the valleys now occupied by the Grassmarket and Princes Street Gardens some 83m (270 feet) below. The hard basaltic core of an extinct volcano, the crag (also known as Castle Rock) resisted the gouging of the ice in a way that the softer surrounding sedimentary material could not. A ridge in a gentle slope to the east of the crag was also left by the glacier, the spine of which is now occupied by the Royal Mile.

Although King Mynyddog is known to have feasted in the hall in Din Eidyn (the stronghold of Eidyn) in the 6thC, a clear picture of the castle can only be drawn from the 11thC. When St Margaret, Queen of Scotland, died here in 1093 there were walls defending the royal residence, and an oratory and church which were built on the summit. The oldest surviving building within the castle, a chapel dedicated to St Margaret, now occupies part of this site. It was well described by John Taylor, Thames waterman and poet, who walked to Scotland in 1618. He wrote in his *Pennyles Pilgrimage*, 'the castle on a loftie rock is so strongly grounded, bounded and founded, that by force of man it can never be confounded'.

The history of Scotland itself is reflected in the castle's turbulent development from fortified royal residence to military stronghold and finally national monument.

In its early years, the castle was a royal residence, but in 1542, on the death of James V, the Palace of Holyroodhouse superseded it in this role. After this, the castle assumed an increasingly military function, with the Old Church becoming an arsenal and the erection of the House of Artillery.

In 1566, however, in what is seen as a symbolic gesture, Mary, Queen of Scots, gave birth to James VI of Scotland (James 1 of England) in a small room within the castle on 19 June.

Edinburgh Castle is the city's most popular tourist attraction but, as the administrative HQ of the Scottish Division and the 52nd Lowland Brigade, it is also a military establishment and there is a guard on the main gate.

Edinburgh Castle

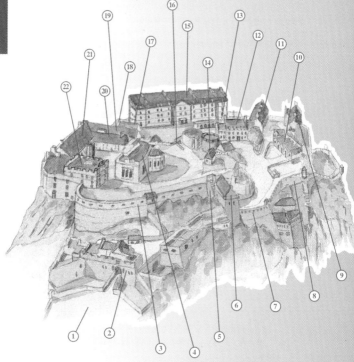

FEATURES WITHIN THE CASTLE AREA

1 Esplanade
2 Gatehouse
3 Forewall & Half Moon Batteries
4 Scottish National War Memorial
5 Lang Stairs
6 Argyle Tower & Portcullis Gate
7 Argyle Battery
8 Mills Mount Battery
9 Scottish United Services Museum
10 Mills Mount Cart Shed
11 Butts Battery
12 Governor's House
13 Royal Scots Dragoon Guards Museum (Carabiniers & Greys)
14 St. Margaret's Chapel
15 New Barracks
16 Foog's Gate
17 Military Prison
18 Durys Battery
19 Royal Scots Museum
20 Queen Anne Building
21 The Great Hall
22 The Palace

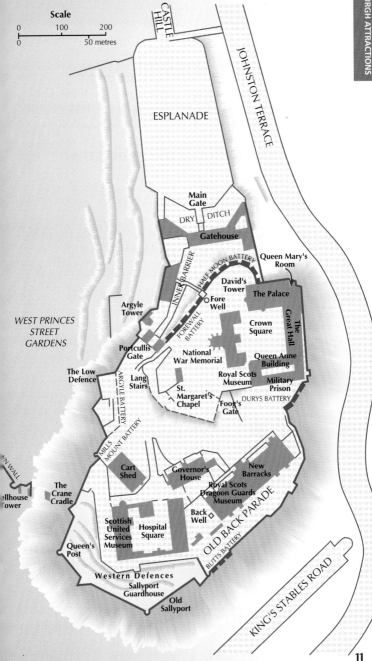

Scale

| 0 | 100 | 200 |

| 0 | 50 metres |

CASTLE HILL

JOHNSTON TERRACE

ESPLANADE

Main Gate

DRY DITCH

Gatehouse

INNER BARRIER

HALF MOON BATTERY

Queen Mary's Room

David's Tower

The Palace

Argyle Tower

Fore Well

FOREWALL BATTERY

Crown Square

The Great Hall

WEST PRINCES STREET GARDENS

Portcullis Gate

National War Memorial

Queen Anne Building

The Low Defence

ARGYLE BATTERY

Lang Stairs

Royal Scots Museum

Military Prison

St. Margaret's Chapel

Foog's Gate

DURYS BATTERY

MILLS MOUNT BATTERY

The Crane Cradle

Cart Shed

Governor's House

New Barracks

Royal Scots Dragoon Guards Museum

ллN WALL

Back Well

ellhouse ower

Scottish United Services Museum

Hospital Square

OLD BACK PARADE

Queen's Post

BUTTS BATTERY

KING'S STABLES ROAD

Western Defences

Sallyport Guardhouse

Old Sallyport

11

The following descriptions of the various castle buildings are arranged as far as possible in the form of a tour, climbing up Hawk Hill and returning via the Lang Stairs.

Esplanade
First created as a parade ground in 1753, it was completed in its present form by 1816. The Esplanade measures about 130m by 90m (140 yards by 100 yards) and is used for various ceremonies and parades, and annually in August for the floodlit Edinburgh Military Tattoo.

Gatehouse
Built between 1886-8 with no strategic pretence, it makes for a rather timid entrance compared to the sturdier stuff beyond the drawbridge. The gateway is surmounted by the Royal Arms of Scotland and flanked by bronze statues of Robert The Bruce and Sir William Wallace.

Portcullis Gate
The initial stage was completed in 1577 on the site of Constable's Tower, destroyed during a siege of the castle in 1573. The original portcullis, open to the elements, quickly rusted away, so in 1584 it was replaced and another two storeys were added to house both the portcullis and the Captain of the Castle. In 1887 it was rebuilt as the Argyle Tower. The present modern portcullis, decorative rather than defensive, is protected by two outer doors and an inner door.

Argyle Battery
Named after the 2nd Duke of Argyle, Commander-in-Chief of Scotland who fought the Jacobites at Sheriffmuir in 1715, the battery consists of six 19thC muzzle-loaders, and is also called the Six Gun Battery. It was built in 1730 for Major General Wade, of military roads and bridges fame.

Mills Mount Battery
Beyond the Argyle Battery to the west, and originally overlooking an area of open fields beyond Nor' Loch, the Mills Mount Battery now affords splendid views of Princes Street and the 18thC New Town. It is from here that the one o'clock gun is fired each day, (except Sundays, Good Friday and Christmas Day) a custom initiated in 1861 to serve as a time signal for ships in the Firth of Forth.

Mills Mount Cart Shed
An 18thC building which once had room for 50 carts, which were used to bring provisions from the town. Later used as a barracks and as an ammunition store, it is now a restaurant.

Butts Battery
Built between 1708–13 to strengthen the defences in response to fears of revolt against the Act of Union.

Military Prison

Built around 1842 to accommodate prisoners from all Scottish units, its cells, although spartan, could be centrally heated. Externally, its handsome design reflects the thought that was given to the castle buildings at that time. The last inmates left in 1923.

French Prisons

The vaults which were built to support the Great Hall have, over the years, been used variously for stores, munitions, barracks and even as a bakehouse. Most notable of their uses was as prisons during the wars with the French and Americans from the mid 1700s until the end of the Napoleonic Wars in 1815. Graffiti made on the stones by the inmates can still be seen (especially at the main entrance).

Mons Meg

This giant siege cannon, the lass wi' the iron mou (mou meaning mouth), is now kept in the castle vaults, away from the ravages of the elements. It was manufactured at Mons in Flanders for the Duke of Burgundy in 1449, and given to James II, his nephew by marriage, in 1457. The cannonballs, each weighing 150kg (330 pounds), could be fired at targets over 1600m (1750 yards) away, but at over 6040kg (6 tons), the gun proved very slow to move around. It was used in the siege of Norham Castle in 1497, but it was retired from military action in the middle of the 16thC. Mons Meg finally burst while firing a salute for the Duke of York (later James VII of Scotland, James II of England) in 1681.

Dury's Battery

Commanding the southern approach to the castle, these defences are named after Theodore Dury, who rebuilt the southern wall between 1708–13.

Edinburgh Castle

Foog's Gate

At the top of Hawk Hill and facing the vast Barrack Block, Foog's Gate was built in the 17thC to provide access to the Upper Ward near the highest point on Castle Rock.

Forewall and Half-Moon Batteries

The Forewall Battery was built in 1544, heightened in 1573, and follows the original line of the castle's eastern defences. From this elevated position it gave a wide range of fire to protect the castle entrance.

Similarly, the Half-Moon Battery, built following the siege of 1573, gave excellent cover over and beyond the area now occupied by the Esplanade.

Palace

This occupies the site of earlier 15thC Royal accommodation, but the present building was remodelled in 1617 for James VI, when the pattern of windows was altered to conform to the classical taste of the time. The last major work was the heightening of the octagonal stair turret in 1820 with an extension topped by a flagstaff.

Inside is the small bedchamber where Mary, Queen of Scots, gave birth in 1566 to James VI (and James I of England after the death of Elizabeth I in 1603), and which was later redecorated for James himself. One side of the room looks out onto the Grassmarket and a completely spurious tradition exists that the infant James was lowered out of this window in a basket to be smuggled to safety, and possibly baptised in his mother's Roman Catholic faith.

The Honours of Scotland – crown, sword and sceptre – are kept in the Crown Room above Mary's rooms. The crown, of Scottish gold, was remodelled for James V by goldsmith James Mossman in 1540, and received a new bonnet and ermine for Queen Elizabeth II in 1953. The sceptre was given to James IV in 1494 by Pope Alexander VI, and the sword presented to him by Pope Julius II in 1507.

The Honours were hidden at various locations at the time of Cromwell's occupation in Scotland, and walled in the castle after the Act of Union in 1707 when the old Scottish parliament was dissolved. They came to light in a chest behind the blocked wall of the Crown Room in 1817, after a search of the castle initiated by Sir Walter Scott.

An exhibition preceding the Crown Room traces the history of the Scottish crown jewels, which are the oldest British royal regalia. The Crown Room also houses the Stone of Destiny which was returned to Scotland from Westminster Abbey in 1996 after 700 years in England. It had been used as a coronation stone for Scottish Kings until it was taken from Scone Palace by Edward I in 1296.

St Margaret's Chapel

The oldest building within the castle walls, occupying the highest point on the crag. It dates from the early 12thC and was most probably built during the reign of David I some time after 1124, and dedicated to his mother.

A small rectangular building with only five windows, it was rediscovered in 1845 after being used as a store and powder magazine for many years.

Great Hall

Occupying the south side of Crown Square, the Great Hall dates from the early 16thC. During the early Middle Ages a hall such as this would have served as a communal living space for all the household, but this gradually changed until its main function was to accommodate great ceremonial occasions. It was for this purpose that James IV built the hall, extending the space available by building the massive sub-structure now known as the French Prisons.

Around 1650 it was converted for use as barracks for Cromwell's troops, being partitioned with walls and floors. Later it served as a hospital from about 1880–7.

The Great Hall is one of the highlights of the castle.

Scottish United Services Museum

This is Scotland's National Museum of the Armed Forces, reopening in the spring of 2000 after a period of refurbishment and the creation of six thematic galleries to illustrate different aspects of Scottish military history.

Royal Scots Dragoon Guards Museum (Carabiniers and Greys)

The Regimental Museum, which traces the history and roots of this regiment back as far as 1678. Formed in 1971 from the amalgamation of three older cavalry units, the Royal Scots Dragoon Guards is now an active tank unit of the British Army.

Tel: 0131 310 5100.
Admission free but charge to enter castle.
Disabled access.

Regimental Museum of the Royal Scots

Known as the Royal Regiment, the Royal Scots is the oldest regiment in the British Army, dating back to 1633 and the reign of Charles I. The museum is housed in a 1900 Drill Hall and contains memorabilia, including silver and medals, illustrating the Regiment's illustrious history.

Tel: 0131 310 5018.
Admission free but charge to enter castle.
Disabled access.

Scottish National War Memorial

The most modern of the castle buildings, and a moving memorial to Scotland's dead in World War I. The original building on this site was the church of St Mary, used during the 16thC to store munitions and later demolished to make way for a barrack block, erected in 1755. It was upon the shell of this building that Sir Robert Lorimer designed the Memorial, which was opened by the Prince of Wales (later King Edward VIII) in 1927. The memorial now also commemorates the dead of World War II and other conflicts.

Lang Stairs

A steep flight of 70 steps which was the main means of entry to the Upper Ward of the castle during the Middle Ages. It adjoins the upper storeys of the Portcullis Gate.

Edinburgh Castle is in the care of Historic Scotland.
Tel: 0131 225 9846.
Open daily Apr–Sep, 09.30–1800; Oct–Mar, 09.30–17.00. Last admission 45 minutes before closing time.
Admission charge.
Reasonable wheelchair access, and toilets for the disabled.
Café and restaurant.

EDINBURGH ZOO

`80 A4`

Founded in the grounds of Corstorphine Hill House in 1913 by Thomas Gillespie and planned by Sir Patrick Geddes, the zoo has always pioneered the principle of keeping animals in surroundings that are as natural as possible. The success of this is seen by the number of species, particularly endangered species, which are breeding here. Indeed, the Scottish Zoological Society, of which Edinburgh Zoo is a part, is decreasing the number of animals kept purely for display and is concentrating on those endangered species which can be sustained as breeding groups. This is done in co-operation with other zoos throughout the world. Environmental education and scientific research go hand-in-hand with the obvious pleasure that seeing animals can bring. The modest entrance gives little indication of the 32ha (80 acres) of sloping parkland over which the zoo extends.

There are over 1000 animals to see including mammals, birds, reptiles and amphibians. Each species is identified by a board giving its name (common and Latin), description, distribution, habitat, diet and behaviour. Keep an eye out for the rare pygmy hippos from West Africa, the guanaco, a wild ancestor of the llama, from the Andes, snow leopards and red pandas from the foothills of the Himalayas, and the Siberian tigers.

There is a chimpanzee house with an artificial termite mound. Wild chimps fashion sticks into tools for poking into termite nests – the termites crawl up the sticks and the chimps lick them off. Here at Edinburgh Zoo the mound contains not termites, but honey, which the chimps may dip for.

The African Plains exhibit is an important feature of the zoo. It is a large undulating area with trees, practically on the summit of Zoo Hill. The view of the animals is unimpeded due to a ha-ha ditch, and one can watch the interaction amongst the groups of zebra, oryx antelope, and ostrich.

A new addition to the zoo in 1999 was the Magic Forest, featuring marmosets and tamarins, the smallest monkeys in the world from the rainforests of South America. Next to the Magic Forest is a Physic Garden with plants that vets have used over the centuries to treat animal injuries and illness. A group of rare Asiatic Lions are also to be found in a new enclosure, located in 1.6ha

(4 acres) of woodland at the top of the zoo. The lions can be viewed from a raised walkway.

Edinburgh Zoo is world renowned for the Penguin Parade (Mar–Oct 14.00), when the penguins walk around with their keepers outside their enclosure. The penguin enclosure itself is the world's largest, and the penguins can be viewed from underwater viewing windows or from a suspension bridge.

African Plains exhibit at Edinburgh Zoo

There are many other special events, features and temporary exhibitions at the zoo.

Entrance is in Corstorphine Road. Tel: 0131 334 9171.
Open daily (including Christmas Day) from 09.00. Closes Apr–Sep 18.00; Oct and Mar 17.00; Nov–Feb 16.30. Admission charge.
Facilities for the disabled.
Café.
Picnics welcome.
No pets allowed.
Website: www.edinburghzoo.org.uk

FORTH RAILWAY BRIDGE

Thomas Bouch was to have built the railway bridge across the Forth. But when his Tay Bridge collapsed so disastrously in the storm of December 1879, with the loss of 90 lives, there was an understandable reluctance to trust his designs, and the task was given instead to Sir John Fowler and Benjamin Baker. With the Tay disaster still fresh in their minds, they built this massive all steel bridge comprising three double cantilevers, over 2.5km (1.5 miles) long in total (there is 1m/3 feet difference in its length between mid-summer and mid-winter) and giving a clearance of 110m/120 yards under the two main spans. A graceful cobweb seen from afar, the enormity of its construction can only be appreciated close to. This tribute to Victorian engineering skill was built between 1882–90, and 7000 gallons of paint are needed to cover its surface area of over 135 acres. Modern paint technology obviates the need for the once notorious continual painting.

FORTH ROAD BRIDGE

No less significant than the rail bridge, since it replaced the infamous ferries which had existed there since 1129. They caused no end of delays during the summer holiday period with long queues of traffic waiting on both banks. This elegant suspension bridge was opened in 1964. The largest in Europe when built, it cost £20 million and took six years to construct.

GEORGIAN HOUSE

82 C3

Charlotte Square was designed by Robert Adam and is to be found in the heart of Edinburgh's New Town. The Georgian house, No. 7, is on the north side of the Square and is a fine example of the houses of the era. The New Town was conceived in the mid 1700s to relieve

Georgian House, situated on the north side of Charlotte Square

the cramped and unsanitary conditions of the Old Town, and resulted in the unique Georgian architecture of the city which remains today.

Three floors of the Georgian House are elegantly furnished as they would have been by the Lamont family, the first owners of the house, in 1796.

A National Trust for Scotland property.
Tel: 0131 226 3318 or 0131 225 2160.
Open Apr– (or Good Friday if earlier) Oct,
Mon–Sat 10.00–17.00, Sun 14.00–17.00. Last admission 16.30. Parties of 20 or more must book in advance.
Admission charge.

GREYFRIARS KIRK

84 E4

Greyfriars Kirk was built between 1602 and 1620 in grounds belonging to the old Franciscan friary in the Grassmarket, which were given to the town for use as a cemetery by Queen Mary in 1562. It was the first church to be built in Edinburgh after the Reformation. Little remains of the original church which was smaller than the present one, with a plain nave and a tower at the west end.

The kirk suffered severe damage early one morning in May 1718, when gunpowder stored by the town council in a tower next to the church exploded. The building was repaired and shortened by constructing a new west wall, and internal galleries were incorporated to compensate for the lack of floor space. However, in November of the same year, the town council decided to erect a new building back to back with the old one, creating a separate new church. This was completed in 1721 after demolishing the remains of the original tower, and a porch was added on the north side to provide access to both churches.

Greyfriars Kirkyard. Many of Edinburgh's notables are buried here, including James Craig, the architect of the New Town.

Fire seriously damaged Old Greyfriars in 1845 and destroyed the furnishings of the new church. In 1929 the two congregations of Old and New Greyfriars united, with the dividing wall between the churches taken down during restoration, which took place from 1931–8.

Events that took place at Greyfriars are perhaps of greater interest than the architecture of the building. It was here on 28 February 1638 that the congregation, together with the merchants and nobles of Edinburgh, gathered to sign the National Covenant to pledge themselves to oppose anyone trying to establish Roman Catholicism in Scotland. The Covenant also called for a free Scottish Parliament, swore loyalty to Charles I, but warned him against interference in the affairs of the church. Copies were signed, sometimes in blood, in churches throughout the country. An original copy of the Covenant is displayed in the Visitor Centre within the church.

Just inside the churchyard entrance is thought to be the grave of Greyfriars Bobby, the famous wee dog whose bronze statue, erected in 1873, stands at the top of Candlemaker Row. This faithful Skye

Greyfriars Bobby

Terrier watched over the grave of his master, John Gray, for 14 years after Gray's death in 1858. Arrested for being unlicensed, the dog was reprieved when his street friends petitioned the Lord Provost. Given the Freedom of the City and an engraved collar, Bobby lived happily until 1872, cared for by locals. He now rests near his master, a gesture suggested by Queen Victoria herself, and one that the majority of visitors to Greyfriars still find more alluring than the bloody episode in Scotland's history which began here.

Greyfriars Place. Tel: 0131 226 5429.
Visitors are welcome to all services.
Programme of concerts.
Disabled access.
Website: www.greyfriarskirk.com
email: greyfriarskirk@compuserve.com

LAURISTON CASTLE

`69 E3`

Lauriston Castle, 8km (5 miles) west of Edinburgh city centre, is a 16thC tower house which was greatly extended in the 19thC. It is remarkable for its carefully preserved Edwardian interiors, and fine collection of furniture and decorative art.

Lauriston Castle, built in the 1590s and extended in the 1820s

The castle was built in the 1590s for Sir Archibald Napier, whose son John invented logarithms. In the 1820s Thomas Allan, who owned the house at the time, employed the architect William Burn to extend the house, which he did in neo-Jacobean style.

Lauriston has been home to many prosperous and well-known people. One of these was the financier John Law, who held high office at the French court in the 1720s.

The last private owners were Mr and Mrs William Robert Reid, who lived at Lauriston between 1902 and 1906. The Reids left the house and contents in trust to the Nation and it is now managed by the City of Edinburgh Council. Lauriston is set in 12ha (30 acres) of peaceful, well-tended gardens and parkland with panoramic views of

21

the Firth of Forth. Special events are held here throughout much of the year.

Cramond Road South, Davidson's Mains. Tel: 0131 336 2060.
Open Apr–Oct, Sat–Thu (closed Fri) 11.00–17.00; Nov–Mar, weekends only 14.00–16.00. Last admission 40 minutes before closing.
Admission is by guided tour only.
Admission charge.
Admission is free to the grounds, open all year 09.00–dusk.

NATIONAL GALLERY OF SCOTLAND and ROYAL SCOTTISH ACADEMY `83 D3`

Both the National Gallery and the Royal Academy are to be found at the bottom of the Mound, which was created from the earth excavated from the building sites of Edinburgh's Georgian New Town in the 18thC.

National Gallery
The neoclassical building was designed by William Henry Playfair (1789–1857) and the foundation stone laid by Prince Albert in 1850. The gallery, with octagonal shaped rooms, opened to the public nine years later. This small but world-renowned collection of western art contains outstanding paintings by the greatest artists from the Renaissance to Post-Impressionism, including Velázquez, El Greco, Titian, Vermeer, Turner, Constable, Monet, and Van Gogh. An altarpiece, painted by Hugo van der Goes in the mid 1400s for the Collegiate Church of Holy Trinity, is a particular treasure: the four panels depict James III and his family with the patron saints. The gallery also houses a major collection of Scottish art since the 16thC, featuring works by William McTaggart, Allan Ramsay, Henry Raeburn and Sir David Wilkie. The gallery's important collection of drawings, including individual sheets and sketchbooks, numbers more than 14,000.

National Gallery

22

*Royal
Scottish
Academy*

The Mound. General enquiries tel: 0131 624 6200.
Recorded information tel: 0131 332 2266.
Open all year (except Christmas Day and Boxing Day), Mon–Sat
10.00–17.00, Sun 14.00–17.00. Extended hours during the Edinburgh
Festival.
Admission free but charges may be made for special loan exhibitions.
The Print Room is open to visitors by arrangement at the front desk.
Disabled access.

Royal Scottish Academy

Designed in 1822 by William Henry Playfair, the Royal Scottish
Academy is typical of the Doric temple style buildings with which he
is associated. Above the front portico is a statue of Queen Victoria
by John Steell RSA, which was added in 1840. The building was first
occupied by the Royal Institution for the Encouragement of the Fine
Arts in Scotland and was known as the Royal Institution.

In 1826 the Scottish Academy was founded to promote the
interests of living artists in Scotland and this work continues today.
A Royal Charter was granted in 1838, and the Royal Scottish
Academy has been resident in this building since 1910. The
Academy is currently made up of 36 academicians and 50 associates,
and new associates are elected from the disciplines of painting,
sculpture, architecture and printmaking. On display are the works

of academicians together with invited artists. The RSA's annual Students' Art Exhibition and Annual Exhibition are held in spring and early summer. Other arts organisations also hold exhibitions here.

The Mound. Tel: 0131 225 6671.
Open Mon–Sat 10.00–17.00, Sun 14.00–17.00.
Admission charge.

NATIONAL LIBRARY OF SCOTLAND

Founded in 1682 as the Library of the Faculty of Advocates, the library is a treasure house of books, maps and manuscripts, with reading rooms open to scholars from home and abroad. The library has illuminated manuscripts, early printed books, historical documents and the letters and papers of Scottish literary figures. Although it is a research and reference library only, regular exhibitions give visitors a fascinating insight into the wealth of its collections.

George IV Bridge. Tel: 0131 226 4531.
Exhibition Hall open Mon–Fri 10.00–17.00, Sun 14.00–17.00.
Admission free.
Disabled access.
Website: www.nls.uk

PALACE OF HOLYROODHOUSE

Situated at the eastern end of the Royal Mile and on the edge of Holyrood Park, the baroque Palace of Holyroodhouse is the Queen's official residence in Scotland. The Royal Apartments are used for state ceremonies, including investitures and official banquets. Adjoining the building is the Holyrood Abbey Church.

What is now a palace probably originated as a guesthouse of the Abbey of Holyrood. The Augustinian monastery was founded by David I in 1128 on the spot where, according to legend, he had a vision of a stag with a cross (holy rood) between its antlers while he was out hunting.

The royal foundation conferred great status upon Holyrood, and it is likely that from the earliest time the accommodation had been designed as suitable for a monarch. In 1174 the bishops and nobles of Scotland met at Holyrood to discuss raising a ransom for William the Lion, captured at Alnwick while trying to recover Northumberland. The Pope's envoy, Vivian, held council here in 1177. During the period 1195–1230 the abbey church was rebuilt on a much grander scale and by 1329 it seems certain that Holyrood was used as a royal residence. With the burial in the choir of David II in 1370, the royal connection was irreversibly made. James II, born at Holyrood in 1430, was crowned here six years later, married here in 1449, and was finally buried here in 1460 after being killed by an exploding canon during the siege of Roxburgh Castle. Royal internments continued at Holyrood until 1566, the year in which Henry Darnley (husband of Mary, Queen of Scots,) was strangled at Kirk o'Field and buried here.

James IV embarked on an extensive building programme in preparation for his marriage to Margaret Tudor in 1503, which included the construction of a gatehouse, later destroyed in 1753. His son James V, crowned at Holyrood in 1524, continued the reconstruction, building the large north west tower containing the Royal Apartments and a new decorative west front between 1528 and 1536. In 1544 the Palace was damaged when the Earl of Hertford sacked Edinburgh.

Holyroodhouse, in history and romance, is strongly associated with Mary, Queen of Scots, the daughter of James V. Mary lived at Holyrood from 1561–67. It was here that she married Henry Darnley, and here that Rizzio, her private secretary, was murdered in 1566.

Further major improvement to the fabric of the palace of Holyrood was undertaken prior to the return to Scotland of James VI (James I of England) in 1633, and for the coronation of his son Charles I in 1633. It was damaged in 1650, this time by fire whilst occupied by Cromwell's troops.

The palace was rebuilt in the new Palladian style, and was completed in 1679, after eight years, the result was sumptuous with elegant plasterwork, fine carved woodwork, and decorative painting. The finest quarried stone from Fife and South Queensferry, Dutch tiles, Italian marble and English and French glass were all used to great effect, and the quality of the interiors was due in no small part to the skills of the craftsmen. It is largely this rebuilt Palace that is seen today.

During the 20thC Holyroodhouse has been the Royal Family's official Scottish home. The Lord High Commissioner also stays here during the annual General Assembly of the Church of Scotland in May.

Palace Interiors:

Great Staircase
The broad stairway has a large stone balustrade, and the walls are embellished with displays of tapestries and fresco paintings. The fine plasterwork of the ceiling, with tiers of flowers and swags, dates from 1678–9 and is by the English plasterers John Houlbert and George Dunsterfield. Life-sized figures of angels blow trumpets from the corners of the ceiling.

Royal Dining Room
Refurbished in Adam style in the late 18thC as a reception room for the Duke of Hamilton, it overlooks the forecourt.

Throne Room
This was originally Charles II's Guardroom. The panelling and ceiling is a copy of 17thC work; the fireplace dates from 1856.

Evening Drawing Room
George V installed the oak panelling, but the ceiling, by Houlbert and Dunsterfield, dates from 1676. The large panels of Brussels tapestries on the walls were sent from Buckingham Palace by Queen Victoria.

Morning Drawing Room

This was once the Privy Chamber and is lavishly decorated. The ceiling is again by Houlbert (1676). Above the green marble chimney piece the overmantle, elaborately carved by Dutch sculptor Jan van Santvoort, encloses a painting by the Dutch artist, Jacob de Wet. Panelling is by the Dutchman Alexander Eizat. The French tapestries have hung in this room since 1796, and the furniture is mainly 18thC.

King's Antechamber

Early panelling in here is also by Eizat, dating from 1677. There is a painting in the overmantle by Jacob de Wet.

King's Bedchamber

The most sumptuously decorated and furnished room in the Great Apartment, with visible manifestation of the wealth and influence of the monarch, Charles II. The ceiling, heavily decorated with foliage and royal emblems, is by Houlbert and Dunsterfield, enclosing an oval painting by de Wet. The chimney piece, carved with lion heads, is by Jan van Santvoort. The panelling and massive state bed date from the 17thC.

Great Gallery

Occupying the whole of the north range, 47m long and 7m wide (150 feet long and 24 feet wide), the picture gallery was created in 1671 for Charles II who wished for a connection between the old Royal Apartment in James V's north-west tower and the grand new apartment in the east. On the wood-panelled walls hang the portraits of more than 80 real and legendary kings of Scotland, from Fergus I (330 BC) to Charles II. The decorated ceiling, by James Baine, dates from 1672 and carries the monogram of Charles II.

Darnley's Rooms

Otherwise known as the Queen's Antechamber and Bedchamber, and located on the first floor of the north west tower, they were occupied by Lord Henry Darnley, husband of Mary, Queen of Scots. Originally, however, they comprised the original King's apartments. The decoration, ceiling and panelling are all 17thC, as is the bed. The Antechamber is hung with 17thC tapestries. A narrow stair connects with Mary's rooms above.

Mary, Queen of Scots, Chambers

Three rooms comprise Mary's Chambers. A plaque in the outer room marks the spot where Rizzio, Mary's private secretary, was believed to have been stabbed to death in 1566. Of particular interest is the wooden ceiling, divided into 16 panels and decorated with motifs which recall the auld alliance between Scotland and France. In the centre are the arms of Mary of Guise, Mary's mother. The ceiling dates from 1532 and survived the fire of 1650.

Abbey Church

The abbey was built between 1195 to 1230, and, in spite of later rebuilding, the remains of the abbey contain original sculptural detail on the processional door leading from the cloisters. A much larger church was built around the walls of the original abbey and then the earlier work was demolished. Flying buttresses were added in the 15thC. Since the coronation of Charles I in 1633, the abbey has suffered from neglect. Although a new roof was installed in 1758 it was never restored when it collapsed, causing considerable damage, ten years later. The remains of the roofless nave is the ruin seen today.

Palace Precincts:

Palace Yard Gates

Built in 1922 as a memorial to Edward VII, they were designed by Sir George Washington Browne and feature lions and unicorns overlooking some fine wrought iron. The gates have images of St Andrew and the Holyrood stag, with prominent thistles.

Palace Yard Gates

Fountain

The ornamental fountain was designed by Robert Matheson and dates from 1859. It was apparently inspired by the Cross Well at Linlithgow Palace, built in 1628.

Sundial

In what was once the walled Privy Garden to the north of the forecourt, is the sundial, designed and carved by John Mylne in 1633, with carvings of various heraldic badges and the crowned initials of Charles I.

Holyrood Park (Queen's Park)

A 263ha (650-acre) oasis of peace not far from the busy city centre. Paths lead to the summit of Arthur's Seat, the cone of an ancient volcano, and at 250m (822 feet) the highest point in the city. The park also encompasses three lochs.

Tel: 0131 556 1096 (24-hour information) or 0131 556 7371.
Open Apr–Oct, 09.30–18.00 (last admission 17.15); Nov–Mar, 09.30–6.30 (last admission 15.45). Closed 2 Apr, 4–16 May, 26 Jun–11 Jul, 25–26 Dec. Occasionally closed at other times. Official conducted tours only.
email: information@royalcollection.org.uk

ROYAL BOTANIC GARDEN
72 A5

This beautifully landscaped garden occupies an area of 28-ha (70 acres) less than a mile north of Princes Street. The gardens are the culmination of work begun by Dr Robert Sibbald, the first Professor of Medicine at Edinburgh University, and Dr Robert Balfour, who established a physic garden just 12m (14 yards) square on a site near Holyroodhouse in 1670. There they grew medicinal plants and herbs. However, they soon needed more space and six years later took over the Trinity Hospital garden, on a site now occupied by Waverley Station. James Sutherland was appointed to care for both gardens; he rapidly became Edinburgh's leading botanist, was made Professor of Botany at the University in 1695, and ultimately Regius Professor of Botany in 1710.

His successor, John Hope, who had studied at the Royal Garden in Paris, continued the development, moving in 1763 to a larger 2-ha (5-acre) site where Haddington Place (Leith Walk) now stands. Furthermore, he secured a permanent income from the Crown for the gardens. Also made Regius Professor, he encouraged his students to research and investigate Scottish plant life, arranging plant collecting not only on the mainland, but also on Orkney, Shetland, and the Western Isles.

Daniel Rutherford followed in 1786, a man more interested in plants as a means to his chemical experiments, but who was fortunate in having exceptional head gardeners: including John Tweedie, who introduced exotic plants – verbena and Chilean jasmine; John McKay, who exchanged plants with the botanic gardens at Kew; and William McNab, who came from Kew and introduced many rare plants and specialised in aquatics, introducing

The Pringle Chinese Collection on the south slopes of Inverleith Hill. Royal Botanic Garden.

species from all around the world. But perhaps Rutherford's greatest success was in organising the move to the present site at Inverleith between 1820 and 1823, a complex and difficult task during which time he lost hardly a single plant or tree.

In 1864 the Experimental Garden of the Royal Caledonian Horticultural Society was transferred here, and 12 years later the grounds surrounding Inverleith House were added. At the end of the 19thC, the gardens were transferred by the Treasury to the First Commissioner of Works and were opened to the public on Sundays for the first time.

During the latter part of the 18thC, under Isaac Bayley Balfour, the Edinburgh Botanic Gardens became an important centre for taxology (classification of living things), especially with regard to the plants of China and the Himalayas.

Today, the garden is one of the world's most important centres for the study of plants, with more than 34,000 living plants and a Herbarium of over 200 million specimens.

Flora Celtica – Scotland 2000

To mark the new Millennium, a major project is underway at the Royal Botanic Garden to increase awareness of the tradition of using the native plants of Scotland. This initiative is supported by the Scottish Millennium Festival Fund.

29

A complete record of the traditional and contemporary uses of plants is planned. The project is unique in the endeavour to involve the Scottish public, who are being asked to make a record of their use of native plants as well as that of their ancestor's. The results of the research will be published in a book and on the Internet and major exhibitions are planned.

Main features of the Royal Botanic Garden:

The largest area of the garden is the arboretum which includes nearly 2000 specimens and stretches around the slopes of Inverleith Hill. In addition to this, the Pringle Chinese Collection, situated on the south facing slope of the hill, includes many plants brought back by George Forest during his trips between 1904 and 1932. The plants are set in a recreated Chinese landscape, which includes boulders, water features and a Chinese Pavilion.

The gardens include an impressive 165m (180 yards) long herbaceous border, sheltered by a beech hedge. There are also demonstration gardens, a winter garden and the azalea lawn; which is a blaze of colour throughout May and June.

The rock garden dates from 1871, and was constructed by James McNab from Kew Gardens and used basalt from the island of Staffa.

There are also ten glasshouses, displaying plants ranging from warm temperate to tropical environments, plus two palm houses: the tropical dating from 1834 and the temperate from 1858.

Entrances on Inverleith Row and Arboretum Place.
Tel: 0131 522 7171. Gardens open daily from 09.30; closing Apr–Aug 19.00; Mar and Sep 18.00; Feb and Oct 17.00; Nov–Jun 16.00.
Glasshouse Experience and Exhibition Hall open from 10.00.
Admission free but voluntary contributions to the Glasshouse Experience and some exhibitions are invited.
Disabled access.
Café.
No animals except guide dogs.
Website: www.rbge.org.uk

The Tropical Palm House

ROYAL MILE

Sloping gently from the castle to the Palace of Holyroodhouse, the Royal Mile is a crowded, historic and romantic jumble of buildings from past centuries. Straddling the crest of a ridge to the east of the Castle Rock, it stretches for a lang Scots mile (1817m or 1984 yards), made up of four successive roads: Castlehill, Lawnmarket, High Street and Canongate. Lawnmarket derives its name from the linen market which traded there, while Canongate was the thoroughfare of the independent burgh of the Canons of Holyrood Abbey.

Lawnmarket Street

There was certainly some kind of fortification on Castle Rock in the 6thC, and as this became more significant a cluster of cottages was built close to the castle gate, at the top of what is now Lawnmarket and the High Street. David I founded the Royal Burgh of Edinburgh. He decided that some order should be brought to the town by dividing the land on either side of the High Street into tofts, narrow strips upon which each citizen was to build a dwelling within a year and a day. In 1376 the population had risen to about 2000, and subsequent division of the tofts created forelands (a land being a building) and backlands. The latter were reached though a narrow close between the forelands or through a pend, or archway, when the buildings actually joined.

In this way the High Street rapidly became built up, as did Canongate, a separate burgh founded by the Canons of Holyrood, who were granted a charter by David I in 1140. Canongate was to remain independent of the city until 1856. Further expansion of the population increased pressure on the space available within the city walls, until the only way left to build was up, and to create the suburbs of Cowgate and Grassmarket. Limited water supply and lack of provision for proper sanitation brought conditions of unimaginable squalor to the city's seething spine.

Royal Mile

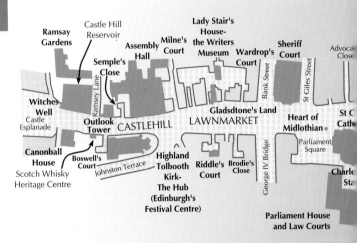

Ramsay
Gardens

Castle Hill
Reservoir

Assembly
Hall

Milne's
Court

Lady Stair's
House-
the Writers
Museum

Wardrop's
Court

Sheriff
Court

Advoca
Close

Semple's
Close

Witches
Well
Castle
Esplanade

Ramsay Lane

Outlook
Tower

CASTLEHILL

LAWNMARKET

Gladsdtone's Land

Bank Street

St Giles Street

Heart of
Midlothian

St C
Cath

Canonball
House

Boswell's
Court

Johnston Terrace

Highland
Tolbooth
Kirk-
The Hub
(Edinburgh's
Festival Centre)

Riddle's
Court

Brodie's
Close

George IV Bridge

Parliament
Square

Charle
Sta

Scotch Whisky
Heritage Centre

Parliament House
and Law Courts

CONTINUATIO

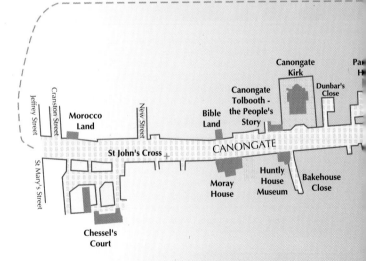

Jeffrey Street

Cranston Street

Morocco
Land

New Street

Canongate
Tolbooth -
the People's
Story

Bible
Land

Canongate
Kirk

Dunbar's
Close

Pa
H

St John's Cross

CANONGATE

St Mary's Street

Moray
House

Huntly
House
Museum

Bakehouse
Close

Chessel's
Court

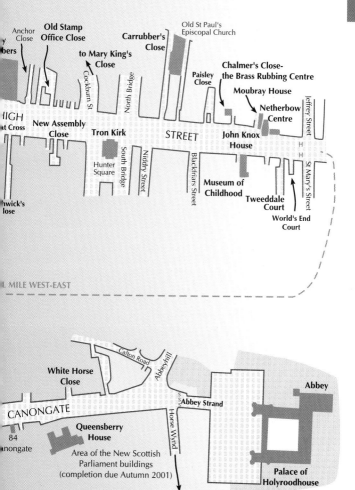

N

Anchor Close
Old Stamp Office Close
Carrubber's Close
Old St Paul's Episcopal Church
to Mary King's Close
Cockburn St
North Bridge
Paisley Close
Chalmer's Close-the Brass Rubbing Centre
Moubray House
Netherbow Centre
Jeffrey Street

HIGH
at Cross
New Assembly Close
Tron Kirk
STREET
John Knox House
bers

Hunter Square
South Bridge
Niddry Street
Blackfriars Street
Museum of Childhood
Tweeddale Court
World's End Court
St Mary's Street

hwick's
lose

L MILE WEST-EAST

White Horse Close
Calton Road
Abbeyhill
Abbey

CANONGATE
Abbey Strand
Horse Wynd

84
anongate
Queensberry House
Area of the New Scottish Parliament buildings (completion due Autumn 2001)

Palace of Holyroodhouse

to Our Dynamic Earth

33

In 1544, during a period known as the Rough Wooing, Henry VIII demanded that Mary, Queen of Scots, (then three years old) should marry his son Edward, to gain the support of the Scottish Lords. An English army, led by the Earl of Hertford, burned their way up the Royal Mile from the Palace of Holyroodhouse, and laid waste to everything else within a 11.25km (7 mile) radius. This was followed by a great rebuilding, with stone replacing wood, slate replacing thatch, and the amalgamation of tofts to accommodate courts enclosed by tenements.

In the 18thC the population crammed within the city walls was some 50,000. The appalling conditions led to crime and disease which reached epidemic proportions.

It was the Lord Provost George Drummond who provided the impetus for building a New Town to the north of the existing city, shortly after his appointment in 1725; building eventually began in 1767, the year after Drummond's death. This resulted in wealthier sections of the community abandoning the Old Town in favour of the New. With only the poor left, the Royal Mile soon degenerated further into an area of slums.

On the night of 15 November 1824 a great fire broke out in a tenement at the top of Old Assembly Close. It rapidly spread along the south side of the High Street to the Exchequer Buildings, destroying everything in its wake.

Improvement Acts in 1827 and 1867 provided for the renovation of the slums and the replacement of some of the narrow closes with ten new streets. Life improved, but it was to be many years before the fashionable returned.

North side
Downhill towards Holyrood:

Witches Well
A cast iron wall fountain marks the spot where over 300 women, thought to be witches, were burnt at the stake between 1479 and 1722. One of these unfortunate women was Dame Euphane MacCalzean, found guilty of using a spell to sink a vessel out of Leith, and trying to destroy King James VI's ship as it entered North Berwick. Another, Agnes Fynnie, was burnt in 1643 after 'depriving 12 people of their speech'.

Ramsay Garden

Outlook Tower, home of the camera obscura

Ramsay Garden

Incorporating the eccentric octagonal house, nicknamed Goose Pie, which poet and publisher Allan Ramsay (1686–1758) built for himself, this inventive example of early town planning was built by Professor Patrick Geddes (1854–1932) as a hall of residence and apartments between 1892–4.

Outlook Tower

The Outlook Tower was reconstructed in 1853, from a 17thC tenement building, as Short's Observatory by the optician Maria Theresa Short, and a camera obscura was installed. The lens and mirror of the original camera obscura were replaced in 1945 with a superior system which, on a clear day, projects a panorama of the City of Edinburgh onto a white concave table to the accompaniment of a running commentary. There are fine views from the rooftop terrace which has the most powerful public telescope in Britain, a history of the camera obscura, a display of holograms and an exhibition of pinhole photographs taken with biscuit tins and drink cans.

Tel: 0131 226 3709.
Open Apr–Oct, Mon–Fri 09.30–18.00, weekends 10.00–18.00; Nov–Mar, daily 10.00–17.00.
Admission charge.

Semple's Close

A 17thC mansion with inscribed door lintels, dated 1638. Lady Sempill, the widow of the 8th Lord Sempill, lived here.

Assembly Hall

This venue is being used as the debating chamber until the new parliamentary building is complete; it was built in 1859 by David Bryce, for the Free Church of Scotland, on the site of the Palace of Mary of Guise, who was the mother of Mary, Queen of Scots.

Milne's Court

Robert Mylne, architect and master mason to Charles II, created this open plan design amidst the crowded closes of the Old Town in 1690. He built a courtyard enclosed by existing buildings on the east and west. James' Court, to the east, is a later copy by James Brownhill. David Hume (1711–76), philosopher and historian lived here, as did James Boswell (1740–95), who chronicled the life of the diarist, Dr Samuel Johnson.

Gladstone's Land

Rebuilt by burgess and merchant Thomas Gledstanes when he acquired the property in 1617. A curved forestair stands beside an arcaded front, enclosing reconstructed shop booths, with round pillars supporting a typically narrow frontage some six storeys tall, culminating in two equal gables. Presented to the National Trust for Scotland by Miss Helen Harrison in 1934, it was sensitively restored by Sir Frank Mears and Robert Hurd to give the feeling of life here in the 1600s, and it remains a superb example of a 17thC tenement house. There is a gallery featuring a changing exhibition of contemporary work and a textile workshop.

Lawnmarket. Tel: 0131 226 5856.
Open Apr–Oct, Mon–Sat 10.00–17.00, Sun 14.00–17.00.
Last admission 16.30.
Admission charge.

Lady Stair's House – the Writers' Museum

Situated in Lady Stair's Close, this house was built in 1622 for Sir William Grey of Pittendrum and purchased in 1719 by Elizabeth, Dowager Countess of Stair. The house was enthusiastically restored by George S Aitken in 1897, and presented to the city in 1907.

Lady Stair's House is now a Writers' Museum and inside there are period room settings and collections of memorabilia, including manuscripts and portraits, relating to the lives and works of Scottish literary figures, notably Robert Burns (1759–96), Sir Walter Scott (1771–1832) and Robert Louis Stevenson (1850–94).

Lawnmarket. Tel: 0131 529 4901.
Open Mon–Sat 10.00–17.00, also Sun 14.00–17.00 during the Festival.
Admission free.
email: enquiries@writersmuseum.demon.co.uk

Wardrop's Court

Adjoining Lady Stair's Close and entered through an archway guarded by four iron dragons, Wardrop's Court was formed when two smaller closes were demolished in the 1840s.

City Chambers

A decorated 18thC building designed by John Adam, enclosing a courtyard on three sides and entered from the High Street through a single storey arcaded screen. Completed in 1761, it incorporated shops, coffee houses, printing presses, and apartments, and was intended as a covered Royal Exchange for merchants to carry out their business. It did not prove popular, however, and the merchants continued to trade on the street and in the taverns as was customary. The council first established their city chambers here in 1811, and finally took over the whole building in 1893, extending it in 1901. On 15 June 1567 Mary, Queen of Scots, spent her last night in Edinburgh here, after her surrender to the Confederate Lords at Carberry Hill. She was taken to Holyrood and from there to Loch Leven Castle as a state prisoner. After escaping and fleeing to England, she was imprisoned by Queen Elizabeth and beheaded at Fotheringhay Castle in 1587.

Mary King's Close

In Cockburn Street a barred gate leads to the remains of the saddest close of all, now incorporated into the side of the City Chambers. It was here that the death toll from the Great Plague in 1645 was so great that the city magistrates ordered it to be sealed off. After fire damage in 1750, the close was built over and incorporated into the Royal Exchange, now in the City Chambers. All that is visible today is a recognisable series of doorways rising part way to the High Street. The close was named after one Mary King who once owned houses in the close.

To visit the buried street, contact Mercat Tours, tel: 0131 225 6591.

Old Stamp Office Close

An attractive close, home of the Scottish Inland Revenue between 1799 and 1821, and also the fashionable Fortune's Tavern, where the Lord High Commissioner to the Church of Scotland held receptions. Flora MacDonald, heroine of Bonnie Prince Charlie's flight after the unsuccessful 1745 rebellion, went to school here.

Carrubber's Close

A walk down the close, past the House of Archbishop Spottiswood (1578, rebuilt 1864) will bring you to Old St Paul's Episcopal Church with its bellcote silhouetted against the sky, but the rest of the building is well and truly hemmed in. In 1880 a new building was begun on the side of the old, which had become ruinous, and continued in stages which culminated in the building of the Warriors' Chapel in 1924. The interior stonework and contrasting levels are quite dramatic, and rich furnishings are particularly notable – especially the altar, the triptych which contains figures by Sebastian Zwink of Oberammergau, and a sculpture of the Madonna and Child by Louis Deuchars.

Paisley Close

A sculpture above the entrance bears the inscription 'Heave awa' chaps, I'm no dead yet', which refers to the rescue of a boy trapped in the debris when a tenement collapsed in 1861, killing 35 occupants.

Chalmer's Close – the Brass Rubbing Centre

This close gives access to the Brass Rubbing Centre which is housed in a fragment of the Gothic Holy Trinity College Church, founded about 1460 by Mary of Gueldres, the wife of James II of Scotland, as a memorial to her husband.

At the centre you can make rubbings from replicas of ancient Pictish crosses, from medieval church brasses, and from rare Scottish brasses. No experience is needed to make a rubbing and materials and instruction are provided.

81 High Street. Tel: 0131 556 4364.
Open Mon–Sat 10.00–17.00 (last rubbing at 15.45); also Sun 14.00–17.00 during the Festival.
Admission free but charge for making rubbings.

Moubray House

Although the frontage was rebuilt around 1630 with a characteristic outside stair, parts of Moubray House date from the early 15thC. Daniel Defoe edited the *Edinburgh Courant* from this building in 1710. Outside is the old Fountain Well, one of the street wells which provided the Old Town with its first piped water.

John Knox House

This is one of the most notable medieval town houses of the Old Town. It has strong associations with John Knox and houses an exhibition about his life and career, but it is not certain he lived here.

John Knox was minister at St Giles (see page 43) for about nine years from 1560. He had been converted from Catholicism in 1542 and become the leader of the Reformers in Scotland. Imprisoned by the French for two years in revenge for the murder of Cardinal Beaton, he returned to Scotland and did more than any other man to establish Protestantism, even to the extent of chastising Mary, Queen of Scots, regarding her Roman Catholic religion and light-heartedness.

The house is picturesque and dates from the late 15thC. Built from polished freestone with an outside stairway and elaborate carvings, it was probably extended in either 1525 or 1544, and remains a prime example of a house with the once common overhanging wooden upper floors with crow-stepped gables.

John Knox House

43/45 High Street. Ticket office is located in the adjoining Netherbow Centre. Tel: 0131 556 9579/2647.
House open Mon–Sat 10.00–16.30.
Admission charge.

Netherbow Centre

The name recalls the old Netherbow Port, the main eastern city gate built in 1513 and demolished in 1764. Studs in the road indicate its actual position. The city wall, which separated Edinburgh from the separate burg of Canongate, ran at right angles to the High Street here. The old bell which hung in the spired city gate building is preserved in the Arts Centre, which features changing exhibitions of contemporary work, and there is also a theatre.

Tel: 0131 556 9579/2647.
Open Mon–Sat 09.30–1700, later when there are evening theatre performances.
Wheelchair access (assisted to theatre).
Café.

39

Bible Land

An extensively restored 17thC tenement built by the Incorporation of Cordwainers, or Shoemakers, and so called because of the fine stone open book plaque above the entrance door.

Canongate Tolbooth – the People's Story

Marked by an overlarge Victorian clock which sticks out over the pavement, the present building dates from 1591, when the tower and courtroom block were built on the site of an earlier tolbooth. Quite picturesque, with its forestair and stair turret, it has variously served as courthouse, prison and municipal centre for the independent burgh of Canongate. It now houses the People's Story museum, which illustrates the lives and work of ordinary people, from the late 18thC to the present, by means of sights, sounds, and smells. The museum has a rare collection of friendly society regalia and trade union banners.

163 Canongate. Tel: 0131 529 4057.
Open Mon–Sat 10.00–17.00; also Sun 14.00–17.00 during the Festival.
Admission free.
Disabled access.

Canongate Tolbooth – The People's Story Museum

THE PEOPLE'S STORY

Canongate Kirk

This is the parish kirk of the Canongate, which includes Holyroodhouse within its boundaries. It was completed two years after James VII (or James II of England) directed a new kirk to be built for the congregation, when he took over the Holyrood Abbey church in 1688 to use as a chapel for the Order of the Thistle.

In the churchyard are memorials to many of Scotland's best-loved sons including the economist Adam Smith (1723–90) and Provost George Drummond who initiated the planning of the city's New Town. It is a fascinating place to explore: look for the grave of Robert Fergusson (1750–74), the poet who inspired Robert Burns. When Burns found his grave neglected and overgrown, he paid for the stone that is now in situ.

Tel: 0131 556 3515.
Open Jun–Sep, Mon–Sat 10.30–16.30.
Visitors welcome to services.
Disabled access.
email: canongate@aol.com

Dunbar's Close

A beautifully recreated formal 17thC garden enclosed by high walls and entered through iron gates. An ideal place to rest when walking the Royal Mile. The garden was laid out in 1978.

Panmure House

Secreted in Panmure Close, this 17thC house with crow-stepped gables was once the house of the Jacobite Earls of Panmure, and more notably Adam Smith from 1778 until his death in 1790.

White Horse Close

An extensively restored but wholly enjoyable 1960s recreation of the original 17thC buildings. The coach for London used to leave from the White Horse Inn, which once stood at the rear of the close. The horses were stabled below.

Abbey Strand

Here was the legal boundary line between Holyrood Abbey and the burg of Canongate. The three Ss in the road are a reminder that debtors could find sanctuary in the 17thC tenements which were within the Abbey precincts. When imprisonment for debt ended in 1880, the need for sanctuary also ended.

South side

Downhill towards Holyrood:

Cannonball House

A cannonball embedded in the stonework of the west wall gives the building its name. Whether it was a shot fired from the castle during the Jacobite siege of 1745 or simply a marker indicating the gravitation head height of the city's first water supply, is not known, although the latter explanation is most likely. It is known that the

building dates from 1630 and was built onto an earlier structure for Alexander Mure.

Boswell's Court

A large tenement built for Thomas Lowthian around 1600. The court is named after the uncle of James Boswell.

Highland Tolbooth Kirk — The Hub (Edinburgh's Festival Centre)

This magnificently detailed neo-Gothic building, built between 1842 and 1844, was designed by James Gillespie Graham and Augustus Pugin, the latter famous for the design of the Houses of Parliament. The church's graceful 74m (243 feet) octagonal spire is the tallest in the city, and is seen to great advantage because of its elevated position at the top the Royal Mile. Tiling, textiles, stained glass and sculpture, the work of renowned artists and craftspeople, have been brought together by architect Benjamin Tindall to create a vibrant cultural centre. The building serves as Edinburgh's Festival centre, known as The Hub (see Edinburgh Festival) and is also used for various educational and arts events. The Hub also has a Festival ticket office, café and shop.

Riddle's Court

Situated in the inner court is the mansion of Bailie John McMorran, built in 1590 and one of the finest surviving examples of a wealthy merchant's house, with richly decorated interiors and a curious curved outside wooden stair. Such was the stature of the mansion, that it was used for a banquet given by the Town Council in honour of James VI and his Queen.

Brodie's Close

Initially evocative of the old Edinburgh, the illusion is shattered when the close opens onto an unsympathetic new building. The close takes its name from Francis Brodie, father of William Brodie. William was a respected Deacon of Wrights and Masons and cabinet-maker by day, but he was a burglar by night. This other life was discovered after a bungled raid on the Excise office at Chessel's Court. Brodie escaped to Holland but was eventually caught and returned. Ironically, he was hanged, along with his accomplice, on gallows of his own design on 1 October 1788. Three brass studs at the corner of George the IV Bridge mark this spot, which is also overlooked by the tavern bearing his name. It is thought Robert Louis Stevenson used Brodie as the inspiration from which he wove *The Strange Case of Dr Jekyll and Mr Hyde*.

Heart of Midlothian

A brass plaque enclosed by a heart-shaped arrangement of cobblestones marks the site of the doorway of the Old Tolbooth or Heart of Midlothian, erected in the 14thC and finally pulled down in 1817.

St Giles' Cathedral

Strictly the High Kirk of the City of Edinburgh, since it was only a cathedral in the true sense between the years 1633–8 and 1661–89, when there was a bishopric here. The title has stuck, perhaps because of its prominent position halfway along the High Street. John Knox directed the Reformation from here, when he was minister at St Giles in the 16thC.

There has been a church here since AD 854, but the present building is mainly medieval, with some Norman work enclosed in a Georgian exterior.

The real delights of St Giles are to be found inside, where much of the original medieval work can be seen; the choir has been noted as the finest piece of late medieval parish church architecture in Scotland. It is home to the Order of the Thistle and honours some of the greatest Scots of the last 300 years. Traditional and modern styles feature in the spectacular stained glass windows.

Tel: 0131 225 9442.
Open Mon-Sat 09.00–1700 (later in summer), Sun 13.00–17.00.
Admission free, donations invited.
Visitors welcome to services.
Restaurant below the church.

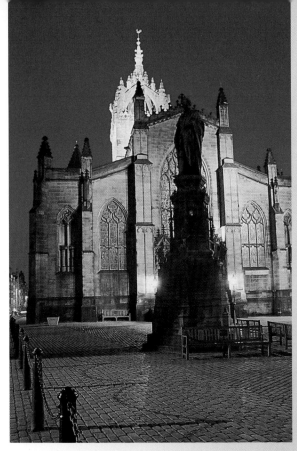

*St Giles'
Cathedral.
John Knox
was minister
here in
16thC.*

Half Hangit Maggie

Margaret Dickson was a much loved 18thC High Street fishwife, who became pregnant by a Kelso innkeeper's son after her husband deserted her. Born prematurely, the child died and Maggie's attempts to conceal the body resulted in her being found guilty under the Concealment of Pregnancy Act of 1690. On 2 September 1724 she was hanged near St Giles. After a scuffle with some medical students who wanted her body for research, she was put in a coffin and taken by her friends to be buried at Musselburgh. But in the graveyard Maggie started moaning, and when the lid was lifted she was found to be alive. Perplexed magistrates had to agree that, having been officially pronounced dead, she could not be sentenced again. She lived another 40 years, known to her friends and all as Half Hangit Maggie.

Mercat Cross

The original was first mentioned in 1365, and since then, it has occupied five separate sites in the High Street, one of which is

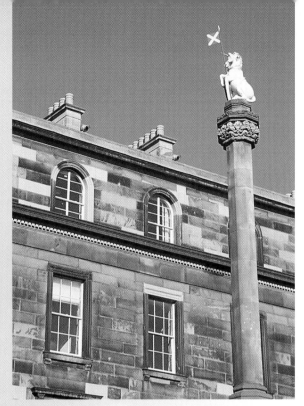

Mercat Cross

marked in the cobbles by the entrance to Old Fishmarket Close. The cross has served as an important focus of events in Scotland's turbulent past; it was from here that Royal Proclamations, such as the dissolution of Parliament, were read three days after their announcement in London (or the time it took to complete the journey on horseback).

Charles II Statue

Situated in Parliament Square, this is a unique life-sized equestrian statue depicting the King as a Roman Emperor. It was cast in lead and supplied by James Smith in 1685.

Parliament House and Law Courts

This complex array of buildings lies behind a neoclassical façade, built by Robert Reid in 1808. It is the home of the Supreme Law Courts of Scotland.

James V established the supreme civil court, the Court of Session, in Edinburgh in 1532. A hundred years later Charles I ordered the town council to build new accommodation to house the Court of Session as well as the Scottish Parliament and the Privy Council. For this purpose the Parliament Hall was built by Sir James Murray, His Majesty's Master of Works, to the west of St Giles. The original building comprised the Parliament Hall and an east wing. Completed in 1639, it was used by the Scottish Parliament until the dissolution of the Parliament at the Act of Union of 1707.

Parliament Hall was where the Scottish Parliament and the Outer House of the Court of Session convened. The Hall is 37m long and 13m wide (123 feet long and 42 feet wide) with a magnificent original open timber roof arching 12m (40 feet) above the floor of the Hall.

Beneath the Parliament Hall is the Laigh (low) Hall, formerly used as a library. It has a central arcade with eight pillars on octagonal bases and a large stone fireplace.

The wonderfully light and airy Signet Library (not open to the public except by written request to the Librarian) has elegant Corinthian columns beneath a saucer dome roof by William Stark.

Tel: 0131 225 2595.
Parliament House is open Mon–Fri 09.00–17.00.

Borthwick's Close

A close which conjures up visions of old Edinburgh. Wander through its irregular arches, over uneven paving slabs hemmed in by high walls, and you will see the 1839 Jacobean style building which was once George Heriot's Hospital School.

New Assembly Close

An 18thC wing of the Commercial Bank building, built by James Gillespie Graham in 1814. It was used as Assembly Rooms between 1736 and 1784, the venue for many dancing assemblies which were an 18thC passion.

Tron Kirk

A finely proportioned and extremely handsome building, it takes its name from the public weighing beam, or tron, which once stood close by. It was built between 1636 and 1647 by John Mylne Junior and John Scott to accommodate the Presbyterian congregation of St Giles, when the latter became a cathedral. Reconstructed between 1785 and 1787 by John Baxter Junior, it was severely damaged in the great fire of 1824 and the original tower was subsequently demolished. Rebuilt to a taller classical design by R & R Dickson in 1828, a remarkably successful marriage of 17thC and 19thC styles was achieved.

Museum of Childhood

Devoted to the history of childhood, this is an enchanting, colourful, noisy place. Dolls, trains, models, games, mechanical amusements, nursery equipment and books from many parts of the world crowd the rooms. Audiovisual displays add to the atmosphere – you can, for instance, listen to 1930s schoolchildren chanting multiplication tables.

42 High Street. Tel: 0131 529 4142/4119.
Open Mon–Sat 10.00–17.00; also Sun 14.00–17.00 during the Festival.
Admission free.

Tweeddale Court

Tweeddale House dates from the 16thC and was built by Neil Lang, Keeper of the Signet. Sir William Bruce bought it in 1664 and in turn sold it in 1670 to the 2nd Earl of Tweeddale. The Scottish Poetry Library is to be found here and is open to anyone who would like to visit or use the library.

World's End Close

The first and last close, when it was just inside the city wall.

Chessel's Court

The well-restored block of mansion flats is Chessel's Buildings, erected in 1748 by Archibald Chessel for the well-to-do. Later used as the Excise Office, it was here that Deacon Brodie was caught stealing in 1788 (see Brodie's Close) and subsequently hanged.

St John's Cross

A cobbled cross on the road indicates the site of St John's Cross, which marked the boundary of land owned by the Order of St John. The Scottish headquarters of the Knights of St John is in St John Street nearby.

Moray House

This fine mansion was built around 1625 for Mary, Dowager Countess of Horne. Charles I was a frequent visitor and Oliver Cromwell is known to have stayed here twice.

Huntly House Museum

This 16thC house, damaged in 1544 when the English attacked Edinburgh, was rebuilt in 1570 with a new frontage and triple gable. It takes its name from George, first Marquess of Huntly, who had lodgings here in 1636. Bought in 1647 by the Incorporation of Hammermen and used as a meeting house, they employed Robert Mylne to enlarge the frontage and convert it into apartments. This work was completed in 1671.

Huntly House still has a wealth of original fittings, panelling and fireplaces. Acquired in 1924 by the City of Edinburgh, it was opened as the principle city museum in 1932. Restoration was executed by Frank C Mears in 1927–32, who replicated the exterior inscribed Latin panels which gave rise to the building's 19thC nickname, the Speaking House. The exhibits and period room settings give a great insight into the past life of Edinburgh. Historical items span the centuries and include the National Covenant, signed in 1638 by the leaders of the Presbyterian Church, and memorabilia relating to Field Marshal Earl Haig, World War I leader. There are also regular temporary local history and decorative art exhibitions.

142 Canongate. Tel: 0131 529 4143.
Open Mon–Sat 10.00–17.00; also Sun 14.00–17.00 during the Festival.
Admission free.
Disabled access.

Bakehouse Close

Entered through a broad arch beneath Huntly House, Bakehouse Close offers a handsome glimpse of Old Edinburgh. At its head is Acheson House, built in 1633 by Secretary of State Archibald Acheson and restored in 1937 by the 4th Marquess of Butte.

Queensberry House

Lord Halton began building this great mansion in 1681, with James Smith as his mason, and sold the completed work to the first Duke of Queensberry in 1686. Used variously as flats, a barracks, people's refuge and a hospital for the elderly, it is best known as the home of the 2nd Duke of Queensberry. A staunch supporter of the Treaty of Union, the Duke is reported to have accepted a bribe of £12,325 to ensure its signing.

ROYAL MUSEUM and MUSEUM OF SCOTLAND

`83 E4`

The Royal Museum houses the International Collection whilst the adjoining Museum of Scotland, opened in 1998, is home to the Scottish Collection.

Royal Museum

The heavy, Venetian Renaissance style exterior gives no clue to the extraordinarily fine and imaginative interior of this building, designed by Captain Francis Fowke and built in three stages between 1866 and 1869. The main hall is a prime example of Victorian skills with slender cast iron pillars (partly replaced with steel in 1955) which support galleried aisles with cast iron balustrades, all beneath a soaring glass roof. Fountains and fishponds are now a delightful feature of this main hall. The whole building is light, elegant and airy, giving it an echo of Joseph Paxton's Crystal Palace building for the Great Exhibition held in London in 1851.

Originally called the Industrial Museum of Scotland, its name was changed to the Royal Scottish Museum in 1904. The University Natural History Collection was transferred to this new building upon its opening, and this provided the basis of the Natural World Collection, which now ranges across the whole of plant and animal life on the planet. The skeleton of a huge blue whale has hung in the mammal hall for over 100 years, and a more recent acquisition is a Sperm Whale nicknamed Moby Dick, which was stranded in the Firth of Forth in 1997. In the new fish gallery there is a shark park, and in a gallery which focuses on environmental and conservation issues, a slide show in the Biodome illustrates the development of life on earth.

Besides the wide ranging Natural World Collection, there are also outstanding collections representing Science and Industry, and the Decorative Arts. A great favourite is the Wylam Dilly, a locomotive which pre-dated Stephenson's more famous Rocket, and occupying the whole of one end of the same hall is a giant water wheel dating from 1862. There is 20thC space exploration equipment, and a new Art and Industry gallery explores the work and relationship between artists, engineers, scientists and craftspeople over the last 150 years with many interactive displays.

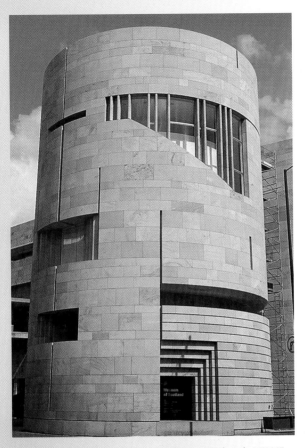

Museum of Scotland

Chambers Street. Tel: 0131 225 7534 or 0131 247 4219 (voice); 0131 247 4027 (text).
Open Mon–Sat 10.00–17.00, but closes Tue 20.00,
Sun 12.00–17.00. Closed 25 December.
Admission charge but free on Tue after 16.30.
Charge includes entry to Museum of Scotland, to which it has interior access on three levels.
Fully accessible for the disabled.
Café and tearoom.
Website: www.nms.ac.uk

Museum of Scotland

A striking, modern, five-storey building built as an annexe to the Royal Museum. The museum traces the history and achievements of Scotland and Scottish people from the country's geological beginnings to the 20thC, drawing on the rich and varied national collections. The 20thC Gallery features exhibits chosen by well-known people to illustrate life in that century: Professor Malcolm Baird, son of Sir John Logie Baird, aptly chose a television. From the rooftop terrace there are spectacular views of the city and beyond.

Chambers Street. Tel: 0131 225 7534 or 0131 247 4422 (voice); 0131 247 4027 (text).
Opening times, admission and access same as Royal Museum.
Tower Restaurant.

SCOTTISH NATIONAL GALLERY OF MODERN ART

81 F3

Set in beautiful wooded parkland, which includes a sculpture garden, the gallery has a superb collection of 20thC painting, graphic art and sculpture. Bonnard, Matisse, Picasso, Miro, Magritte, Giacometti, Feininger, and Lichtenstein are all represented by major works of art. There is also a collection of modern and contemporary Scottish artists including Francis Cadell, George Leslie Hunter and Ian Hamilton Finlay. In the sculpture garden are works by Jacob Epstein, Henry Moore, Barbara Hepworth, and Eduardo Paolozzi.

The large Doric building, originally designed by William Burns in 1825, was converted to its present use in 1984.

Belford Road. General enquiries tel: 0131 624 6200.
Recorded information tel: 0131 332 2266.
Open all year (except Christmas Day and Boxing Day) Mon–Sat 10.00–17.00; also Sun 14.00–17.00.
Extended hours during the Festival.
Admission free but charges may be made for special loan exhibitions.
Disabled access.

Scottish National Gallery of Modern Art

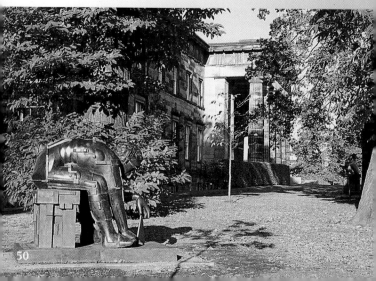

*Scottish
National
Portrait
Gallery*

SCOTTISH NATIONAL PORTRAIT GALLERY   83 D2

Statues of well-known Scots adorn this Gothic red sandstone
building, designed by Sir Rowand Anderson in the 1880s and
thought to have been modelled on the Doge's Palace in Venice. This
is the place to see an outstanding collection of portraits of all those
people who have made their mark on Scottish history right up to the
present day: from Mary, Queen of Scots, to Sean Connery and from
Robert Burns to Mick McGahey.

1 Queen Street. General enquiries tel: 0131 624 6200.
Recorded information tel: 0131 332 2266.
Open all year (except Christmas Day and Boxing Day) Mon–Sat
10.00–17.00, Sun 14.00–17.00. Extended hours during the Festival.
Reference Archive open to visitors by arrangement at the front desk.
Admission free but charges may be made for special loan exhibitions.
Disabled access.

Other Attractions

Adam Pottery
76 Henderson Row. Tel: 0131 557 3978.
A pottery making a wide variety of stoneware and porcelain in colourful reduction-fired glazes. Visitors may watch work in progress. The work of other ceramists is also on sale.

Auld Reekie Tours
Tronkirk, the Royal Mile. Tel: 0131 557 4700.
Underground tour of 200-year-old chamber, where over 70 supernatural occurrences have taken place. Also learn about Edinburgh's grizzly past on the evening ghost and torture tour. Deacon Brodie pub tour takes visitors around Edinburgh's finest pubs for an evening of humour and stories about Edinburgh's creepy past. Witchcraft tour covers the occult, witchcraft and paganism.

Bank of Scotland Museum
Bank of Scotland Head Office, The Mound. Tel: 0131 529 1288.
A small but unusual museum telling the 300-year story of Scotland's first bank in the context of the economic development of the country. Features early adding machines, bank notes and forgeries, bullion chests and gold coins, maps, plans and photographs. Summertime weekday opening only.

Caledonian Brewery
`91 F1`
24 Slateford Road. Tel: 0131 337 1286.
Traditional beers can be tasted at this famous Edinburgh brewery, founded in 1896.

City Art Centre
2 Market Street. Tel: 0131 529 3993.
Situated in a building designed in 1899 by Dunn & Findlay for the Scotsman newspaper as a newsprint store. Sympathetically converted to its present use in 1980, the city's permanent fine art collection is beautifully displayed here. The works, numbering about 3500, are mainly Scottish and date from the 17thC to the present. Works by late 19thC and early 20thC artists are well represented, and contemporary works are continually being added. There are also temporary international exhibitions.

Craigmillar Castle
`95 E4`
Craigmillar Castle Road, off A68. Tel: 0131 661 4445.
Imposing ruins of a massive 14thC tower house enclosed in the early 15thC by an embattled curtain wall. Within are the remains of the stately ranges of apartments dating from the 16th and 17thC. The castle was burned by the Earl of Hertford in 1544. Mary, Queen of Scots, stayed here after the murder of Rizzio, her private secretary.

Edinburgh Butterfly and Insect World
Lasswade, Midlothian. Tel: 0131 663 4932.
An exotic rainforest landscaped with tropical plants, cascading waterfalls and lily ponds provides the setting for hundreds of spectacular tropical butterflies to fly freely around. Visitors can watch them feeding and breeding. There are also many other species, including scorpions, tarantulas and giant stick insects.

Edinburgh Experience `83 F2`
City Observatory, Calton Hill. Tel: 0131 556 4365.
Tells the story of Scotland's capital in a 3-D slide show.

Edinburgh Old Town Weaving Company
555 Castlehill. Tel: 0131 226 1555.
A working mill that demonstrates the production of tartan cloth from sheep to shop, with the opportunity for visitors to try their hand at making tartan on a pedal loom. Kiltmakers are at work, and there is also a Highland Dress exhibition. The building was converted from the former Old Town reservoir.

Edinburgh Printmakers Workshop and Gallery
23 Union Street. Tel: 0131 557 2479.
Edinburgh's main studio for practicing artists who make limited edition prints. Visitors can watch artists at work and see the huge range of etchings, lithographs and screenprints for sale in the gallery.

Fruitmarket Gallery
45 Market Street. Tel: 0131 225 2383.
Originally built in 1938 as a fruit and vegetable market, the gallery is now an acclaimed art gallery with a national and international reputation for diverse and challenging contemporary exhibitions. Art bookshop and café.

Fun Park `86 B2`
Pipe Lane. Tel: 0131 669 1859.
A family entertainment centre on Portobello Promenade with various amusements – dodgems, carousel, merry-go-round, soft play area, full-size ten-pin bowling lanes, snooker and American pool hall.

Gorgie City Farm
51 Gorgie Road. Tel: 0131 337 4202.
The 1-ha (2-acre) farm with various farm animals, herbs, vegetables, and a wildlife garden. The Pet Lodge houses small animals, from rabbits to tortoises, which visitors are welcome to handle. There are special events throughout the year, including craft classes and educational workshops.

Hanover Fine Arts
22a Dundas Street. Tel: 0131 556 2181.
Holds exhibitions of contemporary Scottish artists, including painters, sculptors and potters.

James Pringle Weavers at Leith, Clan Tartan Centre

70–74 Bangor Road. Tel: 0131 553 5161.

With the aid of a computer research facility, the centre can provide visitors with a printed certificate detailing any clan connection, information on the clan chief, its origins, heraldic emblems, plant badge, Highland Dress, and other historic information. The large shop also sells woollens, tartans and clothing.

Laser Quest

28 Bread Street. Tel: 0131 221 0000.

A game of pursuit for all ages, which takes place in a maze filled with pulsating lights and smoke.

Magdalen Chapel

41 Cowgate. Tel: 0131 220 1450.

Built as an almshouse in 1541, the chapel was used by various denominations as an ecclesiastical building, and also as a guildhall by the Incorporation of Hammermen until 1862, when it was sold to the Protestant Institute of Scotland. Since 1965 it has been in the possession of the Scottish Reformation Society and used as their headquarters, with regular services. Features stained glass (the only Scottish medieval examples still in their original location), a bell and clock dating from early 17thC.

Malleny Garden

Balerno, off A70. Tel: 0131 449 2283.

Dominated by four 400-year-old clipped yew trees, this peaceful walled garden features fine herbaceous borders and a large collection of old-fashioned roses. The National Bonsai Collection for Scotland is kept here, and the garden is a National Trust for Scotland property.

Matthew Architecture Gallery

20 Chambers Street. Tel: 0131 650 2306.

An ongoing programme of exhibitions brings the best of contemporary architecture and related arts to the general public.

Mercat Walking Tours

Mercat Cross, High Street. Tel: 0131 661 4541.

Dramatised history and ghost tours of the Royal Mile by guides in costume. Tours visit the wynds and closes of Old Edinburgh and include a visit to the vaults beneath the South Bridge and the world-famous Mary King's Close.

Museum of Fire

Brigade Headquarters, Lauriston. Tel: 0131 228 2401.

A museum telling the history of the oldest municipal fire brigade in the United Kingdom. Housed in the historic headquarters building, it shows the development of fire fighting in an exciting and educational way. Displays a range of fire engines from 1806 onwards, and many other fire related items. Open by written appointment only.

Nelson Monument

`83 F2`

32 Calton Hill. Tel: 0131 556 2716.
One of the first monuments to Admiral Nelson, built between 1807 and 1815. The Tower is shaped like a telescope, with a time-ball on the top. The latter is lowered as the one o'clock gun is fired at Edinburgh Castle, every day except Sunday. Nelson's Trafalgar signal is flown annually on 21 October. Situated on Calton Hill, there are spectacular views from the top.

New Town Conservation Centre

13A Dundas Street. Tel: 0131 557 5222.
Exhibitions and information about the restoration of Edinburgh's Georgian New Town.

Newhaven Heritage Museum

`73 D1`

24 Pier Place. Tel: 0131 551 4165.
This museum is situated in the historic fishmarket overlooking the harbour. It tells the story of Newhaven and its people, the Society of Free Fishermen and the development of this tightly knit community. Find out about fishing and other sea trades, customs and superstitions. There are reconstructed sets of fishwives and fishermen, and first-hand written and spoken accounts of their lives.

Royal Commonwealth Pool

`94 A1`

21 Dalkeith Road. Tel: 0131 667 7211.
Olympic size swimming pool, together with diving, flume and baby teaching pools. There is also a soft play area and a fitness studio.

Royal Observatory Visitor Centre

`93 E4`

Blackford Hill. Tel: 0131 668 8405.
Although built in 1894, the observatory is right up-to-date with CD-ROMs, interactive displays and exhibits about space and astronomy. The telescope is one of the largest in Scotland, and there are panoramic views of the city from the rooftop.

St Cuthbert's Parish Church

5 Lothian Road. Tel: 0131 229 1142.
The seventh church on this site. Legend has it that St Cuthbert had a small cell church here at the head of the Nor' Loch on land given to him by King David I. The present church was built in 1894 to a design by Hippolyte Blanc, but retained the 1790 tower. The interior was revamped in 1990 by Stewart Tod. Notable features of the church are Renaissance style stalls, marble communion table, mural, and stained glass by Tiffany.

St Mary's Episcopal Cathedral

`82 B4`

Palmerston Place. Tel: 0131 225 6293.
Built in the 1870s by Sir George Gilbert Scott, this is a huge neo-Gothic church with three spires. Choral evensong is held here every day.

Royal Observatory

Scotch Whisky Heritage Centre

83 D3

354 Castlehill. Tel: 0131 220 0441.
Illustrates the history of Scotch Whisky, as well as providing a tour of the whisky making process.

Scott Monument

83 E3

East Princes Street Gardens. Tel: 0131 529 4068.
A monument to Sir Walter Scott in Princes Street Gardens, built in 1844 and decorated with figures from Scott's novels. It has panoramic views of the city from the top, which is 61.5m (200 feet) and 287 steps above ground level.

Scottish Agricultural Museum

76 A5

Royal Highland Showground, Ingliston, Newbridge. Tel: 0131 333 2674.
Situated on the Royal Highland Showground at Ingliston, this museum provides an insight into the history of Scottish rural life and agriculture.

Scottish Tartans Museum

The Scotch House, 39-41 Princes Street. Tel: 0131 556 1252.
Contains some of the rarest Highland artefacts in the world as well as a clan database.

*Scott
Monument*

ScottishTelecom World of Communications
Level 3, Saltire Court, 10 Cambridge Street. Tel: 0131 473 3939.
A free interactive exhibition for adults and children alike, exploring
the world of communications.

Stills Gallery
23 Cockburn Street. Tel: 0131 225 9876.
Photographic gallery of Scottish and international contemporary
photographers.

Talbot Rice Gallery
Old College, South Bridge. Tel: 0131 650 2210.
The University of Edinburgh's Old Masters collection of paintings and
temporary contemporary art exhibitions, housed in Old College, the
oldest surviving part of the University.

Edinburgh Festival

For three weeks, beginning in mid August each year, Edinburgh plays host to what is probably the greatest and most prestigious arts festival in the world. The official Edinburgh International Festival is supported by a number of other festivals including the boisterous

fringe festival which spills over onto the streets, giving the city a colourful, carnival atmosphere. Filled to overflowing with some of the world's most talented artists and performers, audiences arrive in droves from all over the world. Many of Edinburgh's visitor attractions extend their opening hours during the festival, and the major museums and art galleries, as well as numerous smaller venues, mount special exhibitions.

The Edinburgh Military Tattoo takes place at the same time as the official festival and its matchless setting against the floodlit backdrop of the castle adds pageantry and occasion to the calendar of events. The sounds of the massed pipes and drums echo over the city and the noise of cannon fire can be heard three miles away in Portobello.

The Film Festival, which also runs concurrently, has become world renowned and is often the venue for UK premiers. There is also a Jazz and Blues Festival which is held during the ten days leading up to the main events, and a Book Festival which has built up a fine reputation.

EDINBURGH INTERNATIONAL FESTIVAL

The festival was the idea of impresario Rudolf Bing and H Harvey Wood, the then Director of the British Council in Scotland. It came to fruition in 1947, during a gloriously warm August, set against the background of rationing and post-war austerity. The opening concert was given by the Orchestre des Concerts Colonne of Paris and critics acclaimed the new festival as a success.

Music

The Usher Hall is the main concert venue and the Opening Concert is held there, followed throughout the three weeks by orchestral concerts, chamber music, choral works, and piano recitals. The beautiful Queen's Hall also sees a series of concerts by smaller ensembles and soloists. Other venues include the Reid Concert Hall and St Ceclia's Hall. The finale is the spectacular Bank of Scotland Fireworks Concert, at the Ross Bandstand in Princes Street Gardens with the Scottish Chamber Orchestra.

Opera and Music Theatre

Classic and modern opera by international artists as well as performances by Scottish Opera, the Scottish Chamber Orchestra, and the Royal Scottish National Orchestra at the Edinburgh Festival Theatre, Edinburgh Playhouse and the Royal Lyceum Theatre.

Dance

The Edinburgh Playhouse and Edinburgh Festival Theatre stage classical ballet and modern dance by internationally renowned choreographers and companies.

Finale of the festival is the Bank of Scotland Fireworks Concert.

Theatre

The best of theatre from all over the globe graces the stages of the King's Theatre and the Royal Lyceum Theatre with world and UK premiers, and work by the Traverse Theatre company.

THE FRINGE

Eight theatre companies turned up uninvited at the inaugural International Festival in 1947 and the Fringe was born. Now it is usual for over 500 companies to give around 14,000 performances of 1600 shows in the space of three weeks. Performances inevitably go on around the clock, and late night licensed premises dominate the festival scene. The present fringe is no longer impromptu. Since the 1950s the Festival Fringe Office has produced a programme, sold tickets and offered advice to those wishing to take part.

Exciting, adventurous, ridiculous, speculative and outrageous, the fringe exudes creative energy and encompasses comedy, revue, children's shows, music and dance, as well as drama. Many of Britain's leading comedians, performers, and actors enjoyed their first

*Fringe
Sunday*

success here. Groups rely on publicising their events by handing out leaflets and performing on the streets in the competition for audiences. Try not to miss Fringe Sunday, always the second Sunday of the festival. It is a giant open air event and a feast of entertainment for all the family in Holyrood Park.

THE HUB – EDINBURGH'S FESTIVAL CENTRE `83 D3`

348 Castlehill, Edinburgh, EH1 2NE. Tel: 0131 473 2011.
Box Office tel: 0131 473 2000. Open 09.30–17.30 – extended hours when festivals are taking place.
Opened in July 1999, the Hub provides a ticket and information centre for all Edinburgh's festivals, a programme of education events, a café, and function and rehearsal space. The Main Hall is used for the Festival Club in August. Accessible for those with physical, visual and hearing impairment.

The Hub building is open every day (except Christmas Day) 08.00–01.00.
Café Hub tel: 0131 473 2067.
email: thehub@eif.co.uk

How to Book Festival Tickets

Programme and ticket order forms are usually available during April from the Hub and you can then book by post or fax (fax: 0131 473 2003). Telephone and personal counter bookings at the Hub Box Office (tel: 0131 473 2000) begin about ten days later. Payment can be made by cash £ sterling, a cheque drawn on a UK bank, major credit/debit cards, or Festival Gift vouchers. Email reservations can be made from the festival website at www.eif.co.uk

During the festival period only, tickets are on sale to personal callers at the Usher Hall, the Queen's Hall, the Edinburgh Festival Theatre, the Edinburgh Playhouse and the Royal Lyceum Theatre. Unsold tickets for other venues will go on sale one hour before the start of performances.

Tickets for the Fireworks Concert are obtained by postal ballot (May closing date), although a limited number of tickets will be on

*The Hub –
Edinburgh's
Festival
Centre*

sale at the Hub counter about a week before the concert. Telephone the Box Office for details of date and time.

There is a range of discounted festival tickets available for young people, students, unemployed, senior citizens and groups. Unsold tickets will be sold at half price on the day of the performance from 13.00 at the Hub (two per person).

Facilities for the Disabled

A brochure with full information about facilities for people with disabilities is available from the Festival Office. Tel: 0131 473 2052 (voice) or 0131 473 2098 (text).

Festival Club

The Hub, Castlehill. Tel: 0131 473 2011.

Provides the opportunity to meet friends and mingle with artists, catch up on the latest reviews, eat, drink and relax between shows. Open 08.00–02.00. Membership available for a day, a week, two weeks, or for the entire festival period. Discounts apply for membership of seven days or more. Book in advance when reserving festival tickets, although a limited number of day tickets will be available each day.

Edinburgh Festival Fringe

180 High Street, Edinburgh EH1 1QS. Tel: 0131 226 5257.

Programme and ticket order forms are usually available in June, and you can then book by post immediately. To order a fringe programme telephone 09065 500 678 (UK only, charge of call covers post and packing). Personal counter bookings and telephone credit card bookings are taken from mid-June.

Box office tel: 0131 226 5138.
email: admin@edfringe.com
Website: www.edfringe.com

Fringe Club

Situated at Old Assembly Close, just off the Royal Mile. Membership free to participants of the fringe. Enquiries to the Festival Fringe office tel: 0131 226 5257.

The Fringe Club is the nerve centre for performers' professional development, hosting a full schedule of events including masterclasses, debates and trade shows for people taking part in the fringe. Performers are provided with unique networking opportunities, professional advice and the chance of working with some of the most important actors and directors in the British theatre.

EDINBURGH MILITARY TATTOO

An event officially separate from the festival, but now an inseparable part of the whole occasion – a spectacular, exciting, noisy and sometimes moving display each evening (except Sun), ending with a fireworks display on the late Saturday performances. The Tattoo first began in 1950 and still thrills the crowds with mock battles, highland dancing, gymnastics, pageantry, horseriding and, of course, music of the Massed Pipes and Drums and the Massed Military Bands. The venue is the Castle Esplanade. The tattoo ends with one spotlight on a lone piper on the battlements, playing a farewell lament.

Tattoo Box Office: 33/34 Market Street. Tel: 0131 225 1188.
Personal counter sales begin from early July.
Open Mon-Fri 10.00–16.30, Sat 10.00–12.30; open on performance days until the start of the performance. Postal and fax bookings accepted from the beginning of January at the Tattoo Office, 32 Market Street, Edinburgh EH1 1QB. Fax: 0131 225 8627. Telephone bookings are taken on the Box Office number from about mid July.
Access to the Tattoo is difficult but there are some facilities for wheelchair patrons and those with hearing difficulties.
email: edintattoo@edintatto.co.uk
Website: www.edintattoo.co.uk

EDINBURGH INTERNATIONAL FILM FESTIVAL

From modest beginnings in 1947, when it concentrated mainly on documentary films, the Film Festival (running concurrently with the main festival) now has a worldwide reputation for its wide range of subject matter – from experimental and pop videos to new Hollywood feature films. Film directors often appear personally to explain their new work.

88 Lothian Road. Tel: 0131 228 4051.
Programme and booking information usually available mid July when the free Preview is published.
email: info@edfilmfest.org.uk.
Website: www.edfilm.fest.org.uk

EDINBURGH BOOK FESTIVAL

Another dimension to the Festival, with over 300 Scottish and International authors taking part in a full literary programme of more than 400 events for adults and children. It takes place during the first two weeks of the main festival.

137 Dundee Street. Tel: 0131 228 5444.
Programme available from the end of June.
email: admin@edbookfest.co.uk

EDINBURGH GALLERIES ASSOCIATION

This association publishes the Gallery Guide in August, with information about the exhibitions taking place during the festival. Available from the International Festival Office. Details also on the Edinburgh Gallery Guide website: www.edinburgh-galleries.co.uk

EDINBURGH INTERNATIONAL JAZZ AND BLUES FESTIVAL

This is one of the longest established jazz festivals in Europe, and is held in August during the ten days preceding the Edinburgh Festival. A wide variety of artists from traditional to avant-garde play at concert hall and cabaret venues throughout the city. For programme and booking information tel: 0131 553 4000.

Edinburgh's other festivals:

Edinburgh International Science Festival (Apr). Tel: 0131 220 3977.

Shoot and Roots – Folk Festival (Apr). Tel: 0131 554 3092.

Scottish International Children's Festival (May). Tel: 0131 225 8050.

Edinburgh's Hogmanay (Dec–Jan). Tel: 0131 557 3990.

Web information:
Information about Edinburgh International Festival events and access to websites of other Festivals: www.edinburghfestivals.co.uk

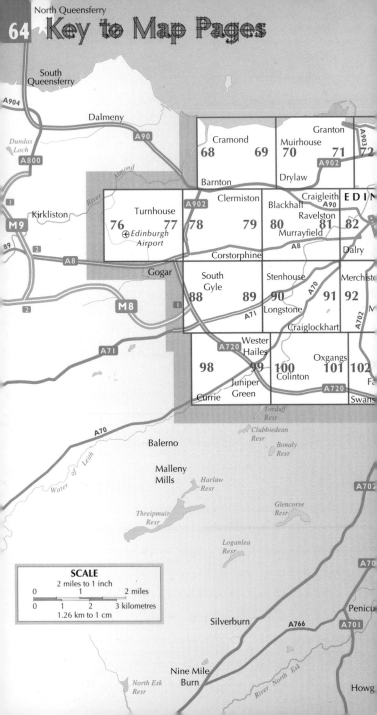

South
Queensferry

A904

Dalmeny

A90

*Dundas
Loch*

A800

River Almond

Cramond

68 **69**

Barnton

Granton

Muirhouse

70 **71**

A903

72

A902

Drylaw

Craigleith

E D I N

Kirkliston

M9

89

2

Turnhouse

76 **77**

⊕ *Edinburgh
Airport*

A902

Clermiston

78 **79**

Blackhall

Ravelston

80 **81**

Murrayfield

A90

82

Dalry

A8

Corstorphine

A8

Gogar

South
Gyle

88 **89**

M8

2

Stenhouse

90 **91**

Longstone

Craiglockhart

A70

A71

Merchisto

92 **M**

A702

1

A71

Wester
Hailes

A720

98 **99**

Currie

Juniper
Green

100
Colinton

Oxgangs

101 **102**

A720

Fa

Swans

*Torduff
Resr*

*Clubbiedean
Resr*

*Bonaly
Resr*

Balerno

Malleny
Mills

*Harlaw
Resr*

Water of Leith

*Threipmuir
Resr*

*Glencorse
Resr*

A702

*Loganlea
Resr*

A70

SCALE

2 miles to 1 inch

0   1   2 miles

0   1   2   3 kilometres

1.26 km to 1 cm

Silverburn

A766

A701

Penicu

Nine Mile
Burn

*North Esk
Resr*

River North Esk

Howg

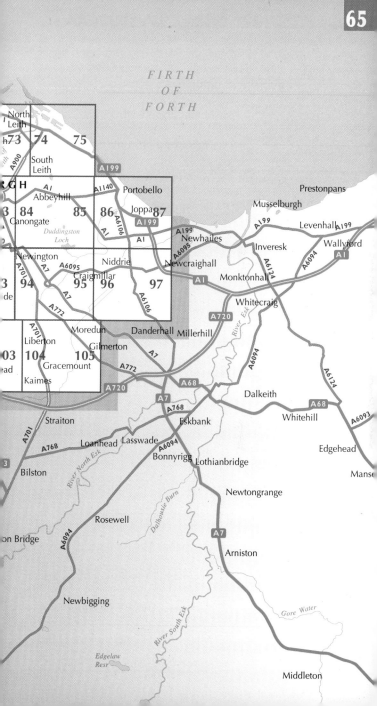

FIRTH
OF
FORTH

North
Leith
73 74 75
h73
A900
South
Leith
A199
RGH
A1
A1140
Portobello
Prestonpans
Abbeyhill
Musselburgh
3 84 85 86 Joppa 87
Canongate
A6106
A199
Levenhall
A199
Duddingston
Loch
A1
A1
Newhailes
Wallyford
A199
A6095
Inveresk
A6094
A1
Newington
A701
A7
A6095
Niddrie
Newcraighall
A7
94 Craigmillar 95 96 97
Monktonhall
3
de
A6106
A1
Whitecraig
A772
A720
River Esk
Moredun
Danderhall
Millerhill
Liberton
A701
Gilmerton
A7
A6094
103 104 105
A772
A6124
Gracemount
Kaimes
A68
A720
A7
Dalkeith
A68
A6093
Straiton
A7
A768
Whitehill
A701
A768
Loanhead Lasswade
Eskbank
Bonnyrigg Lothianbridge
Edgehead
3
River North Esk
A6094
Manse
Bilston
Newtongrange
Dalhousie Burn
Rosewell
A7
on Bridge
A6094
Arniston
Newbigging
Gore Water
River South Esk
Edgelaw
Resr
Middleton

	Motorway
	Dual carriageway
	Main through route
	Main link road
	Other road
	Lane / Drive
	Shopping area
	Bus route
→	One way street
○	Traffic lights
	Walkway
	Path
	Picturesque road
⇌	Railway / Main station
⊕ X74	Airport coach terminal / Bus terminus
P T	Car park / Taxi rank
ℹ ♦♦	Tourist information centre / Toilet
★ MGM ★ King's	Cinema / Theatre or Public hall
○ ●	Museum or Gallery / Post Office

	Dense built-up area
	Open residential area
	Industrial area
	Open land
	Park
	Woodland
	Sport / Recreation area
	Cemetery
EH5	Postal boundary
	Council boundary
🔆 🔆	Viewpoint
≋ ⌐	Swimming pool / Golf course
B T	Bowling green / Tennis court
▲ ┳	Principal hotel / Tower block
🔺 🚐 △	Sailing centre / Caravan / Camping site
✚ Ⓟ Ⓕ	Hospital / Police / Fire station
★ +	Library / Church
△ ▲	Primary / Secondary school
▭ Ⓡ⁰	Public building / Consulate

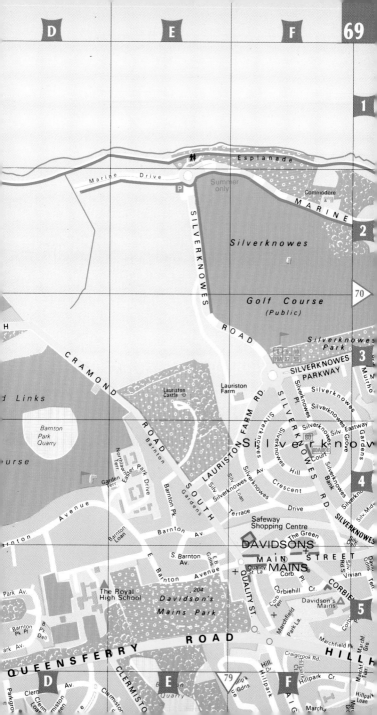

1

Esplanade

Marine   Drive

P

Summer
only

Commodore

M A R I N E

Silverknowes

2

Golf Course
(Public)

70

R O A D

SILVERKNOWES

*Silverknowes
Park*

SILVERKNOWES
PARKWAY

3

Murho

H

C R A M O N D

Lauriston
Castle

Lauriston
Farm

LAURISTON FARM RD.

Silverknowes

Silverknowes Pl.

Silverknowes

Silverknowes Eastway

Silv.

d Links

R O A D

Barnton
Park Quarry

Barnton

Northlawkster Terr.

Easter Park Drive

Barnton Pk.

Garden
Terr.

S i l v e r k n o w e s

Silverknowes Hill

Silverknowes
Court

80
80A 80B

Silverknowes
Bank

Silverknowes

4

urse

A v e n u e

SOUTH

Barnton
Gardens

Silv.

Silverknowes Av.

Silverknowes Loan

Silverknowes
Terrace

Crescent

Drive

SILVERKNOWES RD.

Silv. Mid

Silv. Marsh

arnton

Barnton
Loan

Barnton   Av.

Safeway
Shopping Centre

The Green

Silv.
Rd S.

Silv. Vivian

Dav
Gdns

Park Av.

S. Barnton
Av.

E. B. Gdns

E.
Barnton

DAVIDSONS

MAIN   **STREET**

CORBIE

CORBIE

The Royal
High School

S. Barnton
Av.

Avenue

Quality
St La.

Corb.

MAINS

Corb.

Corbiehill Cr.

Corbiehill

Davidson's
Mains

Davidson's
Mains Park

204

QUALITY ST.

Cro
Terr.

Marchfield
Park La.

5

Barnton
Pk. Pl.

B
Pk.
Dell

R O A D

Hill.
Dr

Marchfield Pk.

Marchfield Gro.

H I L L

Park Av.

QUEENSFERRY

CLERMISTO

Barton
Quarry

79

Clk.
Gdns

Hillpark Cr.

A I G

Hillpar
Loan

Marchfi

Marchfi

Mai
Grd

Park grov

Clerm

Clermiston
Loan

Clermiston Mean

Clermisto

A B C

1

Granton Point

Long
Craig Rd.
Long
Craig
Rigg

W

G r a n t o n

Craigroyston Ho.

Muirhouse

'84

D R I V E

N E

West Shore Road

Gypsy

Brae

Granton
Ho.

G a s   W o r k

2

Civil Service
Sports Ground

W E S T

B

B

G

Br.

M. Gdns

Vale Pk.

Salvesen
Terr.

Salv. Gdns.

Pennywell
Villas
Pennywell
Cotts.

69

Muirhouse
Mains

Salvesen

Salv.
Cr.

Salvesen
Gdns.

PARKWAY

Muirhouse
Parkway

Pennywell
Pl.

W. Pilton
Dr.

W. Pilton Ln.

W. Pilton St.

W. Pilton Gr.

West

M U I R H O U S E

May Ct.

Fidra Ct.

Penn. Medway

Pennywell
Gro.

Pirniehall

W. Pilton Lea

Craigmuir

3

rknowes

Oxcars
Ct.

Birnie's
Ct.

Muirho.
Ct.

Gunnet
Ct.

81

81A 81B

Pennywell
Gardens

14 28

Northview
Ct.

Crescent
Bank

W. Pilton
Crossway

Inchmickery
Ct.

Muirho.
Gdns.

Martello
Ct.

Pennywell Loan

Muirho. Cr.

Penn.
Terr.

West
Pilton
Rise

West
Pilton
Bank

West
Pilton

West
Pilton

West
Pilton
Park

**West
Pilton**

AY

Muirho.

Muirhouse
Drive

Muirhouse
Green
Pk.

Muirho.
Way

Muirho.

A

V.

Muirho.

W P View

Inchview

Ferry
Rd.
Gdns

Ferry Rd.

Ferry Rd.
Gro.

Ferry

Ferry

Roa

R O

4

nowes

Silverknowes

Silv. Eastway

Silv.
Gardens

Muirhouse
Park

Silverknowes
Brae

Silv. Green

Muir
Ho.

Muirhouse
Park

Muirhouse
Terr.

Muirhouse
Bank

Muirhouse
Green

Muirhouse

Craigroyston

EH4

F E R R Y

P

Easter Drylaw

E Drylaw
Way

RO

SILVERKNOWES RD. EAST

Silv. Midway

Silverknowes
View

Silv.
Southway

Silv.

Muirho.

E E T

David
Ho.

Silv.
Neuk

Wester Drylaw Place

Wester
Drylaw

GROATHILL   ROAD   NORTH

Easter

E. Drylaw

E. Drylaw
Gardens

E. Dry
Loan

E. Drylaw
Av.

E. Drylaw
Avenue

Easter

5

CORBIEHILL

Rd's.
Vivian

B

Davidson's
Terr.

Corbiehill
Terr.

Corbiehill
Gro.

Corbiehill
Cr.

Corbiehill
Av.

CORBIEHILL   ROAD

Drylaw
Ho.

Drylaw
Ho. Gdns.

Drylaw Ho. Padd.

W. Drylaw

D r y l a w

Drylaw

W. Drylaw
Av.

Ferryhill

Easter

Drylaw

htfield Pk.

H o. Hill
Brae

Ho. Hill
Gro.

H o. Hill
Green

House o'Hill Cr.

House o' Hill Row

House o'Hill Road

Houseo'Hill

House o' Hill
Gdns.

W E S T E R D R Y L A W D R I V E

Drylaw
Gdns.

Drylaw
Crescent

W. Drylaw
Row

Goat

H I L L H O U S E   R O A D

Matchf.
Gro.

Matchf.
Pk.

80

13 13A

Drylaw

A

PH

PH

B

Whitehall

Drylaw
Green
Ct.

C

T E L F O R D

Hillpar
Loan

Hillpark
Way

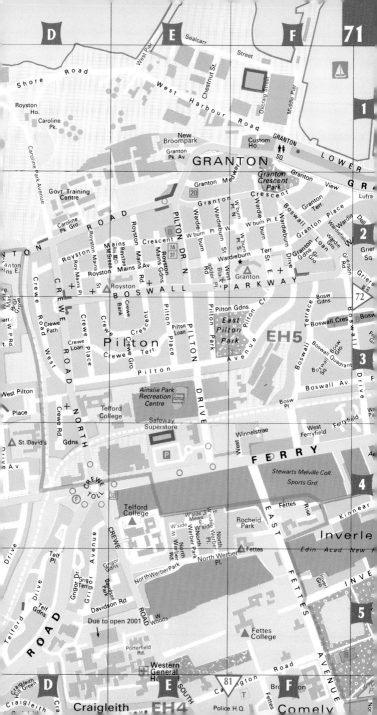

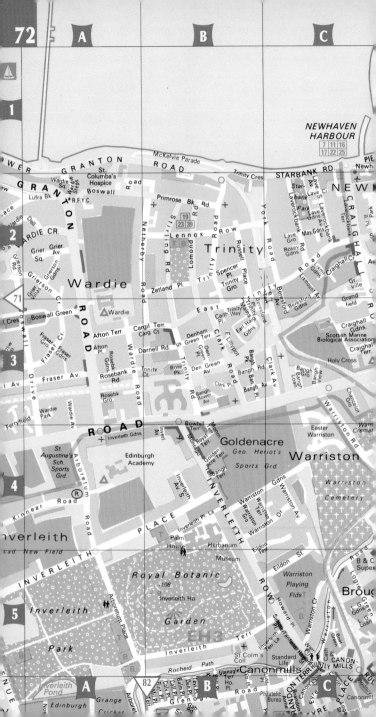

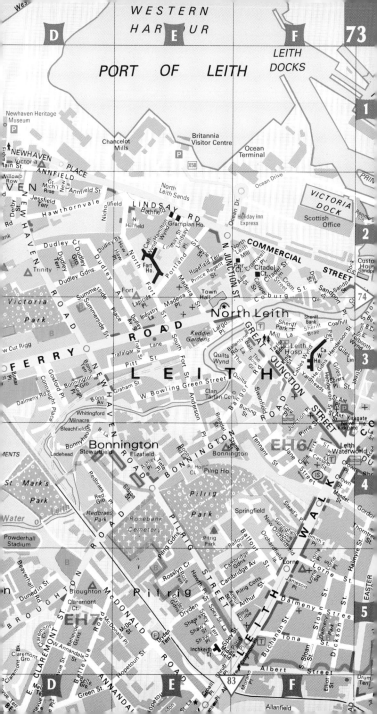

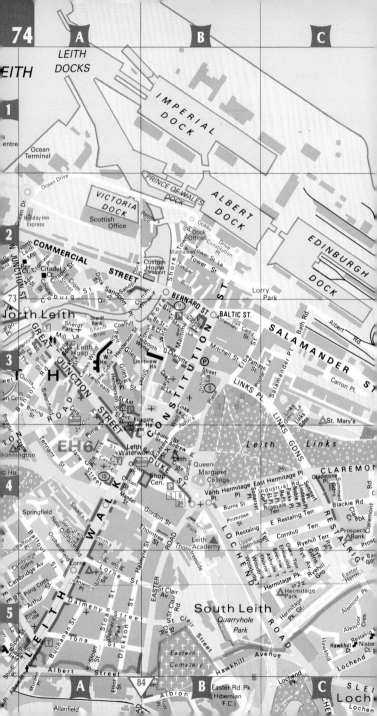

1

2

3

Marine

Esplanade

Sewage
Works

4

SEAFIELD

Seafield
Cemetery &
Crematorium

Seat St

Seafield

ROAD

ARK

Seafield Pl

Pirniefield

Boothacre La

Pirniefield Bank

Seaforth

Seafield Av

Pirniefield
Terr
Rd

Bank
Pl

Bank Terr

Prospect Bank Pl

Pirniefield Gdns

Pirniefield Gro

Pirniefield Place

✚ Eastern
General
Hospital

Craigentinny Av. North

Seafield
Recreation
Ground

Seafield Way

FILLYSIDE RD

Seafield Way

stalrig

Restalrig

Circus

Ct

Findlay Gdns

Findlay
Cotts

Findlay Medway

Findlay Gro

Findlay
Avenue

57'

131/2A

Craigentinny

Golf Course

Nantwich
Dr

AVENUE FILLYSIDE DRIVE

Fillyside Terr

5

Home

SEA

Restalrig
Square

D R I V E

Sleigh Gdns

CRAI

E

(Public)

85

Fillyside Av.

F

RESTALRIG

Gdns

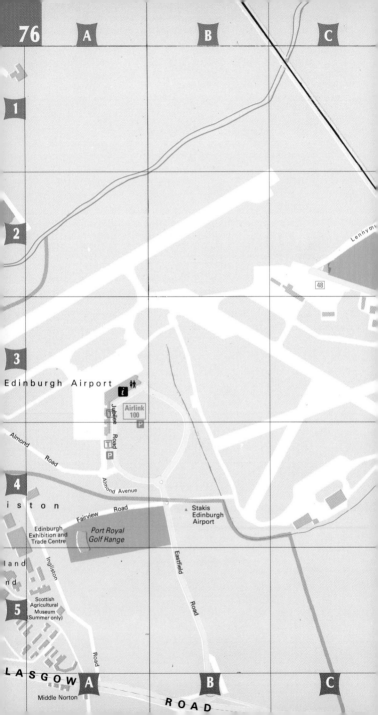

1

2

Lennymu

48

3

Edinburgh Airport

Airlink
100
P

Jubilee
T

Road

Almond
Road

T
P

Almond Avenue

4

i s t o n

Fairview Road

Stakis
Edinburgh
Airport

Edinburgh
Exhibition and
Trade Centre

Port Royal
Golf Range

l a n d
n d

Ingliston

Scottish
Agricultural
Museum
(Summer only)

5

Eastfield Road

Road

LASGOW A B C

Middle Norton

R O A D

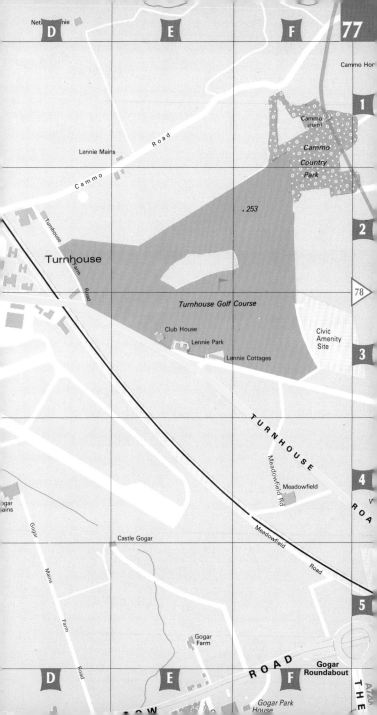

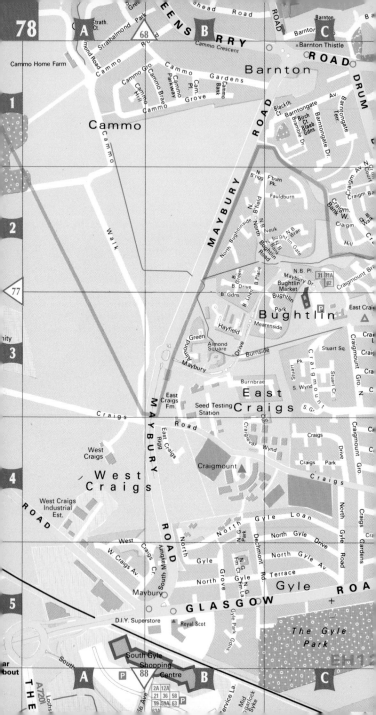

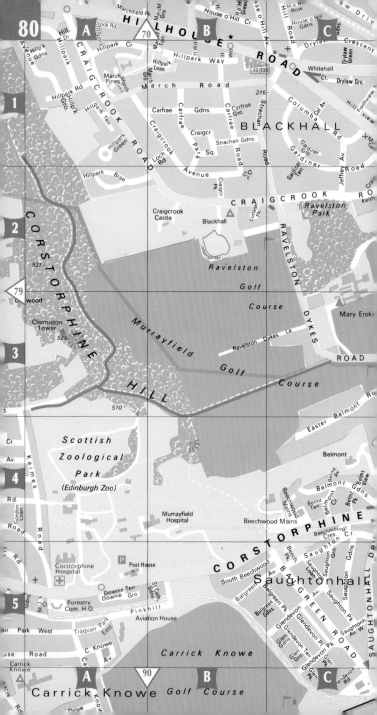

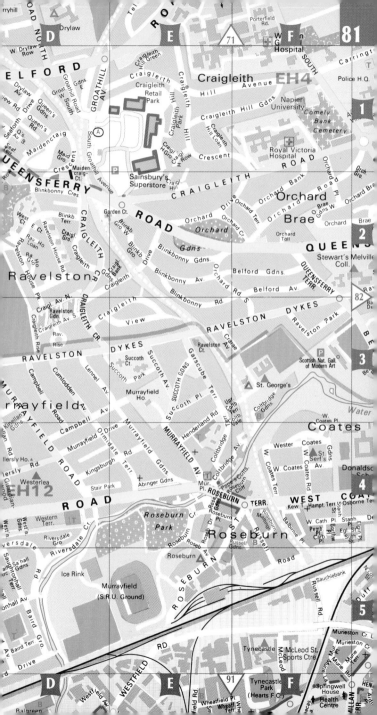

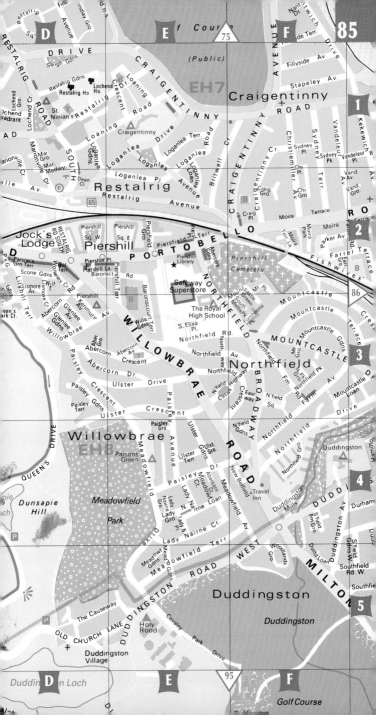

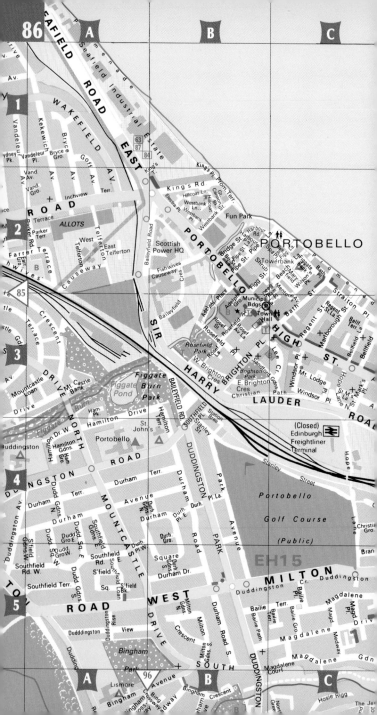

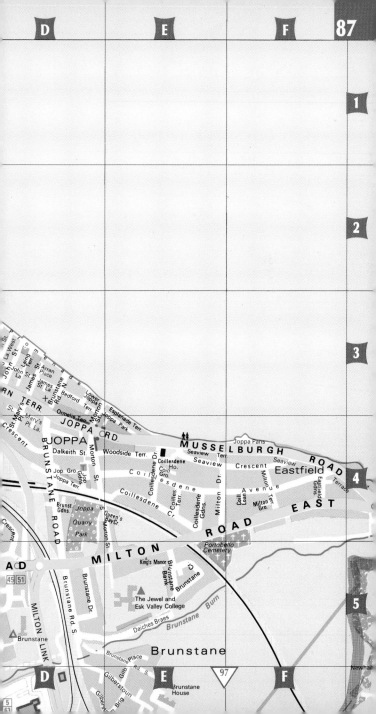

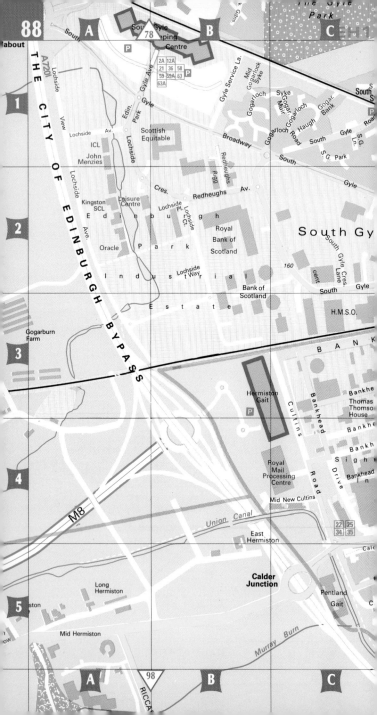

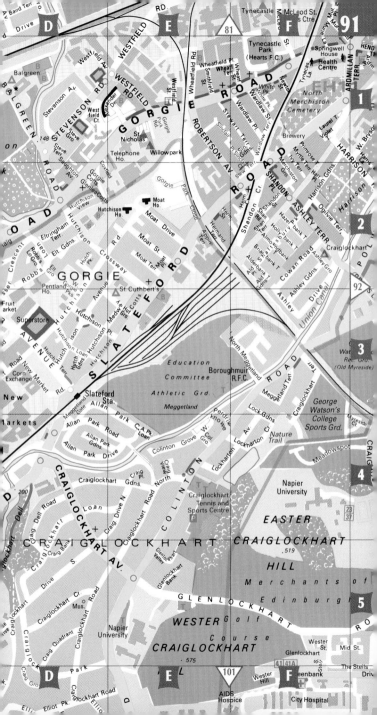

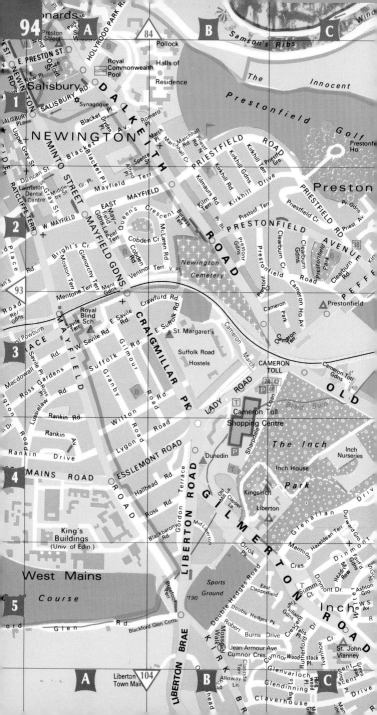

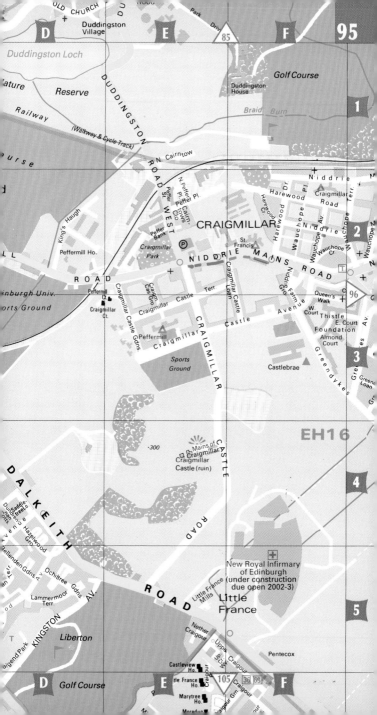

A   B   C

1

2

3

4

5

Dudddingston
VE
Magdalene
Medw
DUDDINGSTON
Magda
Gd
Magdalene
Court
Bingham
Park
86
North
Greens
Hosie Rigg
The
Lismore
Bingham C Avenue
Bingham Crescent
South
Parrotshot
The Jewel
Corbiewynd
Bingham
Broadway
Bingham
Cross-
way
Bingham
Pl.
Bingham
Bldg
Bingham
Drive
Jewel
Park
Vexhim Park
Bingham
Way
Row
Bingham
Medway
PARK
South
Parrotshot
Niddrie Mill Cr.
Mains
Terrace
Cleekim Rd.
Cleekim Ct.
ddrie
Mains
Hay
Hay
Niddrie Mill Dr.
Niddrie Mill Av.
Cleekim Dr.
Peacocktail Ct.
New
Ind.
Blackchapel
Ct.
raigmillar
Road
Pe Terr.
Road
Road
Hay PI.
Hay
Drive
Hay
Drive
Mains
Drive
Niddrie Mill Gro.
N Mill PI.
N Terr.
N Mill
Av.
Blackchapel
Rd.
Quarry
Cotts.
Hay
Terr.
Hay
Sq.
Wauchope
NIDDRIE
Niddrie
Cleekimmin Rd
Cleekimfield
NIDDRIE
MAINS
ROAD
Mar.
Gro.
NEWCRAIG
Wauchope
Ct.
N
MAINS
S
Niddrie Marischal Rd
Mar.
Gro.
THE
Wisp Green
Wisp
T
AD
Chapel
Ct.
Mar.
Gdns.
Mar
Marischal
Pl.
Mar
Niddrie Marischal
Niddrie Marischal Ct.
J. Kane Centre
WISP
ueen
Walk
95
Greendykes
Av.
Niddrie Mar
Mar
Green
N
House Pk
N House
Gro.
Gt Car.
St
Gt Car.
St
Niddrie
Burn
E. Court
oundation
Almond
Court
Greendykes
Road
Greendykes Terr.
Greendykes
Niddrie
Mar
Dr.
Greendykes
N House
Ho. Av.
Niddrie
House
Dr.
Niddrie
Policies
reendykes
Greend
Loan
Greendykes
21
N House
Gdns.
Greendykes Gdns.
Wauchope
Ho.
Greendykes
Ho.
Road
H16
Bankfield
M
I
L
L
E
R
H
I
L
L
THE
WISP
Cau
A   B   C

A
Edmonstone
Cottage
B
Edmonstone
Mains
Toscana
Court
C
Woolr
Edmonstone
Edmonstons

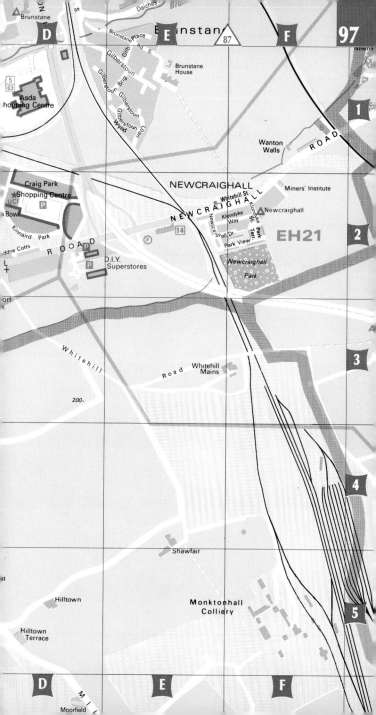

Brunstane

Newna

Brunstane Place

Daiches

Brun

87

Brunstane House

Gilberstoun Brig

Gilberstoun

Gilberstoun Loan

Gilberstoun Wynd

5
63

Asda
hopping Centre

1

Wanton Walls

R O A D

NEWCRAIGHALL

Miners' Institute

Craig Park
Shopping Centre

UCI

NEWCRAIGHALL

Whitehill St.

Newcraighall

EH21

Klondyke Way

Klondyke Park St.

Newcraighall Dr.

Kinnaird Park

R O O A D

ddrie Cotts

2

F

14

Park View

Newcraighall
Park

D.I.Y.
Superstores

P

P

ort

Whitehill

Road

Whitehill
Mains

3

200·

4

Shawfair

Hilltown

Monktonhall
Colliery

5

Hilltown
Terrace

M I

Moorfield

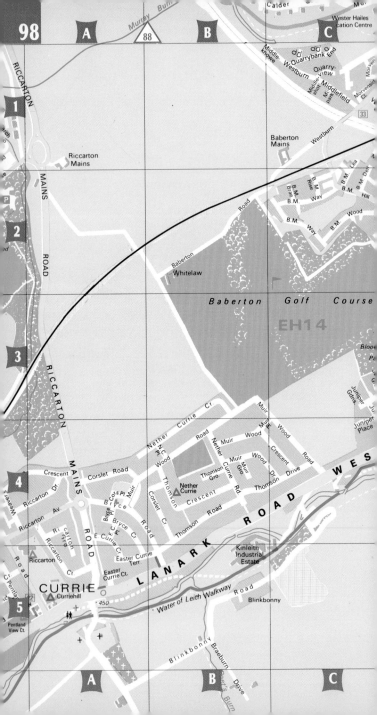

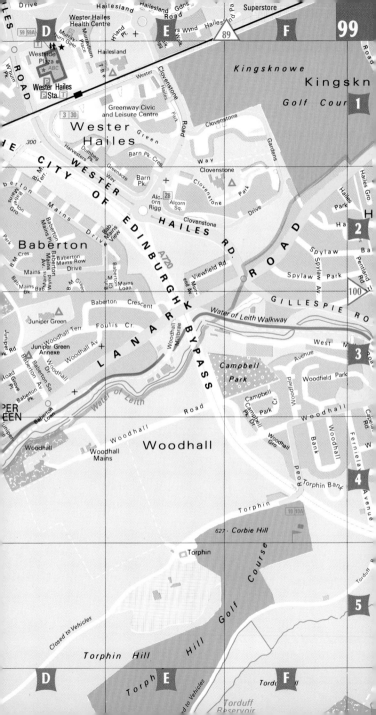

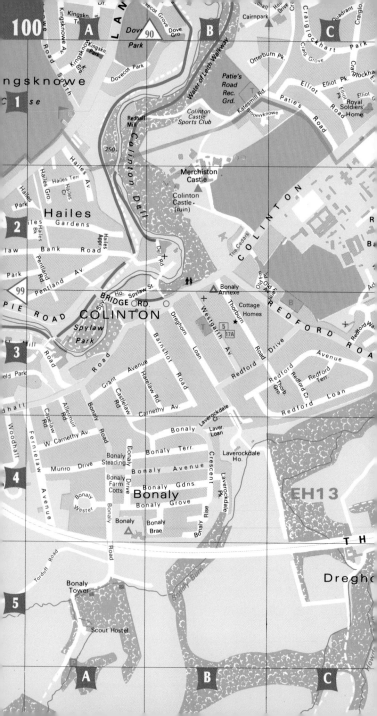

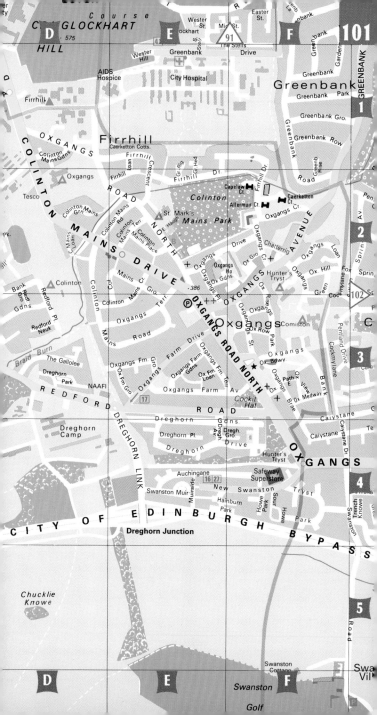

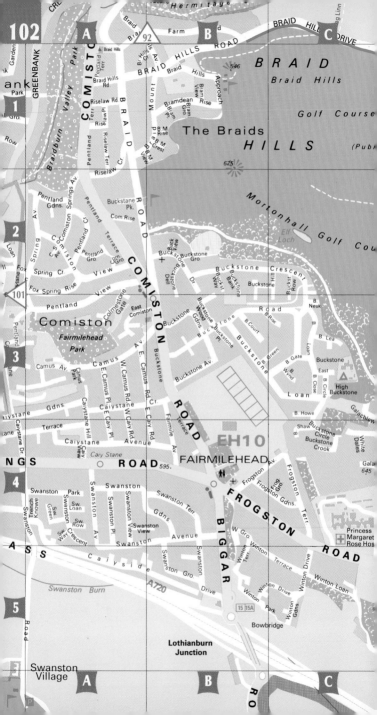

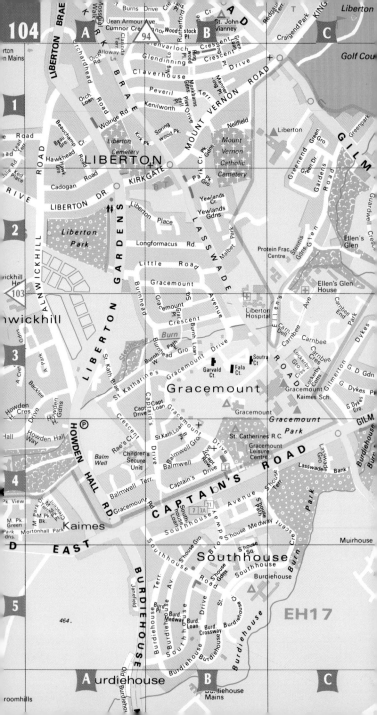

Index to Streets

Post Town Abbreviations

Dalk.	Dalkeith	Muss.	Musselburgh
Jun.Grn.	Juniper Green	Newbr.	Newbridge

District Abbreviations

Cram.	Cramond	Newcr.	Newcraighall
David.	Davidson Mains	Wool.	Woolmet
Inglis.	Ingliston		

General Abbreviations

Acad.	Academy	Fld.	Field	N.	North
All.	Alley	Flds.	Fields	Par.	Parade
App.	Approach	Fm.	Farm	Pk.	Park
Arc.	Arcade	G.P.O.	General Post Office	Pl.	Place
Av.	Avenue	Gall.	Gallery	Pt.	Port
Bdy.	Broadway	Gdn.	Garden	Quad.	Quadrant
Bk.	Bank	Gdns.	Gardens	R.C.	Roman Catholic
Bldgs.	Buildings	Gra.	Grange	R.F.C.	Rugby Football
Bri.	Bridge	Grd.	Ground		Club
Cem.	Cemetery	Grn.	Green	Rd.	Road
Cen.	Central, Centre	Grns.	Greens	Ri.	Rise
Cft.	Croft	Gro.	Grove	S.	South
Ch.	Church	H.Q.	Headquarters	Sch.	School
Circ.	Circle	Ho.	House	Sq.	Square
Clo.	Close	Hos.	Houses	St.	Saint, Street
Coll.	College	Hosp.	Hospital	Sta.	Station
Cor.	Corner	Hts.	Heights	Ter.	Terrace
Cotts.	Cottages	Ind.	Industrial	Twr.	Tower
Crem.	Crematorium	Junct.	Junction	Vills.	Villas
Cres.	Crescent	La.	Lane	Vw.	View
Ct.	Court	Ln.	Loan	W.	West
Cts.	Courts	Lo.	Lodge	Wd.	Wood
Dr.	Drive	Lwr.	Lower	Wds.	Woods
E.	East	Mem.	Memorial	Wf.	Wharf
Esp.	Esplanade	Mkt.	Market	Wk.	Walk
Est.	Estate	Ms.	Mews	Wr.	Wester
Ex.	Exchange	Mt.	Mount	Yd.	Yard

Abbey La. EH8	84	B2	Adams Well EH13	100	C2	Albert St. EH7	73	F5
Abbey Strand EH8	84	A3	Adelphi Gro. EH15	86	B3	Albert Ter. EH10	92	B2
Abbey St. EH7	84	B2	Adelphi Pl. EH15	86	B3	Albion Pl. EH7	84	B1
Montrose Ter.			Admiral Ter. EH10	92	C1	Albion Rd. EH7	84	B1
Abbeyhill EH8	84	A3	Admiralty St. EH6	73	F2	Albion Ter. EH7	84	B1
Abbeyhill Cres. EH8	84	A2	Advocates Clo. EH1	83	E3	Albyn Pl. EH2	82	C2
Abbeymount EH8	84	A2	*High St.*			Alcorn Rigg EH14	99	E2
Abbotsford Ct. EH10	92	B2	Affleck Ct. EH12	78	B4	Alcorn Sq. EH14	99	E2
Abbotsford Cres.	92	B2	*Craigievar Wynd*			Alderbank Gdns.	91	F2
EH10			Afton Pl. EH5	72	A3	EH11		
Abbotsford Pk. EH10	92	B2	Afton Ter. EH5	72	A3	Alderbank Pl. EH11	91	F2
Abercorn Av. EH8	85	E3	Agnew Ter. EH6	73	D3	Alderbank Ter. EH11	91	F2
Abercorn Cotts. EH15	85	E5	*Connaught Pl.*			Alemoor Cres. EH7	74	C5
The Causeway			Ainslie Pl. EH3	82	B2	Alemoor Pk. EH7	74	C5
Abercorn Ct. EH8	85	E4	Airlie Pl. EH3	83	D1	Alexander Dr. EH11	91	D1
Abercorn Cres. EH8	85	D3	Aitchison's Pl. EH15	86	B2	Alfred Pl. EH9	94	A2
Abercorn Dr. EH8	85	D3	*Figgate St.*			Allan Pk. Cres. EH14	91	D3
Abercorn Gdns. EH8	85	E2	Aitkenhill EH11	90	C2	Allan Pk. Dr. EH14	91	D4
Abercorn Gro. EH8	85	D3	Alan Breck Gdns.	79	E2	Allan Pk. Gdns.	91	D4
Abercorn Rd. EH8	85	D3	EH4			EH14		
Abercorn Ter. EH15	86	C3	Albany La. EH1	83	E2	Allan Pk. Ln. EH14	91	E4
Abercromby Pl. EH3	83	D2	Albany St. EH1	83	E2	Allan Pk. Rd. EH14	91	D4
Abinger Gdns. EH12	81	E4	Albany St. La. EH1	83	E2	Allan St. EH4	82	B1
Academy Pk. EH6	74	B4	Albert Pl. EH7	83	F1	Allandale EH13	100	A3
Academy St. EH6	74	B4	Albert Rd. EH6	74	C3	*Spylaw St.*		

Allanfield EH7 84 A1
Allermuir Ct. EH13 101 F2
Allermuir Rd. EH13 100 A3
Alloway Ln. EH16 104 A1
Almond Av. EH12 76 A4
Almond Bk. Cotts. 68 B3
EH4
Whitehouse Rd.
Almond Ct. EH4 68 A5
Almond Ct. EH16 95 F3
Almond Grn. EH12 78 B3
Almond Rd. EH12 76 A4
Almond Sq. EH12 78 B3
Almondbank Ter. 91 F2
EH11
Alnwickhill Ct. EH16 103 F3
Alnwickhill Cres. 103 F3
EH16
Alnwickhill Dr. EH16 103 F3
Alnwickhill Gdns. 103 F3
EH16
Alnwickhill Gro. 103 F3
EH16
Alnwickhill Ln. EH16 103 F3
Alnwickhill Pk. EH16 104 A3
Alnwickhill Rd. 104 A3
EH16
Alnwickhill Ter. 103 F3
EH16
Alnwickhill Vw. 103 F3
EH16
Alva Pl. EH7 84 B2
Alva St. EH2 82 B3
Alvanley Ter. EH9 92 C1
Whitehouse Ln.
Anchorfield EH6 73 E2
Lindsay Rd.
Anderson Pl. EH6 73 E3
Andrew Wd. Ct. EH6 72 C1
Newhaven Main St.
Angle Pk. Ter. EH11 92 A1
Ann St. EH4 82 B2
Annandale St. EH7 83 E1
Annandale St. La. 83 F1
EH7
Annfield EH6 73 D2
Annfield St. EH6 73 D2
Antigua St. EH1 83 F1
Anworth Vills. EH12 89 F1
Saughton Rd. N.
Appin Ter. EH14 91 E2
Arboretum Av. EH4 82 B1
Arboretum Pl. EH3 72 A5
Arboretum Rd. EH3 72 A4
Archibald Pl. EH3 83 D4
Arden St. EH9 93 D1
Ardmillan Pl. EH11 92 A1
Ardmillan Ter. EH11 91 F1
Ardmillan Ter. La. 92 A1
EH11
Ardmillan Ter.
Ardshiel Av. EH4 79 E2
Argyle Cres. EH15 86 C3
Argyle Pk. Ter. EH9 93 E1
Argyle Pl. EH9 93 E1
Argyle St. EH6 73 E2
Argyll Ter. EH11 82 B4
Arnott Gdns. EH14 90 B5
Arran Pl. EH15 87 D3
Arthur Pl. EH6 73 F5
Arthur St.
Arthur St. EH6 73 F5
Arthur St. La. EH6 73 F5
Ashley Dr. EH11 91 F3
Ashley Gdns. EH11 91 F3
Ashley Gro. EH11 91 F2
Ashley Pl. EH6 73 E4
Ashley Ter. EH11 91 F2
Ashton Gro. EH16 94 C5

Ashton Vills. EH15 87 D4
Brunstane Rd.
Ashville Ter. EH6 74 C5
Assembly St. EH6 74 B3
Atholl Cres. EH3 82 B4
Atholl Cres. La. EH3 82 B4
Atholl Pl. EH3 82 B4
Atholl Ter. EH11 82 B4
Auchingane EH10 101 E4
Auchinleck Brae EH6 72 C2
Auchinleck Ct.
Auchinleck Ct. EH6 72 C2
Auchinleck's Brae 69 F5
EH4
Main St.
Avenue Vills. EH4 82 A1
Avon Gro. EH4 68 A4
Avon Pl. EH4 68 A4
Avon Rd. EH4 68 A4
Avondale Pl. EH3 82 C1

B
Baberton Av., 99 D3
Jun.Grn. EH14
Baberton Cres., 99 D3
Jun.Grn. EH14
Baberton Ln., 99 D4
Jun.Grn. EH14
Baberton Mains Av. 99 D2
EH14
Baberton Mains Bk. 99 D2
EH14
Baberton Mains Brae 98 C2
EH14
Baberton Mains Ct. 99 E2
EH14
Baberton Mains Cres. 99 D2
EH14
Baberton Mains Dell 98 C2
EH14
Baberton Mains Dr. 99 D2
EH14
Baberton Mains Gdns. 98 C1
EH14
Baberton Mains Grn. 99 D2
EH14
Baberton Mains Gro. 99 D2
EH14
Baberton Mains Hill 98 C2
EH14
Baberton Mains Lea 98 C2
EH14
Baberton Mains Ln. 99 E2
EH14
Baberton Mains Pk. 99 D2
EH14
Baberton Mains Pl. 99 D2
EH14
Baberton Mains Ri. 98 C2
EH14
Baberton Mains Row 99 D2
EH14
Baberton Mains Ter. 99 D2
EH14
Baberton Mains Vw. 99 E2
EH14
Baberton Mains Way 98 C2
EH14
Baberton Mains Wd. 98 C2
EH14
Baberton Mains 99 D2
Wynd EH14
Baberton Pk., 99 D3
Jun.Grn. EH14
Baberton Rd., 98 B2
Currie EH14
Baberton Sq., 99 D3
Jun.Grn. EH14

Back Dean EH4 82 A3
Back Row EH14 91 D4
Back Sta. Rd. EH15 95 E2
Peffer St.
Backlee EH16 104 A3
Baileyfield Cres. 86 B3
EH15
Baileyfield Rd. EH15 86 B3
Bailie Gro. EH15 86 C5
Bailie Path EH15 86 B5
Bailie Pl. EH15 86 C5
Bailie Ter. EH15 86 B5
Bajlie Ter. EH15 86 B5
Baird Av. EH12 81 D5
Baird Dr. EH12 91 D1
Baird Gdns. EH12 81 D5
Baird Gro. EH12 81 D5
Baird Ter. EH12 81 D5
Bakehouse Clo. EH8 83 F3
Canongate
Baker's Pl. EH3 82 C1
Kerr St.
Balbirnie Pl. EH12 81 F4
Balcarres Ct. EH10 92 C4
Balcarres St. EH10 92 A4
Balderston Gdns. 94 C5
EH16
Balderston Gdns. N. 94 C5
EH16
Balfour Pl. EH6 73 E4
Balfour St. EH6 73 F4
Balfron Ln. EH4 79 D2
Balgreen Av. EH12 80 B5
Balgreen Gdns. EH12 80 B5
Balgreen Pk. EH12 80 B5
Balgreen Rd. EH11 91 D1
Balgreen Rd. EH12 80 C5
Ballantyne La. EH6 73 F3
Ballantyne Rd. EH6 73 F3
Balmoral Pl. EH3 82 C1
Balmwell Av. EH16 104 B4
Balmwell Gro. EH16 104 B4
Balmwell Pk. EH16 104 B4
Balmwell Ter. EH16 104 A4
Baltic St. EH6 74 B3
Bangholm Av. EH5 72 B3
Bangholm Bower Av. 72 B3
EH5
Bangholm Gro. EH5 72 C3
Bangholm Ln. EH5 72 C3
Bangholm Pk. EH5 72 B3
Bangholm Pl. EH5 72 B3
Bangholm Rd. EH5 72 B3
Bangholm Ter. EH3 72 B4
Bangholm Vw. EH5 72 C3
Bangholm Vills. EH5 70 B4
Ferry Rd.
Bangor Rd. EH6 73 E3
Bank St. EH1 83 E3
Bankhead Av. EH11 89 D3
Bankhead Bdy. EH11 88 C3
Bankhead Crossway 88 C3
N. EH11
Bankhead Crossway 88 C4
S. EH11
Bankhead Dr. EH11 88 C3
Bankhead Ln. EH11 89 D4
Bankhead Medway 89 D3
EH11
Bankhead Pl. EH11 89 D3
Bankhead St. EH11 89 D4
Bankhead Ter. EH11 88 C4
Bankhead Way EH11 88 C4
Barclay Pl. EH10 92 C1
Barclay Ter. EH10 92 C1
Barn Pk. EH14 99 E2
Barn Pk. Cres. EH14 99 E1
Barnshot Rd. EH13 100 B3
Barntalloch Ct. EH12 78 B4
Craigievar Wynd

Barnton Av. EH4 69 D4
Barnton Av. W. EH4 68 B4
Barnton Brae EH4 68 B4
Barnton Ct. EH4 68 B5
Barnton Gdns. EH4 69 E4
Barnton Gro. EH4 68 B5
Barnton Ln. EH4 69 E4
Barnton Pk. EH4 69 E4
Barnton Pk. Av. EH4 68 C5
Barnton Pk. Cres. EH4 68 B5
Barnton Pk. Dell EH4 69 D5
Barnton Pk. Dr. EH4 68 C5
Barnton Pk. Gdns. EH4 68 C5
Barnton Pk. Gro. EH4 68 C5
Barnton Pk. Pl. EH4 69 D5
Barnton Pk. Vw. EH4 68 B5
Barnton Pk. Wd. EH4 68 B5
Barntongate Av. EH4 78 C1
Barntongate Dr. EH4 78 C1
Barntongate Ter. EH4 78 C1
Baronscourt Rd. EH8 85 D2
Baronscourt Ter. EH8 85 E2
Barony Pl. EH3 83 E1
Barony St. EH3 83 E1
Barony Ter. EH12 79 E4
Bath Pl. EH15 86 C2
Bath Rd. EH6 74 C3
Bath St. EH15 86 C3
Bath St. La. EH15 86 C3
Bath St.
Bathfield EH6 73 E2
Baxter's Pl. EH1 83 F2
Leith Wk.
Beach La. EH15 86 C2
Beauchamp Gro. EH16 104 A1
Beauchamp Rd. EH16 104 A1
Beaufort Rd. EH9 93 E2
Beaverbank Pl. EH7 72 C5
Beaverhall Rd. EH7 73 D5
Bedford Ct. EH4 82 B1
Bedford St. EH4 82 B1
Bedford Ter. EH15 87 D3
Beechmount Cres. EH12 80 C4
Beechmount Pk. EH12 80 C5
Beechwood Mains EH12 80 C4
Beechwood Ter. EH6 74 C5
Belford Av. EH4 81 F2
Belford Bri. EH4 82 A3
Belford Gdns. EH4 81 F2
Belford Ms. EH4 82 A3
Belford Pk. EH4 82 A3
Belford Pl. EH4 82 A3
Belford Rd. EH4 82 A3
Belford Ter. EH4 82 A3
Belford Rd.
Belgrave Cres. EH4 82 A2
Belgrave Cres. La. EH4 82 A2
Belgrave Gdns. EH12 79 F4
Belgrave Ms. EH4 82 A2
Belgrave Pl. EH4 82 A2
Belgrave Rd. EH12 79 F4
Belgrave Ter. EH12 79 F5
Belhaven Pl. EH10 92 C4
Belhaven Ter. EH10 92 C4

Bell Pl. EH3 82 C1
Bellenden Gdns. EH16 95 D5
Bellevue EH3 83 E1
Bellevue EH7 83 E1
Bellevue Cres. EH3 83 E1
Bellevue Gdns. EH7 73 D5
Bellevue Gro. EH7 83 E1
Bellevue La. EH7 83 E1
Bellevue Pl. EH7 83 E1
Bellevue Rd. EH7 83 E1
Bellevue St. EH7 83 E1
Bellevue Ter. EH7 83 E1
Bellfield La. EH15 86 C3
Bellfield St. EH15 86 C3
Bellfield Ter. EH15 86 C3
Bells Brae EH4 82 B3
Bell's Mills EH4 82 A3
Bell's Wynd EH1 83 E3
High St.
Belmont Av. EH12 80 C4
Belmont Cres. EH12 80 C4
Belmont Gdns. EH12 80 C4
Belmont Pk. EH12 80 C4
Belmont Rd., Jun.Grn. EH14 98 C3
Belmont Ter. EH12 80 C4
Belmont Vw. EH12 80 C4
Belvedere Pk. EH6 72 C2
Beresford Av. EH5 72 C2
Beresford Gdns. EH5 72 C3
Beresford Pl. EH5 72 B3
Beresford Ter. EH5 72 C2
Bernard St. EH6 74 B2
Bernard Ter. EH8 83 F5
Berry Sq. EH15 86 B2
Figgate St.
Biggar Rd. EH10 102 B4
Bingham Av. EH15 96 A1
Bingham Bdy. EH15 96 A1
Bingham Cres. EH15 96 B1
Bingham Crossway EH15 96 B1
Bingham Dr. EH15 96 B1
Bingham Medway EH15 96 A1
Bingham Pl. EH15 96 A1
Bingham St. EH15 96 A1
Bingham Way EH15 96 A1
Birch Ct. EH4 78 C1
Birnies Ct. EH4 70 A3
Blackadder Pl. EH5 71 E2
Blackbarony Rd. EH16 94 B4
Blackchapel Clo. EH15 96 C2
Blackchapel Rd. EH15 96 C2
Blacket Av. EH9 94 A1
Blacket Pl. EH9 94 A1
Blackford Av. EH9 93 E3
Blackford Bk. EH9 93 E3
Blackford Glen Rd. EH16 93 F5
Blackford Hill EH9 93 D4
Blackford Hill Gro. EH9 93 E4
Blackford Hill Ri. EH9 93 E4
Blackford Hill Vw. EH9 93 E4
Blackford Rd. EH9 93 D2
Blackfriars St. EH1 83 F3
Blackie Rd. EH6 74 C4
Blackthorn Ct. EH4 78 C1

Blackwood Cres. EH9 93 F1
Blaeberry Gdns. EH4 78 C1
Blair St. EH1 83 E3
Blantyre Ter. EH10 92 B2
Bleachfield EH6 73 D4
Blenheim Pl. EH7 83 F2
Blinkbonny Av. EH4 81 E2
Blinkbonny Cres. EH4 81 D2
Blinkbonny Gdns. EH4 81 E2
Blinkbonny Gro. EH4 81 E2
Blinkbonny Gro. W. EH4 81 E2
Blinkbonny Rd. EH4 81 E2
Blinkbonny Rd., Currie EH14 98 B5
Blinkbonny Ter. EH4 81 D2
Boat Grn. EH3 72 C5
Bogsmill Rd. EH14 90 C5
Bonaly Av. EH13 100 A4
Bonaly Brae EH13 100 B4
Bonaly Cres. EH13 100 B4
Bonaly Dr. EH13 100 A4
Bonaly Fm. Cotts. EH13 100 A4
Bonaly Gdns. EH13 100 A4
Bonaly Gro. EH13 100 A4
Bonaly Ri. EH13 100 B4
Bonaly Rd. EH13 100 A3
Bonaly Steading EH13 100 A4
Bonaly Ter. EH13 100 B4
Bonaly Wr. EH13 100 A4
Bonar Pl. EH6 73 D3
Bonnington Av. EH6 73 D3
Bonnington Gro. EH6 73 D3
Bonnington Rd. EH6 73 E4
Bonnington Rd. La. EH6 73 E4
Bonnington Ter. EH6 73 D3
Bonnyhaugh EH6 73 D4
Bonnyhaugh La. EH6 73 D4
Boothacre Cotts. EH6 75 D4
Seafield Pl.
Boothacre La. EH6 75 D4
Boroughloch Bldgs. EH8 83 F5
Boroughloch La.
Boroughloch La. EH8 83 F5
Boroughloch Sq. EH8 83 F5
Boroughloch La.
Borthwick Pl. EH12 81 F4
Borthwick's Clo. EH1 83 E3
High St.
Boswall Av. EH5 71 F3
Boswall Cres. EH5 71 F3
Boswall Dr. EH5 71 F3
Boswall Gdns. EH5 71 F2
Boswall Grn. EH5 72 A3
Boswall Gro. EH5 71 F3
Boswall Ln. EH5 71 F2
Boswall Ms. EH5 71 F2
Boswall Ln.
Boswall Parkway EH5 71 E2
Boswall Pl. EH5 71 F3
Boswall Quad. EH5 71 F3
Boswall Rd. EH5 72 A2
Boswall Sq. EH5 71 F3
Boswall Ter. EH5 71 F3
Bothwell St. EH7 84 A1
Bowhill Ter. EH3 72 B3
Bowie's Clo. EH6 74 B3

Bowling Grn., The   73 F3
EH6
Bowmont Pl. EH8   83 F5
Boyd's Entry EH1   83 F3
St. Mary's St.
Boy's Brigade Wk.   83 E5
EH3
Brae Pk. EH4   68 A4
Braeburn Dr.,   98 B5
Currie EH14
Braefoot Ter. EH16   94 B5
Braehead Av. EH4   68 A5
Braehead Bk. EH4   68 A5
Braehead Cres. EH4   68 A5
Braehead Dr. EH4   68 A5
Braehead Gro. EH4   68 A5
Braehead Ln. EH4   68 A5
Braehead Pk. EH4   68 A5
Braehead Rd. EH4   68 A5
Braehead Row EH4   68 A5
Braehead Av.
Braehead Vw. EH4   68 A5
Braepark Rd. EH4   68 A4
Braid Av. EH10   92 C4
Braid Cres. EH10   92 B5
Braid Fm. Rd. EH10   92 B5
Braid Hills App.   102 B1
EH10
Braid Hills Av. EH10   92 B5
Braid Hills Cres.   102 A1
EH10
Braid Hills Dr. EH10   93 D5
Braid Hills Dr. EH16   103 E1
Braid Hills Rd. EH10   102 A1
Braid Mt. EH10   102 B2
Braid Mt. Crest   102 B2
EH10
Braid Mt. Ri. EH10   102 B2
Braid Mt. Vw. EH10   102 B2
Braid Rd. EH10   92 B5
Braidburn Cres.   92 B5
EH10
Braidburn Ter. EH10   92 B5
Bramble Dr. EH4   78 C1
Bramdean Gro.   102 B1
EH10
Bramdean Pl. EH10   102 B1
Bramdean Ri. EH10   102 B1
Bramdean Vw.   102 B1
EH10
Brand Dr. EH15   86 C5
Brand Gdns. EH15   87 D4
Brand Pl. EH8   84 B2
Abbeyhill
Brandfield St. EH3   82 B5
Brandon St. EH3   83 D1
Brandon Ter. EH3   83 D1
Bread St. EH3   82 C4
Bread St. La. EH3   82 C4
Breadalbane St. EH6   73 E3
Breadalbane Ter.   82 B4
EH11
Brewery La. EH6   73 F3
Great Junct. St.
Briarbank Ter. EH11   91 F2
Brickfield EH15   86 B2
Pipe St.
Brickwork Clo. EH6   73 F3
Giles St.
Bridge End EH16   94 C3
Bridge Pl. EH3   82 C1
Bridge Rd. EH13   100 A3
Bridge St. EH15   86 B2
Bridge St. La. EH15   86 B2
Briery Bauks EH8   83 F4
Bright Ter. EH11   82 B4
Brighton Pl. EH15   86 B3
Brighton St. EH1   83 E4
Bright's Cres. EH9   94 A2

Bristo Pl. EH1   83 E4
Bristo Port EH1   83 E4
Bristo Sq. EH8   83 E4
Britwell Cres. EH7   85 E2
Broad Wynd EH6   74 B3
Broombank Ter.   89 E2
EH12
Broomburn Gro.   89 F1
EH12
Broomfield Cres.   89 F2
EH12
Broomhall Av. EH12   89 E2
Broomhall Bk. EH12   89 E1
Broomhall Cres.   89 E1
EH12
Broomhall Dr. EH12   89 D1
Broomhall Gdns.   89 E1
EH12
Broomhall Ln. EH12   89 E1
Broomhall Pk. EH12   89 E1
Broomhall Pl. EH12   89 E1
Broomhall Rd. EH12   89 E1
Broomhall Ter. EH12   89 D1
Broomhouse Av.   89 E3
EH11
Broomhouse Bk.   89 F3
EH11
Broomhouse Cotts.   89 F3
E. EH11
Broomhouse Cotts.   89 E3
W. EH11
Broomhouse Ct.   89 F3
EH11
Broomhouse Cres.   89 F3
EH11
Broomhouse Dr.   89 E2
EH11
Broomhouse Gdns.   89 F2
EH11
Broomhouse Gdns.   89 F2
E. EH11
Broomhouse Gdns.   89 E2
W. EH11
Broomhouse Gro.   89 F3
EH11
Broomhouse Ln.   89 F3
EH11
Broomhouse Mkt.   89 F3
EH11
Broomhouse   89 F2
Medway EH11
Broomhouse Pk.   89 E3
EH11
Broomhouse Path   89 E3
EH11
Broomhouse Pl. N.   89 E3
EH11
Broomhouse Pl. S.   89 F3
EH11
Broomhouse Rd.   89 E2
EH11
Broomhouse Rd.   89 F2
EH12
Broomhouse Row   89 F2
EH11
Broomhouse Sq.   89 F3
EH11
Broomhouse St. N.   89 E3
EH11
Broomhouse St. S.   89 F4
EH11
Broomhouse Ter.   89 F2
EH11
Broomhouse Wk.   89 F3
EH11
Broomhouse Way   89 F3
EH11
Broomhouse Wynd   89 F3
EH11

Broomlea Cres.   89 E1
EH12
Broompark Rd.   89 E1
EH12
Broomside Ter.   89 F1
EH12
Broomview Ho.   89 E4
EH11
Broomyknowe EH14   100 B1
Brougham Pl. EH3   83 D5
Brougham St. EH3   83 D5
Broughton Mkt. EH3   83 E2
Broughton Pl. EH1   83 E1
Broughton Pl. La.   83 E1
EH1
Broughton Pl.
Broughton Rd. EH7   73 D5
Broughton St. EH1   83 E1
Broughton St. La.   83 E2
EH1
Brown St. EH8   83 F4
Brown St. La. EH8   83 F4
Brown St.
Brown's Clo. EH8   84 A3
Canongate
Brown's Pl. EH1   83 D4
Vennel
Bruce St. EH10   92 C4
Brunstane Bk. EH15   87 E5
Brunstane Cres.   87 E5
EH15
Brunstane Dr. EH15   87 D5
Brunstane Gdns.   87 D4
EH15
Brunstane Gdns. Ms.   87 D4
EH15
Brunstane Gdns.
Brunstane Rd. EH15   87 D4
Brunstane Rd. N.   87 D3
EH15
Brunstane Rd. S.   87 D5
EH15
Brunswick Pl. EH7   83 F1
Brunswick Rd. EH7   84 A1
Brunswick St. EH7   83 F1
Brunswick St. La.   83 F1
EH7
Brunswick Ter. EH7   84 A1
Brunswick Rd.
Brunton Gdns. EH7   84 A1
Montgomery St.
Brunton Pl. EH7   84 A1
Brunton Ter. EH7   84 A1
Bruntsfield Av. EH12   92 C1
Bruntsfield Cres.   92 C1
EH10
Bruntsfield Gdns.   92 C1
EH10
Bruntsfield Pl. EH10   92 B2
Bruntsfield Ter.   92 C1
EH10
Bryce Av. EH7   86 A1
Bryce Cres., Currie   98 A4
EH14
Bryce Gdns.,   98 A4
Currie EH14
Bryce Rd.
Bryce Gro. EH7   86 A1
Bryce Pl., Currie   98 A4
EH14
Bryce Rd., Currie   98 A4
EH14
Bryson Rd. EH11   92 A1
Buccleuch Pl. EH8   83 E5
Buccleuch St. EH8   83 F5
Buccleuch Ter. EH8   83 F5
Buchanan St. EH6   73 F5
Buckingham Ter.   82 A2
EH4

Buckstane Pk. EH10 102 A2
Buckstone Av. EH10 102 B3
Buckstone Bk. EH10 102 B2
Buckstone Circle 102 C4
EH10
Buckstone Clo. 102 C3
EH10
Buckstone Ct. EH10 102 B3
Buckstone Cres. 102 B2
EH10
Buckstone Crook 102 C4
EH10
Buckstone Dell 102 B2
EH10
Buckstone Dr. EH10 102 B2
Buckstone Gdns. 102 B3
EH10
Buckstone Gate 102 C3
EH10
Buckstone Grn. 102 B3
EH10
Buckstone Gro. 102 B2
EH10
Buckstone Hill EH10 102 B2
Buckstone Howe 102 C3
EH10
Buckstone Lea EH10 102 C3
Buckstone Ln. EH10 102 B3
Buckstone Ln. E. 102 C3
EH10
Buckstone Neuk 102 C3
EH10
Buckstone Pl. EH10 102 B3
Buckstone Ri. EH10 102 C3
Buckstone Rd. EH10 102 B3
Buckstone Row 102 C2
EH10
Buckstone Shaw 102 C4
EH10
Buckstone Ter. 102 B3
EH10
Buckstone Vw. 102 B2
EH10
Buckstone Way 102 B2
EH10
Buckstone Wd. 102 B3
EH10
Buckstone Wynd 102 C3
EH10
Buckstoneside EH10 102 C4
Buckstone Circle
Bughtlin Dr. EH12 78 B2
Bughtlin Gdns. EH12 78 B3
Bughtlin Grn. EH12 78 B2
Bughtlin Ln. EH12 78 B3
Bughtlin Mkt. EH12 78 C2
Bughtlin Pk. EH12 78 C3
Bughtlin Pl. EH12 78 B2
Bull's Clo. EH8 84 A3
Burdiehouse Av. 104 B5
EH17
Burdiehouse Cres. 104 B5
EH17
Burdiehouse 104 B5
Crossway EH17
Burdiehouse Dr. 104 B5
EH17
Burdiehouse Ln. 104 B5
EH17
Burdiehouse 104 B5
Medway EH17
Burdiehouse Pl. 104 B5
EH17
Burdiehouse Rd. 104 A5
EH17
Burdiehouse St. 104 B5
EH17
Burdiehouse Ter. 104 B5
EH17

Burgess St. EH6 74 B3
Burgess Ter. EH9 94 B2
Burghtoft EH17 105 E4
Burlington St. EH6 73 F3
Burnbrae EH12 78 B3
Burnhead Cres. 104 A2
EH16
Burnhead Gro. EH16 104 B3
Burnhead Ln. EH16 104 B3
Burnhead Path E. 104 B3
EH16
Burnhead Path W. 104 B3
EH16
Burns St. EH6 74 B4
Burnside EH12 78 B3

C
Cables Wynd EH6 73 F3
Cables Wynd Ho. 73 F3
EH6
Caddell's Row EH4 68 B2
Cadiz St. EH6 74 B3
Cadogan Rd. EH16 104 A2
Cadzow Pl. EH7 84 B2
Caerketton Cotts. 101 E1
EH13
Caerketton Ct. EH13 101 F2
Caerlaverock Ct. 78 C4
EH12
Craigievar Wynd
Cairnmuir Rd. EH12 79 F3
Cairntows Clo. EH16 95 E2
Caithness Pl. EH5 72 B3
Caiy Stane EH10 102 A4
Caiyside EH10 102 A5
Caystane Av. EH10 102 A4
Caiystane Cres. 102 A3
EH10
Caiystane Dr. EH10 101 F4
Caiystane Gdns. 101 F3
EH10
Caiystane Hill EH10 102 A3
Caiystane Ter. EH10 101 F4
Caiystane Vw. EH10 102 A4
Calder Ct. EH11 89 D4
Calder Cres. EH11 88 C5
Calder Dr. EH11 89 D5
Calder Gdns. EH11 88 C5
Calder Gro. EH11 89 D5
Calder Pk. EH11 89 D5
Calder Pl. EH11 89 D5
Calder Rd. EH11 89 F4
Calder Rd. Gdns. 90 B3
EH11
Calder Vw. EH11 89 D5
Caledonian Cres. 82 A5
EH11
Caledonian Pl. EH11 82 A5
Caledonian Rd. 82 C5
EH11
Calton Hill EH1 83 F2
Calton Hill EH7 83 F2
Calton Rd. EH8 83 E3
Cambridge Av. EH6 73 E5
Cambridge Gdns. 73 E5
EH6
Cambridge St. EH1 82 C4
Cambridge St. La. 82 C4
EH1
Cambusnethan St. 84 C2
EH7
Cameron Cres. EH16 94 C3
Cameron Ho. Av. 94 C2
EH16
Cameron March 94 B3
EH16
Cameron Pk. EH16 94 B3
Cameron Ter. EH16 94 C3

Cameron Toll EH16 94 B3
Cameron Toll Gdns. 94 C3
EH16
Cammo Bk. EH4 78 B1
Cammo Brae EH4 78 B1
Cammo Cres. EH4 78 B1
Cammo Gdns. EH4 78 B1
Cammo Gro. EH4 78 A1
Cammo Hill EH4 78 A1
Cammo Parkway 78 B1
EH4
Cammo Pl. EH4 78 B1
Cammo Rd. EH4 78 A1
Cammo Rd. EH12 77 D2
Cammo Wk. EH4 78 A1
Campbell Av. EH12 81 D4
Campbell Pk. Cres. 99 F3
EH13
Campbell Pk. Dr. 99 F3
EH13
Campbell Rd. EH12 81 D3
Campbell's Clo. EH8 84 A3
Calton Rd.
Camus Av. EH10 102 A3
Camus Pk. EH10 102 A3
Canaan La. EH10 92 C3
Candlemaker Row 83 E4
EH1
Candlemaker's Cres. 105 F3
EH17
Candlemaker's Pk. 105 F3
EH17
Canning St. EH3 82 B4
Canning St. La. EH3 82 B4
Cannon Wynd EH6 73 E2
Canon St. EH3 72 C5
Canonmills
Canon La. EH3 83 D1
Canon St. EH3 83 D1
Canongate EH8 83 F3
Canonmills EH3 72 C5
Capelaw Ct. EH13 101 F2
Capelaw Rd. EH13 100 A4
Captain's Dr. EH16 104 B4
Captain's Ln. EH16 104 B3
Captain's Rd. EH17 104 B4
Captain's Row 104 B4
EH16
Carberry Pl. EH12 81 F4
Carfrae Gdns. EH4 80 B1
Carfrae Gro. EH4 80 B1
Carfrae Pk. EH4 80 B1
Carfrae Rd. EH4 80 B1
Cargil Ct. EH5 72 A3
Cargil Ter. EH5 72 A3
Carlton St. EH4 82 B2
Carlton Ter. EH7 84 A2
Carlton Ter. Brae EH7 84 A2
Carlton Ter. La. EH7 84 A2
Carlton Ter. Ms. EH7 84 A2
Carlyle Pl. EH7 84 B2
Carnbee Av. EH16 104 C3
Carnbee Cres. EH16 104 C3
Carnbee Dell EH16 104 C3
Carnbee End EH16 104 C3
Carnbee Pk. EH16 104 C3
Carnegie Ct. EH8 83 F4
Carnegie St. EH8 83 F4
Carnethy Av. EH13 100 A3
Caroline Gdns. 79 F4
EH12
Caroline Pk. EH5 71 D1
Caroline Pk. Av. EH5 71 D1
Caroline Pk. Gro. 71 D2
EH5
Caroline Pl. EH12 79 F4
Caroline Ter. EH12 79 E3
Carpet La. EH6 74 B3
Bernard St.

Carrick Knowe Av. 80 A5 EH12
Carrick Knowe Dr. 89 F1 EH12
Carrick Knowe Gdns. 90 A1 EH12
Carrick Knowe Gro. 90 A1 EH12
Carrick Knowe Hill 90 A1 EH12
Carrick Knowe Ln. 89 F1 EH12
Carrick Knowe 89 F1 Parkway EH12
Carrick Knowe Pl. 90 A1 EH12
Carrick Knowe Rd. 90 A2 EH12
Carrick Knowe Ter. 90 A1 EH12
Carrington Cres. EH4 71 E5 *Crewe Rd. S.*
Carrington Rd. EH4 81 F1
Carron Pl. EH6 74 C3
Carrubber's Clo. EH1 83 E3 *High St.*
Casselbank St. EH6 73 F4
Cassel's La. EH6 73 F4
Castle Av. EH12 89 E1
Castle Esp. EH1 83 D4
Castle St. EH2 82 C3
Castle Ter. EH1 82 C3
Castle Ter. EH3 82 C3
Castle Wynd N. EH1 83 D4
Castle Wynd S. EH1 83 D4 *Johnston Ter.*
Castlehill EH1 83 D3
Castlelaw Rd. EH13 100 A3
Castleview Ho. EH17 95 E5
Cathcart Pl. EH11 82 A5
Cathedral La. EH1 83 E2
Catherine Pl. EH3 72 C5
Cattle Rd. EH14 90 C3
Causeway, The EH15 85 D5
Causewayside EH9 93 F1
Cavalry Pk. Dr. EH15 85 E5
Cedars, The EH13 100 B2
Chalmers Bldgs. EH3 82 B5 *Fountainbridge*
Chalmers Clo. EH1 83 F3 *High St.*
Chalmers Cres. EH9 93 E1
Chalmers St. EH3 83 D5
Chamberlain Rd. 92 C2 EH10
Chambers St. EH1 83 E4
Chancelot Cres. EH6 72 C3
Chancelot Gro. EH5 72 C3
Chancelot Ter. EH6 72 C3
Chapel Ct. EH16 95 F2
Chapel La. EH6 74 B3 *Maritime St.*
Chapel St. EH8 83 E5
Chapel Wynd EH1 83 D4 *West Port*
Charles St. EH8 83 E4
Charles St. La. EH8 83 E4
Charlesfield EH8 83 E4 *Bristo Sq.*
Charlotte La. EH2 82 C3
Charlotte Sq. EH2 82 C3
Charterhall Gro. EH9 93 E3
Charterhall Rd. EH9 93 E4
Chatterrig EH13 101 F2
Chessels Ct. EH8 83 F3
Chesser Av. EH14 90 C3
Chesser Cotts. EH11 91 D2 *Gorgie Rd.*
Chesser Ct. EH14 90 C2

Chesser Cres. EH14 91 D3
Chesser Gdns. EH14 90 C2
Chesser Gro. EH14 90 C3
Chesser Ln. EH14 90 C3
Chester St. EH3 82 B3
Chestnut St. EH5 71 E1
Cheyne St. EH4 82 B1
Christian Cres. EH15 86 C4
Christian Gro. EH15 86 C4
Christian Path EH15 86 B3
Christiemiller Av. 85 F1 EH7
Christiemiller Gro. 85 F2 EH7
Christiemiller Pl. EH7 85 F2
Chuckie Pend EH3 82 C4 *Morrison St.*
Church Hill EH10 92 C2
Church Hill Dr. EH10 92 C2
Church Hill Pl. EH10 92 C2
Circus Gdns. EH3 82 C2
Circus La. EH3 82 C1
Citadel Ct. EH6 73 F2
Citadel Pl. EH6 73 F2 *Commercial St.*
Citadel St. EH6 73 F2
City of Edinburgh 101 F4 Bypass, The EH10
City of Edinburgh 88 A1 Bypass, The EH12
City of Edinburgh 100 C4 Bypass, The EH13
City of Edinburgh 99 D1 Bypass, The EH14
Clackmae Gro. 103 F1 EH16
Clackmae Rd. EH16 103 F1
Clapper La. EH16 94 B4
Clapperton Pl. EH7 84 B2 *Lower London Rd.*
Clarebank Cres. EH6 74 C4
Claremont Bk. EH7 83 E1
Claremont Ct. EH7 73 D5
Claremont Cres. EH7 73 D5
Claremont Gdns. EH6 74 C4
Claremont Gro. EH7 73 D5
Claremont Pk. EH6 74 C4
Claremont Rd. EH6 74 C4
Clarence St. EH3 82 C1
Clarendon Cres. EH4 82 B2
Clarinda Ter. EH16 94 B5
Clark Av. EH5 72 C3
Clark Pl. EH5 72 B3
Clark Rd. EH5 72 B3
Claverhouse Dr. 104 A1 EH16
Clearburn Cres. EH16 94 C2
Clearburn Gdns. 94 C2 EH16
Clearburn Rd. EH16 94 C2
Cleekim Dr. EH15 96 C2
Cleekim Rd. EH15 96 C2
Cleikiminfield EH15 96 C2
Cleikiminrig EH15 96 C2
Clerk St. EH8 83 F5
Clermiston Av. EH4 79 F2
Clermiston Cres. EH4 79 E1
Clermiston Dr. EH4 79 E2
Clermiston Gdns. 79 E2 EH4
Clermiston Grn. EH4 79 E1
Clermiston Gro. EH4 79 E2
Clermiston Hill EH4 79 E1
Clermiston Ln. EH4 79 E1
Clermiston Medway 79 E1 EH4
Clermiston Pk. EH4 79 E1
Clermiston Pl. EH4 79 E2
Clermiston Rd. EH12 79 F4

Clermiston Rd. N. 79 F1 EH4
Clermiston Ter. EH12 79 F4
Clermiston Vw. EH4 79 F1
Clerwood Bk. EH12 79 E3
Clerwood Gdns. 79 E3 EH12
Clerwood Gro. EH12 79 F3
Clerwood Ln. EH12 79 E3
Clerwood Pk. EH12 79 E3
Clerwood Pl. EH12 79 F3
Clerwood Row EH12 79 E3
Clerwood Ter. EH12 79 F3
Clerwood Vw. EH12 79 F3
Clerwood Way EH12 79 E3
Clifton Sq. EH15 86 B3 *Baileyfield Rd.*
Clifton Ter. EH12 82 B4
Clinton Rd. EH9 92 C2
Clockmill La. EH8 84 C2
Clovenstone Dr. 99 E2 EH14
Clovenstone Gdns. 99 E1 EH14
Clovenstone Pk. 99 E2 EH14
Clovenstone Rd. 99 E1 EH14
Cluny Av. EH10 92 C4
Cluny Dr. EH10 92 C4
Cluny Gdns. EH10 92 C4
Cluny Pl. EH10 93 D4
Cluny Ter. EH10 92 C4
Clyde St. EH1 83 E2
Coalhill EH6 73 F3
Coates Cres. EH3 82 B4
Coates Gdns. EH12 82 A4
Coates Pl. EH3 82 B4
Coatfield La. EH6 74 B3
Cobbinshaw Ho. 89 D5 EH11
Cobden Cres. EH9 94 A2
Cobden Rd. EH9 94 A2
Cobden Ter. EH11 82 B4
Coburg St. EH6 73 F2
Cochran Pl. EH7 83 E1 *East London St.*
Cochran Ter. EH7 83 E1
Cochrane Pl. EH6 74 C4
Cockburn St. EH1 83 E3
Cockmylane EH10 101 F3
Coffin La. EH11 82 A5
Coillesdene Av. EH15 87 E4
Coillesdene Cres. 87 E4 EH15
Coillesdene Dr. 87 E4 EH15
Coillesdene Gdns. 87 E4 EH15
Coillesdene Gro. 87 E4 EH15
Coillesdene Ln. EH15 87 E4
Coillesdene Ter. 87 E4 EH15
Coinyie Ho. Clo. EH1 83 F3 *Blackfriars St.*
Colinton Gro. EH14 91 E4
Colinton Gro. W. 91 E4 EH14
Colinton Mains 101 D3 Cres. EH13
Colinton Mains Dr. 101 D1 EH13
Colinton Mains 101 D1 Gdns. EH13
Colinton Mains Grn. 101 D2 EH13
Colinton Mains Gro. 101 E2 EH13

Colinton Mains Ln. 101 D2
EH13
Colinton Mains Pl. 101 E2
EH13
Colinton Mains Rd. 101 D2
EH13
Colinton Mains Ter. 101 E2
EH13
Colinton Rd. EH10 92 A3
Colinton Rd. EH13 100 B2
Colinton Rd. EH14 91 E4
College Wynd EH1 83 E4
Cowgate
Collins Pl. EH3 82 C1
Colmestone Gate 102 A3
EH10
Coltbridge Av. EH12 81 E4
Coltbridge Gdns. 81 F3
EH12
Coltbridge Millside 81 E4
EH12
Coltbridge Av.
Coltbridge Ter. EH12 81 E4
Coltbridge Vale EH12 81 E3
Columba Av. EH4 80 C1
Columba Rd. EH4 80 C1
Colville Pl. EH3 82 C1
Comely Bk. EH4 82 A1
Comely Bk. Av. EH4 82 A1
Comely Bk. Gro. EH4 82 A1
Comely Bk. Pl. EH4 82 B1
Comely Bk. Pl. Ms. 82 B1
EH4
Comely Bk. Rd. EH4 82 A1
Comely Bk. Row EH4 82 B1
Comely Bk. St. EH4 82 A1
Comely Bk. Ter. EH4 82 B1
Comely Grn. Cres. 84 B2
EH7
Comely Grn. Pl. EH7 84 B2
Comiston Dr. EH10 92 A5
Comiston Gdns. 92 B4
EH10
Comiston Gro. 102 A2
EH10
Comiston Pl. EH10 92 B4
Comiston Ri. EH10 102 A2
Comiston Rd. EH10 102 A1
Comiston Springs 102 A2
Av. EH10
Comiston Ter. EH10 92 B4
Comiston Vw. EH10 102 A2
Commercial St. EH6 73 F2
Commercial Wf. EH6 74 B2
Connaught Pl. EH6 73 D3
Considine Gdns. EH8 85 D2
Considine Ter. EH8 85 D2
Constitution Pl. EH6 74 B2
Constitution St. EH6 74 B4
Convening Ct. EH4 82 A2
Dean Path
Cooper's Clo. EH8 84 A3
Canongate
Cooper's Ct. EH8 84 A3
Gentle's Entry
Corbiehill Av. EH4 70 A5
Corbiehill Cres. EH4 69 F5
Corbiehill Gdns. EH4 70 A5
Corbiehill Gro. EH4 70 A5
Corbiehill Pk. EH4 69 F5
Corbiehill Pl. EH4 69 F5
Corbiehill Rd. EH4 69 F5
Corbiehill Ter. EH4 69 F5
Corbieshot EH15 96 C1
Corbiewynd EH15 96 C1
Cornhill Ter. EH6 74 C4
Cornwall St. EH1 82 C4
Cornwallis Pl. EH3 83 D1
Coronation Wk. EH3 83 D5

Corporation Bldgs. 73 F3
EH6
Sheriff Brae
Corrennie Dr. EH10 92 C4
Corrennie Gdns. 92 C5
EH10
Corslet Cres., 98 B4
Currie EH14
Corslet Pl., Currie 98 A4
EH14
Corslet Rd., Currie 98 A4
EH14
Corstorphine Bk. Av. 79 D4
EH12
Corstorphine Bk. Dr. 79 D4
EH12
Corstorphine Bk. Ter. 79 D4
EH12
Corstorphine High St. 79 E5
EH12
Corstorphine Hill 79 F4
Av. EH12
Corstorphine Hill 79 F4
Cres. EH12
Corstorphine Hill 79 F4
Gdns. EH12
Corstorphine Hill 79 F4
Rd. EH12
Corstorphine Ho. 79 F5
Av. EH12
Corstorphine Ho. 79 F5
Ter. EH12
Corstorphine Pk. 79 F5
Gdns. EH12
Corstorphine Rd. 80 B5
EH12
Corunna Pl. EH6 73 F3
Cottage Grn. EH4 68 B4
Cottage Homes 100 B3
EH13
Cottage Pk. EH4 80 B2
Couper St. EH6 73 F2
Cowan Rd. EH11 91 F2
Cowan's Clo. EH8 83 F5
Cowgate EH1 83 E4
Cowgatehead EH1 83 E4
Coxfield EH11 91 D2
Craigcrook Av. EH4 80 B1
Craigcrook Gdns. 80 C2
EH4
Craigcrook Gro. EH4 80 B2
Craigcrook Pk. EH4 80 B2
Craigcrook Pl. EH4 80 C2
Craigcrook Rd. EH4 80 A1
Craigcrook Sq. EH4 80 B1
Craigcrook Ter. EH4 80 C1
Craigend Pk. EH16 95 D5
Craigentinny Av. EH7 85 F2
Craigentinny Av. N. 75 E4
EH6
Craigentinny Cres. 85 F2
EH7
Craigentinny Gro. 85 F2
EH7
Craigentinny Pl. EH7 85 F2
Craigentinny Rd. EH7 85 E1
Craighall Av. EH6 72 C2
Craighall Bk. EH6 72 C2
Craighall Cres. EH6 72 C2
Craighall Gdns. EH6 72 C3
Craighall Rd. EH6 72 C2
Craighall Ter. EH6 72 C3
Craighill Gdns. EH10 92 A5
Craighouse Av. EH10 92 A4
Craighouse Gdns. 92 A4
EH10
Craighouse Pk. EH10 92 A4
Craighouse Rd. EH10 92 A4
Craighouse Ter. EH10 92 A4

Craigievar Ct. EH12 78 B4
Craigievar Wynd
Craigievar Sq. EH12 78 B4
Craigievar Wynd 78 B4
EH12
Craiglea Dr. EH10 92 A5
Craiglea Pl. EH10 92 A5
Craigleith Av. N. EH4 81 D3
Craigleith Av. S. EH4 81 D3
Craigleith Bk. EH4 81 E2
Craigleith Cres. EH4 81 D2
Craigleith Dr. EH4 81 D2
Craigleith Gdns. EH4 81 D2
Craigleith Gro. EH4 81 D2
Craigleith Hill EH4 81 E2
Craigleith Hill Av. 81 E1
EH4
Craigleith Hill Cres. 81 E1
EH4
Craigleith Hill Gdns. 81 E1
EH4
Craigleith Hill Grn. 81 E1
EH4
Craigleith Hill Gro. 81 E1
EH4
Craigleith Hill Ln. 81 E1
EH4
Craigleith Hill Pk. 81 E1
EH4
Craigleith Hill Row 81 E1
EH4
Craigleith Ri. EH4 81 D3
Craigleith Rd. EH4 81 E2
Craigleith Vw. EH4 81 D3
Craiglockhart Av. 91 D4
EH14
Craiglockhart Bk. 91 D5
EH14
Craiglockhart Cres. 91 D5
EH14
Craiglockhart Dell Rd. 91 D5
EH14
Craiglockhart Dr. N. 91 D4
EH14
Craiglockhart Dr. S. 91 D5
EH14
Craiglockhart Gdns. 91 D4
EH14
Craiglockhart Gro. 100 C1
EH14
Craiglockhart Ln. 91 D5
EH14
Craiglockhart Pk. 91 D5
EH14
Craiglockhart Pl. 91 E4
EH14
Craiglockhart Quad. 91 D5
EH14
Craiglockhart Rd. 91 D5
EH14
Craiglockhart Rd. N. 91 E5
EH14
Craiglockhart Ter. 91 F3
EH14
Craiglockhart Vw. 91 E4
EH14
Craigmillar Castle Av. 95 E3
EH16
Craigmillar Castle 95 E2
Gdns. EH16
Craigmillar Castle 95 E2
Gro. EH16
Craigmillar Castle Ln. 95 F2
EH16
Craigmillar Castle Rd. 95 E3
EH16
Craigmillar Castle 95 E3
Ter. EH16
Craigmillar Ct. EH16 95 D3

Craigmillar Pk. EH16 94 A3
Craigmount App. 79 D4
    EH12
Craigmount Av. EH12 79 D4
Craigmount Av. N. 78 C2
    EH4
Craigmount Av. N. 78 C2
    EH12
Craigmount Bk. EH4 78 C2
Craigmount Bk. W. 78 C2
    EH4
Craigmount Brae 78 C2
    EH12
Craigmount Ct. EH4 78 C2
Craigmount Cres. 78 C3
    EH12
Craigmount Dr. 78 C3
    EH12
Craigmount Gdns. 78 C4
    EH12
Craigmount Gro. 78 C4
    EH12
Craigmount Gro. N. 78 C3
    EH12
Craigmount Hill EH4 78 C2
Craigmount Ln. 78 C3
    EH12
Craigmount Pk. 78 C4
    EH12
Craigmount Pl. 78 C3
    EH12
Craigmount Ter. 78 C4
    EH12
Craigmount Vw. 78 C3
    EH12
Craigmount Way 79 D2
    EH12
Craigour Av. EH17 105 E1
Craigour Cres. EH17 105 E1
Craigour Dr. EH17 105 E1
Craigour Gdns. 105 E1
    EH17
Craigour Grn. EH17 105 D1
Craigour Gro. EH17 105 E1
Craigour Ln. EH17 105 E1
Craigour Pl. EH17 105 D1
Craigour Ter. EH17 105 E1
Craigs Av. EH12 78 C5
Craigs Bk. EH12 78 C4
Craigs Cres. EH12 78 C4
Craigs Dr. EH12 78 C4
Craigs Gdns. EH12 78 C4
Craigs Gro. EH12 79 D4
Craigs Ln. EH12 79 D4
Craigs Pk. EH12 78 C4
Craigs Rd. EH12 78 A3
Cramond Av. EH4 68 B3
Cramond Bk. EH4 68 B3
Cramond Cres. EH4 68 B3
Cramond Gdns. EH4 68 B3
Cramond Glebe 68 C2
    Gdns. EH4
Cramond Glebe Rd. 68 B1
    EH4
Cramond Glebe Ter. 68 B2
    EH4
Cramond Grn. EH4 68 B2
Cramond Gro. EH4 68 B3
Cramond Pk. EH4 68 B3
Cramond Pl. EH4 68 C3
Cramond Regis EH4 68 B4
Cramond Rd. N. EH4 68 C2
Cramond Rd. S. EH4 69 D3
Cramond Ter. EH4 68 B3
Cramond Vale EH4 68 A3
Cramond Village 68 B1
    EH4
Cranston St. EH8 83 F3
Crarae Av. EH4 81 E3

Craufurdland EH4 68 A4
Crawford Bri. EH7 84 B1
    Bothwell St.
Crawford Rd. EH16 94 A3
Crescent, The EH10 92 B4
Crescent, The EH11 90 B3
    Gorgie Rd.
Crewe Bk. EH5 71 E3
Crewe Cres. EH5 71 D3
Crewe Gro. EH5 71 E3
Crewe Ln. EH5 71 D3
Crewe Path EH5 71 D3
Crewe Pl. EH5 71 D3
Crewe Rd. Gdns. EH5 71 D3
Crewe Rd. N. EH5 71 D2
Crewe Rd. S. EH4 71 E4
Crewe Rd. W. EH5 71 D2
Crewe Ter. EH5 71 D3
Crewe Toll EH4 71 D4
Crichton St. EH8 83 E4
Crichton's Clo. EH8 84 A3
    Canongate
Crighton Pl. EH7 73 F5
Croall Pl. EH7 83 F1
Croft-an-righ EH8 84 A2
Cromwell Pl. EH6 73 F2
Crown Pl. EH6 73 F4
Crown St. EH6 73 F4
Cuddy La. EH10 92 B3
Cultins Rd. EH11 88 C3
Cumberland St. EH3 83 D1
Cumberland St. N. 83 D1
    E. La. EH3
Cumberland St. N. 83 D1
    W. La. EH3
Cumberland St. S. 83 D1
    E. La. EH3
Cumberland St. S. 83 D1
    W. La. EH3
Cumin Pl. EH9 93 F1
Cumlodden Av. EH12 81 D3
Cumnor Cres. EH16 94 B5
Cunningham Pl. EH6 73 F4

D

Daiches Braes EH15 87 E5
Dairsie Pl. EH7 84 B2
    Stanley Pl.
Daisy Ter. EH11 91 F1
    Merchiston Gro.
Dalgety Av. EH7 84 C1
Dalgety Rd. EH7 84 C1
Dalgety St. EH7 84 C2
Dalhousie Ter. EH10 92 B4
Dalkeith Rd. EH16 94 A1
Dalkeith St. EH15 87 D4
Dalmeny Rd. EH6 73 D3
Dalmeny St. EH6 73 F5
Dalry Pl. EH11 82 B4
Dalry Rd. EH11 82 A5
Dalrymple Cres. EH9 93 F2
Dalziel Pl. EH7 84 C2
    London Rd.
Damside EH4 82 A3
Dania Ct. EH11 90 A2
Danube St. EH4 82 B2
Darling's Bldgs. EH3 82 C2
    Saunders St.
Darnaway St. EH3 82 C2
Darnell Rd. EH5 72 A3
Davidson Gdns. EH4 70 A5
Davidson Pk. EH4 71 D5
Davidson Rd. EH4 71 D5
Davie St. EH8 83 F4
Davies Row EH12 79 E5
Dean Bk. La. EH3 82 C1
Dean Bri. EH3 82 B2
Dean Bri. EH4 82 B2

Dean Pk. Cres. EH4 82 B2
Dean Pk. Ms. EH4 82 B1
Dean Pk. St. EH4 82 B1
Dean Path EH4 82 A2
Dean Path Bldgs. EH4 82 B3
    Dean Path
Dean St. EH4 82 B1
Dean Ter. EH4 82 B2
Deanery Clo. EH7 85 D2
Deanhaugh St. EH4 82 C1
Dechmont Rd. EH12 78 B4
Delhaig EH11 91 D2
Dell Rd. EH13 100 B2
Denham Grn. Av. 72 B3
    EH5
Denham Grn. Pl. 72 B3
    EH5
Denham Grn. Ter. 72 B3
    EH5
Derby St. EH6 73 D2
Devon Pl. EH12 82 A4
Dewar Pl. EH3 82 B4
Dewar Pl. La. EH3 82 B4
Dick Pl. EH9 93 E2
Dickson St. EH6 73 F5
Dickson's Clo. EH1 83 F3
    High St.
Dickson's Ct. EH8 83 E4
    Bristo Sq.
Dinmont Dr. EH16 94 C5
Distillery La. EH11 82 B4
    Dalry Rd.
Dochart Dr. EH4 79 D2
Dock Pl. EH6 73 F2
Dock St. EH6 73 F2
Dorset Pl. EH11 92 B1
Double Hedges Pk. 94 B5
    EH16
Double Hedges Rd. 94 B5
    EH16
Douglas Cres. EH12 82 A3
Douglas Gdns. EH4 82 A3
Douglas Gdns. Ms. 82 A3
    EH4
Douglas Ter. EH11 82 B4
Doune Ter. EH3 82 B2
Dovecot Bk. EH16 90 B5
Dovecot Ln. EH14 90 B5
Dovecot Pk. EH14 100 A1
Dovecot Rd. EH12 89 E1
Downfield Pl. EH11 82 A5
Downie Gro. EH12 80 A5
Downie Ter. EH12 80 A5
Dreghorn Av. EH13 101 E4
Dreghorn Dr. EH13 101 E4
Dreghorn Gdns. 101 E3
    EH13
Dreghorn Gro. EH13 101 E4
Dreghorn Link EH13 101 E4
Dreghorn Ln. EH13 100 B3
Dreghorn Pk. EH13 101 D3
Dreghorn Pl. EH13 101 E4
Drum Av. EH17 105 E3
Drum Brae Av. 79 D3
    EH12
Drum Brae Cres. 79 D2
    EH4
Drum Brae Dr. EH4 79 D2
Drum Brae Gdns. 79 D3
    EH12
Drum Brae Gro. EH4 79 D2
Drum Brae Neuk 79 D3
    EH12
Drum Brae N. EH4 78 C1
Drum Brae Pk. EH12 79 D3
Drum Brae Pk. App. 79 D3
    EH12
Drum Brae Pl. EH12 79 D3
Drum Brae S. EH12 79 D3

Drum Brae Ter. EH4	79	D2
Drum Brae Wk. EH4	78	C2
Drum Cotts. EH17	105	F4
Drum Cres. EH17	105	F3
Drum Pk. Yd. EH7	84	B1
Albion Rd.		
Drum Pl. EH17	105	F3
Drum St. EH17	105	E3
Drum Ter. EH7	84	B1
Drumdryan St. EH3	82	C5
Drummond Pl. EH3	83	D1
Drummond St. EH8	83	F4
Drumsheugh Gdns.	82	B3
EH3		
Drumsheugh Pl. EH3	82	B3
Queensferry St.		
Dryden Gdns. EH7	73	E5
Dryden Pl. EH9	94	A1
Dryden St. EH7	73	E5
Dryden Ter. EH7	73	E5
Drylaw Av. EH4	81	D1
Drylaw Cres. EH4	80	C1
Drylaw Gdns. EH4	70	B5
Drylaw Grn. EH4	80	C1
Drylaw Gro. EH4	80	C1
Drylaw Ho. Gdns.	70	B5
EH4		
Drylaw Ho. Paddock	70	B5
EH4		
Duart Cres. EH4	79	D2
Dublin Meuse EH3	83	D2
Dublin St. EH1	83	E2
Dublin St. EH3	83	E2
Dublin St. La. N.	83	E1
EH3		
Dublin St. La. S. EH1	83	E2
Duddingston Av.	85	F5
EH15		
Duddingston Cres.	86	C5
EH15		
Duddingston Gdns.	86	A4
N. EH15		
Duddingston Gdns.	86	A5
S. EH15		
Duddingston Gro.	86	A4
E. EH15		
Duddingston Gro.	86	A5
W. EH15		
Duddingston Ln.	85	F5
EH15		
Duddingston	86	C5
Mains Cotts. EH15		
Milton Rd.		
Duddingston Mills	85	F4
EH8		
Duddingston Pk.	86	B4
EH15		
Duddingston Pk. S.	86	B5
EH15		
Duddingston Ri. EH15	86	A5
Duddingston Rd.	85	F4
EH15		
Duddingston Rd.	85	E5
W. EH15		
Duddingston Rd.	95	D1
W. EH16		
Duddingston Row	86	A5
EH15		
Duddingston Sq. E.	86	A4
EH15		
Duddingston Sq.	86	A4
W. EH15		
Duddingston Vw.	86	A5
EH15		
Duddingston Yards	96	B1
EH15		
Duddingston Pk. S.		
Dudley Av. EH6	73	D2
Dudley Av. S. EH6	73	E3

Dudley Bk. EH6	73	D2
Dudley Cres. EH6	73	D2
Dudley Gdns. EH6	73	D2
Dudley Gro. EH6	73	D2
Dudley Ter. EH6	73	D2
Duff Rd. EH11	82	A5
Duff St. EH11	82	A5
Duff St. La. EH11	82	A5
Duke Pl. EH6	74	B4
Duke St. EH6	74	B4
Duke's Wk. EH8	84	C2
Dumbeg Pk. EH14	99	D1
Dumbiedykes Rd.	84	A4
EH8		
Dumbryden Dr.	89	F5
EH14		
Dumbryden Gdns.	90	A4
EH14		
Dumbryden Gro.	89	F5
EH14		
Dumbryden Rd.	90	A5
EH14		
Dun-ard Gdn. EH9	93	E3
Dunbar St. EH3	82	C4
Duncan Pl. EH6	74	B4
Duncan St. EH9	93	F2
Duncans Gait EH14	90	A4
Dundas St. EH3	83	D1
Dundee St. EH11	82	A5
Dundee Ter. EH11	92	A1
Dundonald St. EH3	83	D1
Dundrennan Cotts.	95	D4
EH16		
Dunedin St. EH7	73	D5
Dunlop's Ct. EH1	83	D4
Grassmarket		
Dunollie Ct. EH12	78	C4
Craigievar Wynd		
Dunrobin Pl. EH3	82	C1
Dunsmuir Ct. EH12	79	D5
Dunsyre Ho. EH11	89	D5
Dunvegan Ct. EH4	68	B4
Durar Dr. EH4	79	E2
Durham Av. EH15	86	A4
Durham Dr. EH15	86	B5
Durham Gdns. N.	86	B4
EH15		
Durham Gdns. S.	86	B5
EH15		
Durham Gro. EH15	86	B4
Durham Pl. E. EH15	86	B4
Durham Pl. La. EH15	86	B4
Durham Pl. W. EH15	86	A5
Durham Rd. EH15	86	B4
Durham Rd. S. EH15	86	B5
Durham Sq. EH15	86	A4
Durham Ter. EH15	86	A4
Durward Gro. EH16	94	C4

E

Earl Grey St. EH3	82	C4
Earl Haig Gdns. EH5	72	B3
Earl Haig Homes	90	B2
EH11		
Earlston Pl. EH7	84	B2
East Adam St. EH8	83	F4
East Barnton Av. EH4	69	E5
East Barnton Gdns.	69	E5
EH4		
East Brighton Cres.	86	B3
EH15		
East Broughton Pl.	83	E1
EH1		
Broughton Pl.		
East Caiystane Pl.	102	A3
EH10		
East Caiystane Rd.	102	B3
EH10		

East Camus Pl.	102	A3
EH10		
East Camus Rd.	102	A3
EH10		
East Castle Rd.	92	B1
EH10		
East Champanyie	93	F3
EH9		
East Clapperfield	94	B5
EH16		
East Claremont St.	83	E1
EH7		
East Comiston EH10	102	A3
East Ct. EH4	81	D2
East Ct. EH16	95	F3
East Craigs Rigg	78	B4
EH12		
East Cromwell St.	73	F2
EH6		
East Crosscauseway	83	F5
EH8		
East Fm. of Gilmerton	105	E3
East Fettes Av. EH4	71	E4
East Fountainbridge	82	C4
EH3		
East Hermitage Pl.	74	B4
EH6		
East Kilngate Pl.	105	D4
EH17		
East Kilngate Rigg	105	D4
EH17		
East Kilngate Wynd	105	D4
EH17		
East Lillypot EH5	72	B3
East London St. EH7	83	E1
East Mkt. St. EH8	83	F3
East Mayfield EH9	94	A2
East Montgomery Pl.	84	A1
EH7		
East Newington Pl.	94	A1
EH9		
East Norton Pl. EH7	84	A2
East Parkside EH16	84	A5
East Preston St. EH8	93	F1
East Preston St. La.	93	F1
EH8		
East Preston St.		
East Restalrig Ter. EH6	74	C4
East Savile Rd. EH16	94	A3
East Sciennes St.	93	F1
EH9		
East Scotland St. La.	83	E1
EH3		
East Silvermills La.	82	C1
EH3		
East Suffolk Rd. EH16	94	B3
East Telferton EH7	86	A2
East Trinity Rd. EH5	72	B3
East Way, The EH8	85	F3
East Werberside EH4	71	E4
East Werberside Ms.	71	E4
EH4		
East Werberside Pl.	71	E4
EH4		
Easter Belmont Rd.	80	C4
EH12		
Easter Currie Ct.,	98	A5
Currie EH14		
Easter Currie Cres.,	98	A4
Currie EH14		
Easter Currie Pl.,	98	A4
Currie EH14		
Easter Currie Ter.,	98	A5
Currie EH14		
Easter Dalry Dr.	82	A5
EH11		
Easter Dalry Pl.	82	A4
EH11		

Easter Dalry Rigg EH11   82 A5
Easter Dalry Rd. EH11   82 A4
Easter Dalry Wynd EH11   82 A4
Easter Drylaw Av. EH4   70 C5
Easter Drylaw Bk. EH4   70 C4
Easter Drylaw Dr. EH4   70 C5
Easter Drylaw Gdns. EH4   70 C5
Easter Drylaw Gro. EH4   70 C5
Easter Drylaw Ln. EH4   70 C4
Easter Drylaw Pl. EH4   70 C4
Easter Drylaw Vw. EH4   71 D4
Easter Drylaw Way EH4   70 C4
Easter Haugh EH13   101 E2
Easter Hermitage EH6   74 C5
Easter Pk. Dr. EH4   69 E4
Easter Rd. EH6   74 B5
Easter Rd. EH7   84 A1
Easter Steil EH10   92 A5
Easter Warriston EH7   72 C4
Eastfield Gdns. EH15   87 F4
Eastfield Rd., Newbr. EH28   76 B5
Eden La. EH10   92 C3
Eden Ter. EH10   92 C2
  Newbridge Ter.
Edina Pl. EH7   84 B1
Edina St. EH7   84 A1
Edinburgh Airport EH12   76 A3
Edinburgh Pk. EH12   88 A1
Eglinton Cres. EH12   82 A4
Eglinton St. EH12   81 F4
Egypt Ms. EH10   93 D3
Eildon St. EH3   72 C5
Eildon Ter. EH3   72 B4
Elbe St. EH6   74 B3
Elcho Ter. EH15   87 D3
Elder St. EH1   83 E2
Elder St. E. EH1   83 E2
Electra Pl. EH15   86 B2
Elgin Pl. EH12   82 A4
Elgin St. EH7   84 A1
Elgin St. N. EH7   84 A1
Elgin Ter. EH7   84 A1
Elizafield EH6   73 E4
Ellangowan Ter. EH16   94 C5
Ellen's Glen Rd. EH17   104 C3
Ellersly Rd. EH12   81 D4
Elliot Gdns. EH14   100 C1
Elliot Pk. EH14   100 C1
Elliot Pl. EH14   100 C1
Elliot Rd. EH14   100 C1
Elliot St. EH7   84 A1
Elm Pl. EH6   74 C4
Elm Row EH7   83 F1
Elmwood Ter. EH6   74 C4
Eltringham Gdns. EH14   91 D2
Eltringham Gro. EH14   91 D2
Eltringham Ter. EH14   91 D2
Esdaile Bk. EH9   93 E2
Esdaile Gdns. EH9   93 E2
Esplanade EH4   68 C1

Esplanade Ter. EH15   87 E3
Essendean Pl. EH4   79 E2
Essendean Ter. EH4   79 E2
Essex Brae EH4   68 A4
Essex Pk. EH4   68 A4
Essex Rd. EH4   68 A4
Esslemont Rd. EH16   94 A4
Ethel Ter. EH10   92 B4
Eton Ter. EH4   82 B2
Ettrick Gro. EH10   92 B1
Ettrick Rd. EH10   92 A2
Ettrickdale Pl. EH3   82 C1
Eva Pl. EH9   93 F4
Ewerland EH4   68 A4
Eyre Cres. EH3   83 D1
Eyre Pl. EH3   83 D1
Eyre Ter. EH3   83 D1

F

Fair-a-Far EH4   68 A3
Fair-a-Far Cotts. EH4   68 B3
Fair-a-Far Shot EH4   68 B3
Fairbrae EH11   90 A3
Fairford Gdns. EH16   94 C5
Fairmile Av. EH10   102 B3
Fairview Rd., Newbr. EH28   76 A4
Fala Ct. EH16   104 B3
Falcon Av. EH10   92 C3
Falcon Ct. EH10   92 C3
Falcon Gdns. EH10   92 C3
Falcon Rd. EH10   92 C3
Falcon Rd. W. EH10   92 C3
Falkland Gdns. EH12   79 F2
Farrer Gro. EH7   85 F2
Farrer Ter. EH7   85 F2
Fauldburn EH12   78 C2
Fauldburn Pk. EH12   78 C2
Featherall Av. EH12   79 E5
Featherhall Cres. N. EH12   79 D5
Featherhall Cres. S. EH12   79 D5
Featherhall Gro. EH12   79 E5
Featherhall Pl. EH12   79 E5
Featherhall Rd. EH12   79 E5
Featherhall Ter. EH12   79 E5
Ferniehill Av. EH17   105 E3
Ferniehill Dr. EH17   105 E3
Ferniehill Gdns. EH17   105 F2
Ferniehill Gro. EH17   105 F2
Ferniehill Pl. EH17   105 E3
Ferniehill Rd. EH17   105 E3
Ferniehill Sq. EH17   105 E3
Ferniehill St. EH17   105 F2
Ferniehill Ter. EH17   105 E3
Ferniehill Way EH17   105 F2
Fernielaw Av. EH13   100 A4
Fernieside Av. EH17   105 E2
Fernieside Cres. EH17   105 E2
Fernieside Dr. EH17   105 E1
Fernieside Gdns. EH17   105 E2
Fernieside Gro. EH17   105 E2
Ferry Rd. EH4   70 B4
Ferry Rd. EH5   71 F4
Ferry Rd. EH6   73 D3
Ferry Rd. Av. EH4   70 C4
Ferry Rd. Dr. EH4   71 D3
Ferry Rd. Gdns. EH4   70 C4
Ferry Rd. Gro. EH4   70 C4
Ferry Rd. Pl. EH4   70 C4

Ferryfield EH5   71 F3
Festival Sq. EH3   82 C4
Fettes Av. EH4   82 A1
Fettes Ri. EH4   71 F4
Fettes Row EH3   83 D1
Fidra Ct. EH4   70 A3
Figgate Bk. EH15   86 C2
Figgate La. EH15   86 C2
Figgate St. EH15   86 B2
Fillyside Av. EH7   85 F1
Fillyside Rd. EH7   75 F5
Fillyside Ter. EH7   75 F5
Findhorn Pl. EH9   93 F2
Findlay Av. EH7   75 D5
Findlay Cotts. EH7   75 D5
Findlay Gdns. EH7   75 D5
Findlay Gro. EH7   75 D5
Findlay Medway EH7   75 D5
Fingal Pl. EH9   93 E1
Fingzies Pl. EH6   74 C4
Finlaggan Ct. EH12   78 B4
  Craigievar Wynd
Firrhill Cres. EH13   101 E1
Firrhill Dr. EH13   101 E2
Firrhill Ln. EH13   101 E2
Fishmarket Sq. EH6   73 D1
Fishwives Causeway EH15   85 F2
Flassches Yd. EH12   89 D2
Fleshmarket Clo. EH1   83 E3
  High St.
Forbes Rd. EH10   92 C1
Forbes St. EH8   83 D5
Fords Rd. EH11   90 C2
Forres St. EH3   82 C2
Forrest Hill EH1   83 E4
Forrest Rd. EH1   83 E4
Forrester Pk. Av. EH12   89 E2
Forrester Pk. Dr. EH12   89 E2
Forrester Pk. Gdns. EH12   89 E2
Forrester Pk. Grn. EH12   89 F2
Forrester Pk. Gro. EH12   89 E2
Forrester Pk. Ln. EH12   89 E2
Forrester Rd. EH12   79 E4
Forteviot Ho. EH17   105 D1
Forth St. EH1   83 E2
Forthview Rd. EH4   81 D1
Forthview Ter. EH4   80 C1
Foulis Cres., Jun.Grn. EH14   99 D3
Fountainbridge EH3   82 B5
Fountainhall Rd. EH9   93 E2
Fowler St. EH11   82 A5
Fox Covert Av. EH12   79 F2
Fox Covert Gro. EH12   79 F2
Fox Spring Cres. EH10   101 F2
Fox Spring Ri. EH10   102 A2
Fraser Av. EH5   72 A3
Fraser Cres. EH5   72 A3
Fraser Gdns. EH5   72 A3
Fraser Gro. EH5   72 A3
Fraser Homes EH13   100 A2
  Spylaw Bk. Rd.
Frederick St. EH2   83 D2
Frogston Av. EH10   102 B4
Frogston Gdns. EH10   102 B4
Frogston Gro. EH10   102 C4
Frogston Rd. E. EH17   103 E5

Frogston Rd. W. EH10 102 B4
Frogston Ter. EH10 102 C4
Furcheons Pk. EH8 85 F3

G

Gabriel's Rd. EH2 83 E2
West Register St.
Gabriel's Rd. EH3 82 C1
Galachlaw Shot EH10 102 C3
Galachlawside EH10 102 C3
Gallolee, The EH13 101 D3
Gamekeeper's Ln. EH4 68 B3
Gamekeeper's Pk. EH4 68 B3
Gamekeeper's Rd. EH4 68 B3
Garden Ter. EH4 69 D4
Gardiner Gro. EH4 80 C1
Gardiner Rd. EH4 80 C1
Gardiner Ter. EH4 80 C2
Gardner St. EH7 84 B2
Lower London Rd.
Gardner's Cres. EH3 82 C4
Garscube Ter. EH12 81 E3
Garvald Ct. EH16 104 B3
Gayfield Clo. EH1 83 F1
Gayfield Sq.
Gayfield Pl. EH7 83 F1
Gayfield Pl. La. EH1 83 F1
Gayfield Sq. EH1 83 F1
Gayfield St. EH1 83 F1
General's Entry EH8 83 E4
Bristo Sq.
Gentle's Entry EH8 84 A3
George IV Bri. EH1 83 E3
George Sq. EH8 83 E5
George Sq. La. EH8 83 E5
George St. EH2 82 C3
Gibb's Entry EH8 83 F4
Simon Sq.
Gibson St. EH7 73 E4
Gibson Ter. EH11 82 B5
Gifford Pk. EH8 83 D5
Gilberstoun EH15 97 E1
Gilberstoun Brig EH15 97 D1
Gilberstoun Ln. EH15 97 E1
Gilberstoun Pl. EH15 97 E1
Gilberstoun Wynd EH15 97 E1
Gilchrist's Entry EH1 83 E2
Leith St.
Gilchrist's La. EH1 83 F2
Greenside Row
Giles St. EH6 73 F3
Gillespie Cres. EH10 82 C5
Gillespie Pl. EH10 82 C5
Gillespie Rd. EH13 99 F3
Gillespie St. EH3 82 C5
Gillsland Pk. EH10 92 A2
Gillsland Rd. EH10 92 A2
Gilmerton Dykes Av. EH17 104 C4
Gilmerton Dykes Cres. EH17 104 C3
Gilmerton Dykes Dr. EH17 105 D4
Gilmerton Dykes Gdns. EH17 104 C3
Gilmerton Dykes Gro. EH17 104 C3
Gilmerton Dykes Ln. EH17 104 C4
Gilmerton Dykes Pl. EH17 104 C3

Gilmerton Dykes Rd. EH17 105 D5
Gilmerton Dykes St. EH17 104 C4
Gilmerton Dykes Ter. EH17 105 D4
Gilmerton Dykes Vw. EH17 105 D4
Gilmerton Pl. EH17 105 D4
Gilmerton Rd. EH16 94 B4
Gilmerton Rd. EH17 104 C1
Gilmerton Sta. Rd. EH17 105 E5
Gilmore Pk. EH3 82 B5
Gilmore Pl. EH3 92 B1
Gilmore Pl. La. EH3 82 C5
Gilmour Rd. EH16 94 A3
Gilmour St. EH8 83 F4
Gilmour's Entry EH8 83 F4
Gilmour St.
Gladstone Pl. EH6 74 C4
Gladstone Ter. EH9 93 F1
Glanville Pl. EH3 82 C1
Kerr St.
Glasgow Rd. EH12 78 B5
Glasgow Rd., Newbr. EH28 78 B5
Glebe, The EH4 68 B2
Glebe Gdns. EH12 79 E5
Glebe Gro. EH12 79 E5
Glebe Rd. EH12 79 E5
Glebe Ter. EH12 79 E5
Glen St. EH3 83 D5
Glenallan Dr. EH16 94 C4
Glenallan Ln. EH16 94 C4
Glenalmond Ct. EH11 89 E4
Glencairn Cres. EH12 82 A4
Glendevon Av. EH12 80 C5
Glendevon Gdns. EH12 80 C5
Glendevon Gro. EH12 80 C5
Glendevon Pk. EH12 80 C5
Glendevon Pl. EH12 80 C5
Glendevon Rd. EH12 90 C1
Glendevon Ter. EH12 80 C5
Glendinning Cres. EH16 104 B1
Glenfinlas St. EH3 82 C3
Glengyle Ter. EH3 82 C5
Glenisla Gdns. EH9 93 E3
Glenisla Gdns. La. EH9 93 E3
Glenisla Gdns.
Glenlea Cotts. EH11 91 D2
Glenlee Av. EH8 85 D3
Glenlee Gdns. EH8 85 D3
Glenlockhart Bk. EH14 91 E5
Glenlockhart Rd. EH10 91 F5
Glenlockhart Rd. EH14 91 E5
Glenlockhart Valley EH14 91 E5
Glenogle Pl. EH3 82 C1
Glenogle Rd. EH3 82 C1
Glenogle Ter. EH3 72 B5
Glenorchy Pl. EH1 83 F2
Greenside Row
Glenorchy Ter. EH9 94 A2
Glenure Ln. EH4 79 E2
Glenvarloch Cres. EH16 104 B1
Gloucester La. EH3 82 C2
Gloucester Pl. EH3 82 C2

Gloucester Sq. EH3 82 C2
Gloucester La.
Gloucester St. EH3 82 C2
Goff Av. EH7 86 A1
Gogar Mains Fm. Rd. EH12 77 D4
Gogar Roundabout EH12 77 F5
Gogarloch Bk. EH12 88 C1
Gogarloch Haugh EH12 88 C1
Gogarloch Muir EH12 88 C1
Gogarloch Rd. EH12 88 B1
Gogarloch Syke EH12 88 B1
Goldenacre Ter. EH3 72 B4
Gordon Ln. EH12 79 F4
Gordon Rd. EH12 79 F4
Gordon St. EH6 74 B4
Gordon Ter. EH16 94 B4
Gorgie Cotts. EH11 91 D2
Gorgie Pk. Clo. EH14 91 E2
Gorgie Pk. Rd. EH14 91 E1
Gorgie Rd. EH11 90 B3
Gosford Pl. EH6 73 D3
Gracemount Av. EH16 104 B2
Gracemount Dr. EH16 104 B3
Gracemount Pl. EH16 104 B3
Gracemount Rd. EH16 104 A4
Gracemount Sq. EH16 104 B3
Graham St. EH6 73 E3
Granby Rd. EH16 94 A3
Grandfield EH6 72 C3
Grandville EH6 72 C2
Grange Ct. EH9 93 F1
Causewayside
Grange Cres. EH9 93 E2
Grange Ln. EH9 93 E2
Grange Ln. Gdns. EH9 93 E2
Grange Rd. EH9 93 E1
Grange Ter. EH9 93 E3
Grant Av. EH13 100 A3
Granton Cres. EH5 71 E2
Granton Gdns. EH5 71 F2
Granton Gro. EH5 71 F2
Granton Mains Av. EH4 70 C2
Granton Mains Bk. EH4 70 C2
Granton Mains Brae EH4 70 C3
Granton Mains Ct. EH4 71 D3
Granton Mains E. EH4 71 D2
Granton Mains Gait EH4 70 C2
Granton Mains Vale EH4 70 C2
Granton Mains Wynd EH4 70 C2
Granton Medway EH5 71 E2
Granton Pk. Av. EH5 71 E1
Granton Pl. EH5 71 F2
Granton Rd. EH5 72 A2
Granton Sq. EH5 71 F1
Granton Ter. EH5 71 F2
Granton Vw. EH5 71 F2
Grantully Pl. EH9 94 A2
Granville Ter. EH10 92 B1

Grassmarket EH1 83 D4
Grays Ct. EH8 83 F4
  West Nicolson St.
Gray's Ln. EH10 92 A2
Graysknowe EH14 90 C4
Great Cannon Bk. 86 B2
  EH15
Great Carleton Pl. 96 B3
  EH16
Great Carleton Sq. 96 B3
  EH16
Great Junct. St. EH6 73 F3
Great King St. EH3 83 D2
Great Michael Clo. 73 D1
  EH6
  Newhaven Pl.
Great Michael Ri. 73 D2
  EH6
Great Michael Sq. 69 F5
  EH4
  Main St.
Great Stuart St. EH3 82 B3
Green, The EH4 69 F4
Green St. EH7 83 E1
Green Way, The 89 F5
  EH14
Greenacre EH14 99 E1
Greenbank Av. EH10 92 B5
Greenbank Cres. 102 A1
  EH10
Greenbank Dr. EH10 92 A5
Greenbank Gdns. 101 F1
  EH10
Greenbank Gro. 101 F1
  EH10
Greenbank La. EH10 92 A5
Greenbank Ln. EH10 101 F1
Greenbank Pk. EH10 101 F1
Greenbank Pl. EH10 92 B5
Greenbank Ri. EH10 101 F2
Greenbank Rd. 92 A5
  EH10
Greenbank Row 101 F1
  EH10
Greenbank Ter. 92 B5
  EH10
Greendale Pk. EH4 70 A4
Greendykes Av. 96 A3
  EH16
Greendykes Dr. 96 A3
  EH16
Greendykes Gdns. 96 A3
  EH16
Greendykes Ho. 96 A3
  EH16
Greendykes Ln. 96 A3
  EH16
Greendykes Rd. 96 A3
  EH16
Greendykes Ter. 96 A3
  EH16
Greenend Dr. EH17 104 C2
Greenend Gdns. 104 C2
  EH17
Greenend Gro. EH17 104 C1
Greenhill Ct. EH9 92 C1
Greenhill Gdns. 92 C1
  EH10
Greenhill Pk. EH10 92 C2
Greenhill Pl. EH10 92 C2
Greenhill Ter. EH10 92 C2
Greenlaw Hedge 101 E2
  EH13
Greenlaw Rig EH13 101 E2
Greenmantle Ln. 94 C5
  EH16
Greenpark EH17 104 C1
Greenside Ct. EH1 83 F2
  Greenside Row

Greenside La. EH1 83 F2
Greenside Pl. EH1 83 F2
  Leith Wk.
Greenside Row EH1 83 F2
Greyfriars Pl. EH1 83 E4
  Candlemaker Row
Grierson Av. EH5 72 A2
Grierson Cres. EH5 72 A2
Grierson Gdns. EH5 72 A2
Grierson Rd. EH5 71 F2
Grierson Sq. EH5 72 A2
Grierson Vills. EH5 72 A2
Grigor Av. EH4 71 D5
Grigor Dr. EH4 71 D5
Grigor Gdns. EH4 71 D5
Grigor Ter. EH4 71 D5
Grindlay St. EH3 82 C4
Grindlay St. Ct. EH3 82 C4
Groathill Av. EH4 81 D1
Groathill Gdns. E. 81 D1
  EH4
Groathill Gdns. W. 81 D1
  EH4
Groathill Rd. N. EH4 70 C5
Groathill Rd. S. EH4 81 D1
Grosvenor Cres. 82 A4
  EH12
Grosvenor Gdns. 82 A4
  EH12
Grosvenor St. EH12 82 B4
Grove Pl., Jun.Grn. 99 D3
Grove St. EH3 82 B4
Grove Ter. EH3 82 B4
  Grove St.
Grundie's Well Rd. 105 E3
  EH17
Guardianswood 81 D4
  EH12
Guardwell Cres. 104 C2
  EH17
Gullan's Clo. EH8 83 F3
Gunnet Ct. EH4 70 A3
Guthrie St. EH1 83 E4
Gyle Av. EH12 88 A1
Gyle Pk. Gdns. EH12 78 B5
Gyle Service La. 88 B1
  EH12
Gylemuir Rd. EH12 79 D5
Gypsy Brae EH5 70 C2

H

Haddington Pl. EH7 83 F1
Haddington's Entry 84 A3
  EH8
  Reid's Clo.
Haddon's Ct. EH8 83 F4
  Nicolson St.
Hailes App. EH13 100 A2
Hailes Av. EH13 100 A1
Hailes Bk. EH13 100 A2
Hailes Cres. EH13 100 A2
Hailes Gdns. EH13 99 F2
Hailes Gro. EH13 100 A2
Hailes Pk. EH13 99 F2
Hailes Quarry 89 E5
  Cottage EH14
  Murrayburn Rd.
Hailes St. EH3 82 C5
Hailes Ter. EH13 100 A2
Hailesland Gdns. 89 F5
  EH14
Hailesland Gro. 89 F5
  EH14
Hailesland Pk. EH14 89 F5
Hailesland Pl. EH14 89 F5
Hailesland Rd. EH14 89 F5
Hainburn Pk. EH10 101 E4

Hall Ter. EH12 79 F5
Hallhead Rd. EH16 94 A4
Hallmyre St. EH6 73 F5
Halmyre St. EH6 73 F5
Hamburgh Pl. EH6 73 E2
  Lindsay Rd.
Hamilton Dr. EH15 86 A4
Hamilton Dr. W. 86 A4
  EH15
Hamilton Gdns. 86 A4
  EH15
Hamilton Gro. EH15 86 A4
Hamilton Pk. EH15 86 A3
Hamilton Pl. EH3 82 C1
Hamilton Ter. EH15 86 B3
Hamilton Wynd EH6 73 E2
Hamilton's Folly Ms. 83 F5
  EH8
Hammermen's Entry 83 F3
  EH8
Hampton Pl. EH12 81 F4
  West Catherine Pl.
Hampton Ter. EH12 81 F4
Hanover St. EH2 83 D2
Harbour Pl. EH15 86 B2
Harbour Rd. EH15 86 B2
Harden Pl. EH11 92 A1
Hardwell Clo. EH8 83 F5
Harelaw Rd. EH13 100 A3
Harewood Cres. 95 F2
  EH16
Harewood Dr. EH16 95 F2
Harewood Rd. EH16 95 F2
Harrismith Pl. EH7 84 B1
Harrison Gdns. 91 F2
  EH11
Harrison La. EH11 92 A1
Harrison Pl. EH11 91 F2
Harrison Rd. EH11 91 F1
Hart St. EH1 83 E1
Hart St. La. EH1 83 E1
  Hart St.
Hartington Gdns. 92 B1
  EH10
Hartington Pl. EH10 92 B1
Harvesters Way 99 D1
  EH14
Hatton Pl. EH9 93 E1
Haugh Pk. EH14 90 B4
Haugh St. EH4 82 C1
Hawkhead Cres. 104 A1
  EH16
Hawkhead Gro. 104 A1
  EH16
Hawkhill EH7 74 C5
Hawkhill Av. EH7 74 B5
Hawkhill Ct. EH7 74 C5
Hawthorn Bldgs. EH4 82 B3
  Belford Rd.
Hawthorn Pl. EH17 105 E3
Hawthorn Ter. EH4 82 B3
  Hawthornbank La.
Hawthornbank La. 82 B3
  EH4
Hawthornbank Pl. 73 E2
  EH6
Hawthornbank Ter. 73 E2
  EH6
Hawthornden Pl. 73 E5
  EH7
Hawthornvale EH6 73 D2
Hay Av. EH16 96 A2
Hay Dr. EH16 96 B2
Hay Pl. EH16 96 A2
Hay Rd. EH16 96 A2
Hay Ter. EH16 96 A2
Hayfield EH12 78 B3
Haymarket EH12 82 B4
Haymarket Ter. 82 A4
  EH12

Haymarket Yards 82 A4
EH12
Hazelbank Ter. EH11 91 F2
Hazeldean Ter. 94 C5
EH16
Hazelwood Gro. 95 D4
EH16
Headrigg Row EH16 94 C5
Henderland Rd. 81 E4
EH12
Henderson Gdns. 73 F3
EH6
Henderson Pl. EH3 83 D1
Henderson Pl. La. 82 C1
EH3
Henderson Row EH3 82 C1
Henderson St. EH6 73 F3
Henderson Ter. 92 A1
EH11
Henry Pl. EH8 84 A5
Henry St. EH8 84 A5
Heriot Bri. EH1 83 D4
Heriot Cross EH1 83 D4
Heriot Bri.
Heriot Hill Ter. EH7 72 C5
Heriot Pl. EH3 83 D4
Heriot Row EH3 82 C2
Hermand Cres. EH11 91 F2
Hermand St. EH11 91 E2
Hermand Ter. EH11 91 E2
Hermiston Ct. EH11 89 E4
Hermitage Dr. EH10 92 C5
Hermitage Gdns. 92 C5
EH10
Hermitage Pk. EH6 74 C5
Hermitage Pk. Gro. 74 C5
EH6
Hermitage Pk. S. 74 C5
EH6
Hermitage Pl. EH6 74 B4
Hermitage Ter. 92 C4
EH10
Hermits Cft. EH8 83 F5
High Buckstone 102 C3
EH10
High Riggs EH3 82 C4
High Sch. Yards 83 F4
EH1
High St. EH1 83 E3
Highway, The EH8 85 F3
Hill Pl. EH8 83 F4
Hill Sq. EH8 83 F4
Hill St. EH2 82 C2
Hill St. N. La. EH2 82 C2
Hill St. S. La. EH2 83 D2
Hillcoat Ln. EH15 86 B2
Hillcoat Pl. EH15 86 B2
Hillend Pl. EH8 85 D2
London Rd.
Hillhouse Rd. EH4 69 F5
Hillpark Av. EH4 80 A1
Hillpark Brae EH4 80 A2
Hillpark Ct. EH4 69 F5
Hillpark Cres. EH4 80 A1
Hillpark Dr. EH4 69 F5
Hillpark Gdns. EH4 80 A1
Hillpark Grn. EH4 80 A1
Hillpark Gro. EH4 80 A1
Hillpark Ln. EH4 80 B1
Hillpark Rd. EH4 80 A1
Hillpark Ter. EH4 80 A1
Hillpark Way EH4 80 B1
Hillpark Wd. EH4 80 B1
Hillside Cres. EH7 83 F1
Hillside St. EH7 84 A1
Hilltown Ter. (Wool.), 97 D5
Dalk. EH22
Hillview EH4 80 C1
Hillview Cres. EH12 79 E4

Hillview Dr. EH12 79 D4
Hillview Rd. EH12 79 E4
Hillview Ter. EH12 79 E4
Hollybank Ter. EH11 91 F2
Holyrood Ct. EH8 84 A3
Holyrood Pk. EH16 84 B3
Holyrood Pk. Rd. 94 A1
EH16
Holyrood Rd. EH8 83 F3
Home St. EH3 82 C5
Hope La. EH15 86 C3
Hope La. N. EH15 86 C3
Hope Pk. Cres. EH8 83 F5
Hope Pk. Sq. EH8 83 F3
Meadow La.
Hope Pk. Ter. EH8 83 F5
Hope St. EH2 82 C3
Hope St. La. EH2 82 C3
Hope Ter. EH9 93 D2
Hopefield Ter. EH6 73 E2
Hopetoun Cres. EH7 83 F1
Hopetoun Cres. La. 83 F1
EH7
Hopetoun St. EH7 73 E5
Horne Ter. EH11 82 B5
Horse Wynd EH8 84 A3
Hoseason Gdns. 79 E2
EH4
Hosie Rigg EH15 96 C1
House o' Hill Av. 70 A5
EH4
House o' Hill Brae 70 A5
EH4
House o' Hill Cres. 70 A5
EH4
House o' Hill Gdns. 70 B5
EH4
House o' Hill Grn. 70 A5
EH4
House o' Hill Gro. 70 A5
EH4
House o' Hill Pl. EH4 70 A5
House o' Hill Rd. 70 A5
EH4
House o' Hill Row 70 B5
EH4
House o' Hill Ter. 80 C1
EH4
Howard Pl. EH3 72 C5
Howard St. EH3 72 C5
Howden Hall Ct. 103 F4
EH16
Howden Hall Cres. 103 F3
EH16
Howden Hall Dr. 103 F4
EH16
Howden Hall Gdns. 104 A3
EH16
Howden Hall Ln. 103 F3
EH16
Howden Hall Pk. 103 F4
EH16
Howden Hall Rd. 104 A4
EH16
Howden Hall Way 104 A4
EH16
Howden St. EH8 83 F5
Howe Pk. EH10 101 F4
Howe St. EH3 83 D2
Hugh Miller Pl. EH3 82 C1
Hunter Sq. EH1 83 E3
Hunter's Clo. EH1 83 D4
Huntingdon Pl. EH7 83 F1
Huntly St. EH3 72 C5
Hutchison Av. EH14 91 D3
Hutchison Cotts. 91 D3
EH14
Hutchison Crossway 91 D2
EH14

Hutchison Gdns. 91 D3
EH14
Hutchison Gro. 91 E3
EH14
Hutchison Ln. EH14 91 D3
Hutchison Medway 91 D3
EH14
Hutchison Pk. EH14 91 D2
Hutchison Pl. EH14 91 D3
Hutchison Rd. EH14 91 D3
Hutchison Ter. EH14 91 D3
Hutchison Vw. EH14 91 D2
Hutton Clo. EH8 84 A3
Hutton Rd. EH8 84 A3
Hyvot Av. EH17 105 D3
Hyvot Bk. Av. EH17 105 E3
Hyvot Ct. EH17 105 D4
Hyvot Gdns. EH17 105 D4
Hyvot Grn. EH17 105 D4
Hyvot Gro. EH17 105 D3
Hyvot Ln. EH17 105 D3
Hyvot Pk. EH17 105 D3
Hyvot Ter. EH17 105 D3
Hyvot Vw. EH17 105 D4

I

Imperial Dock EH6 74 B1
Inchcolm Ct. EH4 70 C3
Inchgarvie Ct. EH4 70 C4
Inchmikery Ct. EH4 70 A3
Inchview Ter. EH7 86 A4
India Bldgs. EH1 83 E4
Victoria St.
India Pl. EH3 82 C2
India St. EH3 82 C2
Industrial Rd. EH6 74 B4
Industry Home EH6 73 E3
Industry La.
Industry La. EH6 73 E3
Infirmary St. EH1 83 F4
Inglewood Pl. EH16 104 B1
Inglis Ct. EH1 83 D4
West Port
Inglis Grn. Rigg 90 C4
EH14
Inglis Grn. Rd. EH14 90 C4
Ingliston Rd. (Inglis.), 76 A5
Newbr. EH28
Inveralmond Dr. EH4 68 A3
Inveralmond Gdns. 68 A3
EH4
Inveralmond Gro. 68 A3
EH4
Inverleith Av. EH3 72 B4
Inverleith Av. S. EH3 72 B4
Inverleith Gdns. EH3 72 A4
Inverleith Gro. EH3 71 F5
Inverleith Pl. EH3 71 F5
Inverleith Pl. La. EH3 72 B4
Inverleith Row EH3 72 B4
Inverleith Ter. EH3 72 B5
Inverleith Ter. La. 72 B5
EH3
Iona St. EH6 73 F5
Ivanhoe Cres. EH16 94 C5
Ivy Ter. EH11 91 F1

J

Jackson's Entry EH8 84 A3
Holyrood Rd.
Jamaica Ms. EH3 82 C2
Jamaica St.
Jamaica St. EH3 82 C2
Jamaica St. N. La. 82 C2
EH3
Jamaica St. S. La. 82 C2
EH3

James' Ct. EH1 *Lawnmarket*	83	E3
James Craig Wk. EH1 *Leith St.*	83	E2
James St. EH15	87	D3
James St. La. EH15	87	D3
Jameson Pl. EH6	73	F5
Jane St. EH6	73	F4
Jane Ter. EH7 *Comely Grn. Cres.*	84	B2
Janefield EH17	104	A5
Jawbone Wk. EH3	83	E5
Jean Armour Av. EH16	94	B5
Jeffrey Av. EH4	80	C2
Jeffrey St. EH1	83	F3
Jessfield Ter. EH6	73	D2
Jewel, The EH15	96	C1
Jock's Lo. EH8	85	D2
John St. EH15	87	D3
John St. La. EH15	87	D3
John St. La. E. EH15 *John St. La.*	87	D3
John St. La. W. EH15	87	D3
John's La. EH6	74	B3
John's Pl. EH6	74	B3
Johnston Ter. EH1	83	D4
Joppa Gdns. EH15	87	D4
Joppa Gro. EH15	87	D4
Joppa Pans EH15	87	F4
Joppa Pk. EH15	87	E4
Joppa Rd. EH15	87	D4
Joppa Ter. EH15	87	D4
Jordan La. EH10	92	C3
Jubilee Rd. EH12	76	A3
Junction Pl. EH6	73	F4
Juniper Av., Jun.Grn.	98	C3
Juniper Gdns., Jun.Grn. EH14	98	C3
Juniper Gro., Jun.Grn. EH14	98	C3
Juniper La., Jun.Grn. EH14	98	C3
Juniper Pk. Rd., Jun.Grn. EH14	99	D3
Juniper Pl., Jun.Grn. EH14	98	C4
Juniper Ter., Jun.Grn. EH14	98	C3
Juniperlee, Jun.Grn. EH14	99	D4

K

Kaimes Rd. EH12	80	A4
Katesmill Rd. EH14	100	B1
Kedslie Pl. EH16	103	F2
Kedslie Rd. EH16	103	F2
Keir St. EH3	83	D4
Keith Cres. EH4	80	C2
Keith Row EH4	81	D2
Keith Ter. EH4	81	D2
Kekewich Av. EH7	86	A1
Kemp Pl. EH3	82	C1
Kenilworth Dr. EH16	104	B1
Kenmure Av. EH8	85	D3
Kerr St. EH3	82	C1
Kew Ter. EH12	81	F4
Kilchurn Ct. EH12 *Craigievar Wynd*	78	B4
Kilgraston Ct. EH9	93	D2
Kilgraston Rd. EH9	93	E2
Kilmaurs Rd. EH16	94	B2
Kilmaurs Ter. EH16	94	B2
Kilncroftside EH14	90	C4
Kincaid's Ct. EH1	83	E4
Kinellan Gdns. EH12	81	D4
Kinellan Rd. EH12	81	D4

King Malcolm Clo. EH10	103	D4
King St. EH6	73	F3
Kinghorn Pl. EH6	73	D3
King's Bri. EH3	83	D4
King's Cramond EH4	68	B4
King's Haugh EH16	95	D2
King's Meadow EH16	94	C2
King's Pl. EH15	86	B1
King's Rd. EH15	86	B2
King's Stables La. EH1	83	D4
King's Stables Rd. EH1	82	C3
King's Ter. EH15	86	A2
Kingsburgh Rd. EH12	81	D4
Kingsknowe Av. EH14	90	B5
Kingsknowe Ct. EH14	90	A5
Kingsknowe Cres. EH14	90	B5
Kingsknowe Dr. EH14	90	B5
Kingsknowe Gdns. EH14	100	A1
Kingsknowe Gro. EH14	100	A1
Kingsknowe Pk. EH14	100	A1
Kingsknowe Pl. EH14	90	A5
Kingsknowe Rd. N. EH14	90	B5
Kingsknowe Rd. S. EH14	90	B5
Kingsknowe Ter. EH14	90	B5
Kingston Av. EH16	95	D5
Kinleith Ind. Est. EH14	98	B5
Kinnaird Pk. EH15	97	D2
Kinnear Rd. EH3	71	F4
Kirk Brae EH16	94	B5
Kirk Cramond EH4	68	B2
Kirk Ln. EH12	79	F5
Kirk Pk. EH16	104	A1
Kirk St. EH6	73	F4
Kirkgate EH6 *Leith Wk.*	73	F4
Kirkgate, Currie EH14	98	A5
Kirkgate EH16	104	A2
Kirkhill Dr. EH16	94	B2
Kirkhill Gdns. EH16	94	B1
Kirkhill Rd. EH16	94	B1
Kirkhill Ter. EH16	94	B1
Kirklands EH12 *Ladywell Av.*	89	E2
Kirkwood Pl. EH7 *Lower London Rd.*	84	B2
Kisimul Ct. EH12 *Craigievar Wynd*	78	C4
Kittle Yards EH9	93	F2
Klondyke St. (Newcr.), Muss. EH21	97	F2
Klondyke Way (Newcr.), Muss. EH21	97	E2
Kyle Pl. EH7 *Montrose Ter.*	84	A2

L

Ladehead EH6	73	D4
Ladiemeadow EH12	89	F1
Lady Lawson St. EH3	83	D4

Lady Menzies Pl. EH7	84	B2
Lady Nairne Cres. EH8	85	E4
Lady Nairne Gro. EH8	85	E4
Lady Nairne Ln. EH8	85	E4
Lady Nairne Pl. EH8	85	E4
Lady Rd. EH16	94	B3
Lady Stair's Clo. EH1 *North Bk. St.*	83	E3
Lady Wynd EH1	83	D4
Ladysmith Rd. EH9	93	F4
Ladywell Av. EH12	79	E5
Ladywell Gdns. EH12	89	E1
Ladywell Ho. EH12	79	D5
Ladywell Rd. EH12	79	D5
Laichfield EH14	90	C3
Laichpark La. EH14 *Chesser Ln.*	90	C3
Laichpark Pl. EH14	90	C3
Laichpark Rd. EH14	90	C3
Laing Ter. EH15	87	D3
Lamb's Clo. EH8 *East Crosscauseway*	83	F5
Lamb's Ct. EH6 *Pier Pl.*	72	C1
Lammermoor Ter. EH16	95	D5
Lampacre Rd. EH12	89	F1
Lanark Rd. EH13	99	F2
Lanark Rd. EH14	90	B5
Lanark Rd., Jun.Grn.EH14	99	D3
Lanark Rd. W., Currie EH14	98	A5
Lang Linn Path EH10	93	D5
Langton Rd. EH9	93	F3
Lansdowne Cres. EH12	82	A4
Lapicide Pl. EH6	73	E3
Larbourfield EH11	89	E5
Largo Pl. EH6	73	E3
Lasswade Bk. EH17	104	C4
Lasswade Gro. EH17	104	C4
Lasswade Rd. EH16	104	B2
Lasswade Rd. EH17	105	D4
Latch Pk. EH13	101	D2
Lauder Ln. EH9	93	E2
Lauder Rd. EH9	93	E1
Lauderdale St. EH9	93	D1
Laurel Ter. EH11	91	F1
Laurie St. EH6	74	B4
Lauriston Fm. Rd. EH4	69	E4
Lauriston Gdns. EH3	83	D4
Lauriston Pk. EH3	83	D5
Lauriston Pl. EH3	83	D4
Lauriston St. EH3	83	D4
Lauriston Ter. EH3	83	D4
Laverockbank Av. EH5	72	C2
Laverockbank Cres. EH5	72	C2
Laverockbank Gdns. EH5	72	C2
Laverockbank Gro. EH5	72	C2
Laverockbank Rd. EH5	72	C2
Laverockbank Ter. EH5	72	C2
Laverockdale Cres. EH13	100	B4
Laverockdale Ln. EH13	100	B4

Laverockdale Pk. 100 B4
  EH13
Law Pl. EH15 86 B2
  Pipe St.
Lawnmarket EH1 83 E3
Leadervale Rd. 103 F1
  EH16
Leadervale Ter. 103 F1
  EH16
Leamington Pl. 82 C5
  EH10
  Leamington Ter.
Leamington Rd. EH3 82 B5
Leamington Ter. 82 C5
  EH10
Learmonth Av. EH4 82 A1
Learmonth Ct. EH4 82 A2
Learmonth Cres. 82 A2
  EH4
Learmonth Gdns. 82 A2
  EH4
Learmonth Gdns. La. 82 A2
  EH4
Learmonth Gdns. Ms. 82 B2
  EH4
Learmonth Gro. EH4 82 A1
Learmonth Pk. EH4 82 A1
Learmonth Pl. EH4 82 A1
Learmonth Ter. EH4 82 A1
Learmonth Ter. La. 82 A2
  EH4
Learmonth Vw. EH4 82 B2
  Learmonth Ter.
Lee Cres. EH15 86 C3
Leith Docks EH6 73 F1
Leith Links EH6 74 B4
Leith St. EH1 83 E2
Leith St. Ter. EH1 83 E2
  Leith St.
Leith Wk. EH6 73 F5
Leith Wk. EH7 83 F2
Lennel Av. EH12 81 D3
Lennox Row EH5 72 B2
Lennox St. EH4 82 B2
Lennox St. La. EH4 82 B2
Lennymuir EH12 76 C2
Leopold Pl. EH7 83 F1
Leslie Pl. EH4 82 B1
Leven Clo. EH3 82 C5
  Leven St.
Leven St. EH3 82 C5
Leven Ter. EH3 83 D5
Lewis Ter. EH11 82 B5
Liberton Brae EH16 104 A1
Liberton Dr. EH16 103 F1
Liberton Gdns. 104 A3
  EH16
Liberton Pl. EH16 104 A2
Liberton Rd. EH16 94 B5
Liddesdale Pl. EH3 82 C1
Lily Ter. EH11 91 F2
  Shandon Pl.
Lilyhill Ter. EH8 85 D2
Limefield EH17 105 E4
Limes, The EH10 92 B2
Lindean Pl. EH6 74 C4
Lindsay Pl. EH1 83 E4
  Chambers St.
Lindsay Pl. EH6 73 E2
Lindsay Rd. EH6 73 E2
Lindsay St. EH6 73 E2
Links Gdns. EH6 74 C3
Links Gdns. La. EH6 74 C3
Links La. EH6 74 C3
Links Pl. EH6 74 B3
Lismore Av. EH8 85 D2
Lismore Cres. EH8 85 D2
Little France Ho. 105 D1
  EH17

Little France Mills 95 E5
  EH16
Little King St. EH1 83 E2
Little Rd. EH16 104 A2
Livingstone Pl. EH9 93 E1
Lixmount Av. EH5 72 C2
Lixmount Gdns. EH5 72 C2
Loaning Cres. EH7 85 E1
Loaning Rd. EH7 85 D1
Loch Rd. EH4 80 B1
Lochend Av. EH7 74 C5
Lochend Castle 84 C1
  Barns EH7
Lochend Clo. EH8 84 A3
  Canongate
Lochend Cres. EH7 85 D1
Lochend Dr. EH7 84 C1
Lochend Gdns. EH7 84 C1
Lochend Gro. EH7 85 D1
Lochend Pk. EH7 84 C1
Lochend Quad. EH7 85 D1
Lochend Rd. EH6 74 B4
Lochend Rd. EH7 74 B4
Lochend Rd. S. EH7 84 C1
Lochend Sq. EH7 84 C1
Lochrin Bldgs. EH3 82 C5
Lochrin Pl. EH3 82 C5
Lochrin Ter. EH3 82 C5
  Thornybauk
Lochside Av. EH12 88 A1
Lochside Ct. EH12 88 B2
Lochside Cres. EH12 88 A1
Lochside Pl. EH12 88 B2
Lochside Vw. EH12 88 A1
Lochside Way EH12 88 B2
Lochview Ct. EH8 84 A3
Lockerby Cotts. 104 C3
  EH16
Lockerby Cres. 104 C3
  EH16
Lockerby Gro. EH16 104 C3
Lockharton Av. 91 E4
  EH14
Lockharton Cres. 91 F4
  EH14
Lockharton Gdns. 91 F3
  EH14
Logan St. EH3 83 D1
Loganlea Av. EH7 85 E1
Loganlea Dr. EH7 85 E1
Loganlea Gdns. EH7 85 D1
Loganlea Ln. EH7 85 E1
Loganlea Pl. EH7 85 E2
Loganlea Rd. EH7 85 E1
Loganlea Ter. EH7 85 E1
Logie Grn. Gdns. 72 C5
  EH7
Logie Grn. Ln. EH7 72 C5
Logie Grn. Rd. EH7 72 C5
Logie Mill EH7 72 C5
Lomond Rd. EH5 72 B2
London Rd. EH7 83 F2
London Rd. EH8 84 B2
London St. EH3 83 E1
Long Craig Rigg 70 C1
  EH5
Long Craig Rd. EH5 70 C1
Longformacus Rd. 104 A2
  EH16
Longstone Av. EH14 90 B4
Longstone Cotts. 90 B4
  EH14
  Longstone Rd.
Longstone Cres. 90 B3
  EH14
Longstone Gdns. 90 A3
  EH14
Longstone Gro. 90 B4
  EH14

Longstone Pk. EH14 90 B4
Longstone Rd. EH14 90 A4
Longstone St. EH14 90 B4
Longstone Ter. 90 A3
  EH14
Longstone Vw. 90 A3
  EH14
Lonsdale Ter. EH3 83 D5
Lord Russell Pl. EH9 93 F1
  Causewayside
Lorne Pl. EH6 73 F5
Lorne Sq. EH6 73 F5
Lorne St. EH6 73 F5
Lothian Pl. EH1 82 C4
Lothian Rd. EH3 82 C4
Lothian St. EH1 83 E4
Lovers' Ln. EH9 93 E1
Lower Gilmore Pl. 92 C5
  EH3
Lower Granton Rd. 71 F1
  EH5
Lower Joppa EH15 87 D3
Lower London Rd. 84 B2
  EH7
Lufra Bk. EH5 72 A2
Lussielaw Rd. EH9 94 A4
Lutton Pl. EH8 83 F5
Lygon Rd. EH16 94 A4
Lyne St. EH7 84 B2
Lynedoch Pl. EH3 82 B3
Lynedoch Pl. La. EH3 82 B3

M

Macdowall Rd. EH9 93 F3
Mackenzie Pl. EH3 82 B2
Madeira Pl. EH6 73 E3
Madeira St. EH6 73 E2
Magdala Cres. EH12 82 A4
Magdala Ms. EH12 82 A4
Magdalene Av. EH15 86 C5
Magdalene Ct. EH15 86 C5
Magdalene Dr. EH15 86 C5
Magdalene Gdns. 86 C5
  EH15
Magdalene Ln. EH15 86 C5
Magdalene Medway 86 C5
  EH15
Magdalene Pl. EH15 86 C5
Maidencraig Ct. EH4 81 D1
Maidencraig Cres. 81 D1
  EH4
Maidencraig Gro. 81 D1
  EH4
Main Point EH3 83 D4
Main St. (David.) EH4 69 F5
Mains of Craigmillar 95 E4
  EH16
Malbet Pk. EH16 104 B2
Malta Grn. EH4 82 C1
  St. Bernard's Row
Malta Ter. EH4 82 C1
Manderston St. EH6 73 F4
Mannering Pl. EH16 104 B1
Manor Pl. EH3 82 B3
Manse Rd. EH12 79 E5
Manse St. EH12 79 E5
Mansfield Pl. EH3 83 E1
Mansionhouse Rd. 93 E1
  EH9
March Gait EH4 80 A1
March Gro. EH4 80 B1
March Pines EH4 80 A1
March Rd. EH4 80 A1
Marchfield Gdns. 69 F5
  EH4
  Hillhouse Rd.
Marchfield Gro. EH4 70 A5
Marchfield Pk. EH4 69 F5

Marchfield Pk. La. 69 F5
EH4
Marchfield Ter. EH4 80 B1
Marchhall Cres. 94 B1
EH16
Marchhall Pl. EH16 94 B1
Marchhall Rd. EH16 94 B1
Marchmont Cres. 93 E1
EH9
Marchmont Rd. EH9 93 D1
Marchmont St. EH9 93 D1
Mardale Cres. EH10 92 B2
Marine Dr. EH4 69 D2
Marine Dr. EH5 69 F2
Marine Esp. EH6 75 D3
Marionville Av. EH7 84 C1
Marionville Cres. 85 D1
EH7
Marionville Dr. EH7 85 D1
Marionville Gro. 85 D1
EH7
Marionville Medway 85 D1
EH7
Marionville Pk. EH7 84 C1
Marionville Rd. EH7 84 C2
Marischal Pl. EH4 81 D2
Queensferry Rd.
Maritime La. EH6 74 B3
Maritime St. EH6 74 B3
Market St. EH1 83 E3
Marlborough St. 86 C3
EH15
Marmion Cres. EH16 94 C5
Marshall Pl. EH7 84 B2
Lower London Rd.
Marshall St. EH8 83 E4
Marshall's Ct. EH1 83 F2
Martello Ct. EH4 70 A3
Martin's Ct. EH6 74 B2
Bernard St.
Maryfield EH7 84 A2
Maryfield EH15 86 C2
Maryfield Pl. EH7 84 B2
Mary's Pl. EH4 82 B1
Raeburn Pl.
Marytree Ho. EH17 105 D1
Maurice Pl. EH9 93 E4
Maxwell St. EH10 92 B3
May Ct. EH4 70 A3
Maybank Vills. EH12 79 E4
Victor Pk. Ter.
Maybury Dr. EH12 78 B3
Maybury Rd. EH4 78 B2
Maybury Rd. EH12 78 B5
Mayfield Gdns. EH9 94 A2
Mayfield Gdns. La. 94 A2
EH9
Mayfield Pl. EH12 79 E5
Mayfield Rd. EH9 94 A3
Mayfield Ter. EH9 94 A1
Mayville Gdns. EH5 72 C2
Mayville Gdns. E. 72 C2
EH5
McDonald Pl. EH7 73 D5
McDonald Rd. EH7 73 D5
McDonald St. EH7 73 E5
McKelvie Par. EH5 72 B1
McLaren Rd. EH9 94 B2
McLaren Ter. EH11 82 B4
McLeod St. EH11 81 F5
McNeill St. EH11 82 B5
Meadow La. EH8 83 E5
Meadow Pl. EH9 93 E1
Meadow Pl. La. EH9 93 E1
Meadow Pl. Rd. 79 D5
EH12
Meadowbank EH8 84 B2
Meadowbank Av. 84 C2
EH8

Meadowbank Cres. 84 C2
EH8
Meadowbank Pl. 85 D2
EH8
London Rd.
Meadowbank Ter. 84 C2
EH8
Meadowfield Av. 85 E4
EH8
Meadowfield Ct. 85 E4
EH8
Meadowfield Dr. 85 E4
EH8
Meadowfield Gdns. 85 E5
EH8
Meadowfield Rd. 77 F4
EH12
Meadowfield Ter. 85 E5
EH8
Meadowhouse Rd. 79 F5
EH12
Meadowspot EH10 91 F4
Mearenside EH12 78 B3
Medwin Ho. EH11 89 D5
Meggetland Gate 91 D3
EH14
Meggetland Ter. 91 F3
EH14
Melgund Ter. EH7 83 E1
Melville Cres. EH3 82 B3
Melville Dr. EH9 93 E1
Melville Pl. EH3 82 B3
Queensferry St.
Melville St. EH3 82 B3
Melville St. La. EH3 82 B3
Melville Ter. EH9 93 E1
Mentone Av. EH15 86 C2
Mentone Gdns. EH9 94 A2
Mentone Ter. EH9 94 A3
Merchant St. EH1 83 E4
Candlemaker Row
Merchiston Av. 92 B1
EH10
Merchiston Bk. Av. 92 B2
EH10
Merchiston Bk. 92 B2
Gdns. EH10
Merchiston Cres. 92 B2
EH10
Merchiston Gdns. 92 A3
EH10
Merchiston Gro. 91 F1
EH11
Merchiston Ms. 92 B1
EH10
Merchiston Pk. 92 B1
EH10
Merchiston Pl. EH10 92 B1
Mertoun Pl. EH11 92 A1
Meuse La. EH2 83 E3
Mid Gillsland Rd. 92 A2
EH10
Mid Gogarloch 88 B1
Syke EH12
Mid Liberton EH16 94 B4
Mid New Cultins 88 C4
EH11
Mid Steil EH10 91 F5
Middle Meadow Wk. 83 E5
EH3
Middle Pier EH5 71 F1
Middleby Ct. EH9 94 A2
South Gray St.
Middleby St. EH9 94 A2
Middlefield EH7 73 E5
Middleknowe EH14 98 C1
Middlepark EH14 98 C1
Middleshot EH14 98 C1
Midmar Av. EH10 93 D4

Midmar Dr. EH10 93 D4
Midmar Gdns. EH10 92 C5
Mill La. EH6 73 F3
Millar Cres. EH10 92 B3
Millar Pl. EH10 92 B3
Millar Pl. La. EH10 92 B3
Millbrae Wynd EH14 90 C4
Miller Row EH4 82 B3
Millerfield Pl. EH9 93 E1
Millerhill Rd., Dalk. 96 C4
EH22
Milnacre EH6 73 D3
Milton Cres. EH15 86 B5
Milton Dr. EH15 87 E4
Milton Gdns. N. 86 B5
EH15
Milton Gdns. S. 86 B5
EH15
Milton Gro. EH15 87 F4
Milton Link EH15 87 D5
Milton Rd. EH15 86 C5
Milton Rd. E. EH15 87 D5
Milton Rd. W. EH15 85 F5
Milton St. EH8 84 B2
Milton Ter. EH15 87 F4
Minto St. EH9 94 A1
Mitchell St. EH6 74 B3
Moat EH14 91 E2
Moat Pl. EH14 91 E2
Moat St. EH14 91 E2
Moat Ter. EH14 91 E2
Moira Pk. EH7 85 F2
Moira Ter. EH7 85 F2
Moira Ter. La. EH7 85 F2
Moncreiffe Ho. EH17 105 D1
Moncrieff Ter. EH9 93 F1
Monkbarns Gdns. 104 B1
EH16
Monkwood Ct. EH9 93 E2
Monmouth Ter. EH3 72 B4
Montagu Ter. EH3 72 B4
Montague St. EH8 83 F5
Montgomery St. EH7 83 F1
Montgomery St. La. 83 F1
EH7
Montpelier EH10 92 B1
Montpelier Pk. EH10 92 B1
Montpelier Ter. EH10 92 B1
Montrose Ter. EH7 84 A2
Moray Pk. EH7 84 B1
Moray Pk. Ter. EH7 84 B1
Moray Pl. EH3 82 C2
Moredun Dykes 105 D3
Rd. EH17
Moredun Ho. EH17 105 D1
Moredun Pk. Ct. 105 D2
EH17
Moredun Pk. Dr. 105 D2
EH17
Moredun Pk. Gdns. 105 D1
EH17
Moredun Pk. Grn. 105 E2
EH17
Moredun Pk. Gro. 105 E2
EH17
Moredun Pk. Ln. 105 D2
EH17
Moredun Pk. Rd. 105 D2
EH17
Moredun Pk. St. 105 D2
EH17
Moredun Pk. Vw. 105 E2
EH17
Moredun Pk. Wk. 105 E2
EH17
Moredun Pk. Way 105 D2
EH17
Moredunvale Bk. 105 D1
EH17

Moredunvale Grn. 105 D1
EH17
Moredunvale Gro. 105 D1
EH17
Moredunvale Ln. 105 D1
EH17
Moredunvale Pk. 105 D1
EH17
Moredunvale Pl. 105 D1
EH17
Moredunvale Rd. 105 D1
EH17
Moredunvale Vw. 105 D1
EH17
Moredunvale Way 105 D1
EH17
Morningside Ct. 92 C4
EH10
Morningside Dr. 92 A4
EH10
Morningside Gdns. 92 A4
EH10
Morningside Gro. 92 A4
EH10
Morningside Pk. 92 B3
EH10
Morningside Pl. 92 B3
EH10
Morningside Rd. 92 B2
EH10
Morningside Ter. 92 B3
EH10
Morrison Circ. EH3 82 B4
Morrison Cres. EH3 82 B5
Morrison Link EH3 82 B4
Morrison St. EH3 82 B4
Morton St. EH15 87 D4
Mortonhall Gate 103 E4
EH16
Mortonhall Pk. Av. 103 F4
EH17
Mortonhall Pk. Bk. 104 A4
EH17
Mortonhall Pk. Cres. 104 A4
EH17
Mortonhall Pk. Dr. 104 A4
EH17
Mortonhall Pk. Gdns. 103 F4
EH17
Mortonhall Pk. Grn. 103 F4
EH17
Mortonhall Pk. Gro. 103 F4
EH17
Mortonhall Pk. Ln. 103 F4
EH17
Mortonhall Pk. Pl. 104 A4
EH17
Mortonhall Pk. Ter. 104 A4
EH17
Mortonhall Pk. Vw. 103 F4
EH17
Mortonhall Pk. Way 103 F4
EH17
Mortonhall Rd. EH9 93 E3
Morven St. EH4 79 D2
Morvenside EH14 98 C1
Morvenside Clo. 98 C1
EH14
Mossgiel Wk. EH16 94 B5
Moston Ter. EH9 94 A2
Mound, The EH1 83 D3
Mound, The EH2 83 D3
Mound Pl. EH1 83 D3
Mount Gra. EH9 93 D2
Mount Lo. EH15 86 C3
Mount Vernon Rd. 104 B1
EH16
Mountcastle Bk. 86 A3
EH8

Mountcastle Cres. 85 F3
EH8
Mountcastle Dr. N. 85 F3
EH8
Mountcastle Dr. N. 86 A4
EH15
Mountcastle Dr. S. 86 A4
EH15
Mountcastle Gdns. 85 F3
EH8
Mountcastle Grn. 85 F3
EH8
Mountcastle Gro. 85 F3
EH8
Mountcastle Ln. EH8 85 F3
Mountcastle Pk. EH8 85 F3
Mountcastle Cres.
Mountcastle Pl. EH8 85 F2
Mountcastle Ter. 85 F3
EH8
Mounthooly Ln. 103 D4
EH10
Muir Wd. Cres., 98 B4
Currie EH14
Muir Wd. Dr., 98 B4
Currie EH14
Muir Wd. Gro., 98 B4
Currie EH14
Muir Wd. Pl., 98 B4
Currie EH14
Muir Wd. Rd., 98 A4
Currie EH14
Muirdale Ter. EH4 80 C1
Muirend Av., 99 E2
Jun.Grn. EH14
Muirhouse Av. EH4 70 B4
Muirhouse Av. N. 70 B3
EH4
Muirhouse Bk. EH4 70 B4
Muirhouse Clo. EH4 70 A4
Muirhouse Ct. EH4 70 A3
Muirhouse Cres. EH4 70 B3
Muirhouse Dr. EH4 70 A3
Muirhouse Gdns. 70 A3
EH4
Muirhouse Grn. EH4 70 B4
Muirhouse Gro. EH4 70 A3
Muirhouse Ln. EH4 70 B3
Muirhouse Medway 70 A4
EH4
Muirhouse Pk. EH4 70 A4
Muirhouse Parkway 70 A3
EH4
Muirhouse Pl. E. EH4 70 B4
Muirhouse Pl. W. 70 B4
EH4
Muirhouse Ter. EH4 70 A4
Muirhouse Vw. EH4 70 A3
Muirhouse Way EH4 70 B4
Muirside EH13 101 E4
Mulberry Pl. EH6 73 D3
Newhaven Rd.
Munro Dr. EH13 100 A4
Munro Pl. EH3 72 C5
Canonmills
Murano Pl. EH7 83 F1
Murdoch Ter. EH11 82 B5
Murieston Cres. 81 F5
EH11
Murieston Cres. La. 81 F5
EH11
Murieston La. EH11 81 F5
Murieston Pl. EH11 81 F5
Murieston Rd. EH11 81 F5
Murieston Ter. EH11 81 F5
Murray Cotts. EH12 79 D5
Murrayburn App. 89 E5
EH14
Murrayburn Dr. EH14 89 D5

Murrayburn Gdns. 89 F5
EH14 -
Murrayburn Gate 89 E5
EH14
Murrayburn Grn. 89 F5
EH14
Murrayburn Gro. 89 F5
EH14
Murrayburn Pk. 89 E5
EH14
Murrayburn Pl. 89 E5
EH14
Murrayburn Rd. 89 E5
EH14
Murrayfield Av. 81 E4
EH12
Murrayfield Dr. 81 D4
EH12
Murrayfield Gdns. 81 E4
EH12
Murrayfield Pl. EH12 81 E4
Murrayfield Rd. 81 D3
EH12
Murrays, The EH17 104 C5
Murrays Brae, The 104 C5
EH17
Musselburgh Rd. 87 E4
EH15
Myreside Ct. EH10 91 F4
Myreside Rd. EH10 92 A3
Myrtle Ter. EH11 91 F1

N

Nantwich Dr. EH7 75 F5
Napier Rd. EH10 92 A2
Neidpath Ct. EH12 78 B4
Craigievar Wynd
Nellfield EH16 104 B1
Nelson Pl. EH3 83 D2
Dublin Meuse
Nelson St. EH3 83 D1
Nether Bakehouse 84 A3
EH8
Gentle's Entry
Nether Craigour 95 E5
EH17
Nether Craigwell 83 F3
EH8
Nether Currie Cres., 98 B4
Currie EH14
Nether Currie Pl., 98 B4
Currie EH14
Nether Currie Rd., 98 B4
Currie EH14
Netherbank EH16 103 F3
Netherbank Vw. 103 F3
EH16
Netherby Rd. EH5 72 B2
New Arthur Pl. EH8 83 F4
New Belfield EH8 85 F4
New Bells Ct. EH6 74 B3
New Broompark EH5 71 E1
New Broughton EH3 83 F5
New Cut Rigg EH6 73 D3
New John's Pl. EH8 83 F5
New Lairdship Pl. 89 E3
EH11
New Lairdship Yards 89 E3
EH11
New La. EH6 73 D2
New Mkt. Rd. EH14 91 E4
New Mart Rd. EH14 90 C3
New Orchardfield 73 F4
EH6
New Skinners Clo. 83 E3
EH1
Blackfriars St.
New St. EH8 83 F3

New St. EH17 105 D4
New Swanston 101 E4
 EH10
New Twr. Pl. EH15 86 C2
 Figgate La.
Newbattle Ter. EH10 92 C4
Newcraighall Dr. 97 E2
 (Newcr.), Muss. EH21
Newcraighall Rd. 96 C2
 EH15
Newcraighall Rd., 97 E2
 Muss. EH21
Newhaven Main St. 72 C1
 EH6
Newhaven Pl. EH6 73 D1
Newhaven Rd. EH6 73 D2
Newington Rd. EH9 93 F1
Newkirkgate EH6 73 F4
Newlands Pk. EH9 94 A2
 Mayfield Gdns.
Newtoft St. EH17 105 E4
Newton St. EH11 91 F1
Nichollfield EH6 73 D2
Nicolson Sq. EH8 83 F4
Nicolson St. EH8 83 F4
Niddrie Cotts. EH15 97 D2
Niddrie Fm. Gro. 95 F2
 EH16
Niddrie Ho. Av. 96 A3
 EH16
Niddrie Ho. Dr. 96 B3
 EH16
Niddrie Ho. Gdns. 96 B3
 EH16
Niddrie Ho. Gro. 96 B3
 EH16
Niddrie Ho. Pk. 96 A3
 EH16
Niddrie Ho. Sq. 96 A3
 EH16
 Niddrie Ho. Pk.
Niddrie Mains Ct. 96 B2
 EH16
Niddrie Mains Dr. 95 F2
 EH16
Niddrie Mains Rd. 96 A2
 EH15
Niddrie Mains Rd. 95 E2
 EH16
Niddrie Mains Ter. 95 F2
 EH16
Niddrie Marischal 96 A2
 Cres. EH16
Niddrie Marischal 96 A3
 Dr. EH16
Niddrie Marischal 96 A2
 Gdns. EH16
Niddrie Marischal 96 A3
 Grn. EH16
Niddrie Marischal 96 B2
 Gro. EH16
Niddrie Marischal 96 A2
 Ln. EH16
Niddrie Marischal 96 A2
 Pl. EH16
Niddrie Marischal 96 B2
 Rd. EH16
Niddrie Marischal 96 A2
 St. EH16
Niddrie Mill Av. 96 B2
 EH15
Niddrie Mill Cres. 96 B1
 EH15
Niddrie Mill Dr. 96 B2
 EH15
Niddrie Mill Gro. 96 B2
 EH15
Niddrie Mill Pl. 96 B2
 EH15

Niddrie Mill Ter. 96 B2
 EH15
Niddry St. EH1 83 E3
Niddry St. S. EH1 83 F4
 Cowgate
Nigel Ln. EH16 104 B1
Nile Gro. EH10 92 C3
Nisbet Ct. EH7 74 C5
Noble Pl. EH6 74 C4
North Bk. St. EH1 83 E3
North Bri. EH1 83 E3
North Bri. Arc. EH1 83 E3
 North Bri.
North Bughtlin Bk. 78 C2
 EH12
North Bughtlin Brae 78 C2
 EH12
North Bughtlin Gate 78 C2
 EH12
North Bughtlin Neuk 78 B2
 EH12
North Bughtlin Pl. 78 C2
 EH12
North Bughtlin Rd. 78 B2
 EH12
North Bughtlinfield 78 B2
 EH12
North Bughtlinrig 78 B2
 EH12
North Bughtlinside 78 B2
 EH12
North Cairntow 95 E1
 EH16
North Castle St. EH2 82 C2
North Charlotte St. 82 C3
 EH2
North E. Circ. Pl. 82 C2
 EH3
North Fort St. EH6 73 E2
North Grns. EH15 96 C1
North Gyle Av. EH12 78 C5
North Gyle Dr. EH12 78 C4
North Gyle Fm. Ct. 78 B5
 EH12
North Gyle Fm. La. 78 B5
 EH12
North Gyle Gro. 78 B4
 EH12
North Gyle Ln. EH12 78 B4
North Gyle Pk. EH12 78 B4
North Gyle Rd. EH12 78 C4
North Gyle Ter. 78 B5
 EH12
North Hillhousefield 73 E2
 EH6
North Junct. St. EH6 73 E2
North Leith Mill EH6 73 F2
North Leith Sands 73 E2
 EH6
North Meadow Wk. 83 D5
 EH3
North Meadow Wk. 83 E5
 EH8
North Meggetland 91 F3
 EH14
North Pk. Ter. EH4 82 B1
North Peffer Pl. EH16 95 E2
North Richmond St. 83 F4
 EH8
 West Adam St.
North St. Andrew La. 83 E2
 EH2
 North St. Andrew St.
North St. Andrew St. 83 E2
 EH2
North St. David St. 83 E2
 EH2
North Wk., The 92 C4
 EH10

North Way, The EH8 85 E3
North Werber Pk. 71 E5
 EH4
North Werber Pl. 71 E5
 EH4
North Werber Rd. 71 E4
 EH4
North W. Circ. Pl. 82 C2
 EH3
Northcote St. EH11 82 A5
Northfield Av. EH8 85 E3
Northfield Bdy. EH8 85 E2
Northfield Circ. EH8 85 E3
Northfield Cres. EH8 85 E3
Northfield Dr. EH8 85 F4
Northfield Fm. Av. 85 F4
 EH8
Northfield Fm. Rd. 85 F3
 EH8
Northfield Gdns. 85 F4
 EH8
Northfield Gro. EH8 85 F4
Northfield Pk. EH8 85 F3
Northfield Pk. Gro. 85 F3
 EH8
Northfield Rd. EH8 85 E3
Northfield Sq. EH8 85 F3
Northfield Ter. EH8 85 E3
 Willowbrae Rd.
Northlawn Ter. EH4 69 E4
Northumberland Pl. 83 D2
 EH3
 Northumberland La.
Northumberland 83 D2
 Pl. La. EH3
Northumberland St. 83 D2
 EH3
Northumberland 83 D2
 St. N. E. La. EH3
Northumberland 83 D2
 St. N. W. La. EH3
Northumberland 83 D2
 St. S. E. La. EH3
Northumberland 83 D2
 St. S. W. La. EH3
Northview Ct. EH4 70 B3
Norton Pk. EH7 84 B1

O

Oak La. EH12 79 F2
Oakfield Pl. EH8 83 F4
Oakville Ter. EH6 74 C4
Observatory Grn. 93 F4
 EH9
Observatory Rd. EH9 93 F4
Ocean Dr. EH6 73 F2
Ochiltree Gdns. 95 D5
 EH16
Ogilvie Ter. EH11 91 F2
Old Assembly Clo. 83 E3
 EH1
 High St.
Old Broughton EH3 83 E1
Old Burdiehouse 104 A5
 Rd. EH17
Old Ch. La. EH15 85 D5
Old Dalkeith Rd. 94 C3
 EH16
Old Fm. Av. EH13 100 B2
Old Fm. Pl. EH13 100 B2
Old Fishmarket Clo. 83 E3
 EH1
Old Kirk Rd. EH12 79 F4
Old Mill La. EH8 94 B4
Old Tolbooth Wynd 83 F3
 EH8
Orchard Bk. EH4 81 F2
Orchard Brae EH4 82 A1

Orchard Brae Av. EH4 81 F2
Orchard Brae Gdns. EH4 81 F2
Orchard Brae Gdns. W. EH4 81 F2
Orchard Brae W. EH4 82 A1
Orchard Brae
Orchard Cres. EH4 81 E2
Orchard Dr. EH4 81 E2
Orchard Gro. EH4 82 A1
Orchard Pl. EH4 81 F1
Orchard Rd. EH4 81 F2
Orchard Rd. S. EH4 81 E2
Orchard Ter. EH4 81 F2
Orchard Toll EH4 81 F2
Orchardfield Av. EH12 79 E5
Orchardfield La. EH6 73 F4
Orchardhead Ln. EH16 104 A1
Orchardhead Rd. EH16 104 A1
Ormelie Ter. EH15 87 D3
Ormidale Ter. EH12 81 D4
Ormiston Ter. EH12 79 E5
Orrok Pk. EH16 94 B5
Orwell Pl. EH11 82 A5
Orwell Ter. EH11 82 A5
Osborne Ter. EH12 81 F4
Oswald Ct. EH9 93 E3
Oswald Rd. EH9 93 E3
Oswald Rd. EH12 79 E5
Otterburn Pk. EH14 100 B1
Oxcars Ct. EH4 70 A3
Oxcraig St. EH5 71 F1
Oxford St. EH8 84 A5
Oxford Ter. EH4 82 B2
Oxgangs Av. EH13 101 F2
Oxgangs Bk. EH13 101 F3
Oxgangs Brae EH13 101 F3
Oxgangs Bdy. EH13 101 F3
Oxgangs Cres. EH13 101 F2
Oxgangs Dr. EH13 101 E2
Oxgangs Fm. Av. EH13 101 E3
Oxgangs Fm. Dr. EH13 101 E3
Oxgangs Fm. Gdns. EH13 101 E3
Oxgangs Fm. Gro. EH13 101 E3
Oxgangs Fm. Ln. EH13 101 E3
Oxgangs Fm. Ter. EH13 101 E3
Oxgangs Gdns. EH13 101 E2
Oxgangs Grn. EH13 101 F2
Oxgangs Gro. EH13 101 F2
Oxgangs Hill EH13 101 F2
Oxgangs Ln. EH13 101 F2
Oxgangs Medway EH13 101 F3
Oxgangs Pk. EH13 101 F3
Oxgangs Path EH13 101 F3
Oxgangs Brae
Oxgangs Path E. EH13 101 F3
Oxgangs Pl. EH13 101 E2
Oxgangs Ri. EH13 101 F2
Oxgangs Rd. EH10 101 F4
Oxgangs Rd. EH13 101 F4
Oxgangs Rd. N. EH13 101 E3
Oxgangs Rd. N. EH14 101 D1

Oxgangs Row EH13 101 F3
Oxgangs St. EH13 101 F3
Oxgangs Ter. EH13 101 E3
Oxgangs Vw. EH13 101 F3

P
Paddockholm, The EH12 79 F5
Paisley Av. EH8 85 E3
Paisley Cres. EH8 85 D3
Paisley Dr. EH8 85 E4
Paisley Gdns. EH8 85 D3
Paisley Gro. EH8 85 E4
Paisley Ter. EH8 85 D3
Palmerston Pl. EH12 82 A3
Palmerston Pl. La. EH12 82 B4
Palmerston Pl.
Palmerston Rd. EH9 93 E1
Panmure Pl. EH3 83 D5
Pape's Cotts. EH12 81 E4
Park Av. EH15 86 B4
Park Cres. EH16 104 B2
Park Gdns. EH16 104 B1
Park Gro. EH16 104 B2
Park Pl. EH6 72 C2
Park Rd. EH6 72 C2
Park Ter. (Newcr.), Muss. EH21 97 F2
Park Vw. (Newcr.), Muss. EH21 97 E2
Parker Av. EH7 85 F2
Parker Rd. EH7 85 F2
Parker Ter. EH7 86 A2
Parkgrove Av. EH4 79 D1
Parkgrove Bk. EH4 79 D1
Parkgrove Cres. EH4 79 D1
Parkgrove Dr. EH4 78 C1
Parkgrove Gdns. EH4 79 D1
Parkgrove Grn. EH4 79 D1
Parkgrove Ln. EH4 79 D1
Parkgrove Neuk EH4 79 D1
Parkgrove Path EH4 79 E1
Parkgrove Ter.
Parkgrove Pl. EH4 79 D1
Parkgrove Rd. EH4 79 D1
Parkgrove Row EH4 79 D1
Parkgrove St. EH4 79 E1
Parkgrove Ter. EH4 79 D1
Parkgrove Vw. EH4 79 D1
Parkhead Av. EH11 89 F4
Parkhead Cres. EH11 89 F4
Parkhead Dr. EH11 89 F4
Parkhead Gdns. EH11 89 F4
Parkhead Gro. EH11 89 F4
Parkhead Ln. EH11 90 A4
Parkhead Pl. EH11 89 F4
Parkhead St. EH11 89 F4
Parkhead Ter. EH11 90 A4
Parkhead Vw. EH11 89 F4
Parkside Pl. EH8 84 A5
Parkside Ter. EH16 84 A5
Parkvale Pl. EH6 74 C4
Parliament Pl. EH6 73 F3
Parliament St.
Parliament Sq. EH1 83 E3
Parliament Sq. EH6 73 D1
Newhaven Pl.
Parliament St. EH6 73 F3
Parrotshot EH15 96 C1
Parsons Grn. Ter. EH8 85 D2
Patie's Rd. EH14 100 C1
Patrick Geddes Steps EH1 83 D4
Patriothall EH3 82 C1
Hamilton Pl.

Pattison St. EH6 74 B3
Peacock Ct. EH6 73 D1
Newhaven Pl.
Peacocktail Clo. EH15 96 C2
Pearce Av. EH12 79 D4
Pearce Gro. EH12 79 D4
Pearce Rd. EH12 79 D4
Peatville Gdns. EH14 90 B5
Peatville Ter. EH14 90 B5
Peel Ter. EH9 94 A2
Peffer Bk. EH16 95 E2
Peffer Pl. EH16 95 E2
Peffer St. EH16 95 E2
Peffermill Ct. EH16 95 D2
Peffermill Rd. EH16 94 C3
Peggy's Mill Rd. EH4 68 A4
Pembroke Pl. EH12 81 F4
Pennywell Cotts. EH4 70 B2
Pennywell Ct. EH4 70 B3
Pennywell Gdns. EH4 70 A3
Pennywell Gro. EH4 70 B3
Pennywell Medway EH4 70 B3
Pennywell Pl. EH4 70 B3
Pennywell Rd. EH4 70 B3
Pennywell Vills. EH4 70 B2
Pentland Av. EH13 100 A3
Pentland Cres. EH10 102 A2
Pentland Dr. EH10 101 F3
Pentland Gdns. EH10 102 A2
Pentland Gro. EH10 102 A2
Pentland Rd. EH13 100 A2
Pentland Ter. EH10 102 A1
Pentland Vw. EH10 102 A3
Pentland Vills., Jun.Grn. EH14 98 C4
Juniper Av.
Perdrixknowe EH14 91 E3
Persevere Ct. EH6 73 F2
Perth St. EH3 82 C1
Peveril Ter. EH16 104 B1
Picardy Pl. EH1 83 E2
Pier Pl. EH6 72 C1
Piersfield Gro. EH8 85 E2
Piersfield Pl. EH8 85 E2
Piersfield Ter. EH8 85 E2
Piershill La. EH8 85 D2
Piershill Pl. EH8 85 D2
Piershill Sq. E. EH8 85 E2
Piershill Sq. W. EH8 85 D2
Piershill Ter. EH8 85 E2
Pillars, The EH17 105 D2
Pilrig Cotts. EH6 73 F5
Pilrig Gdns. EH6 73 E5
Pilrig Glebe EH6 73 F5
Pilrig Ho. Clo. EH6 73 E4
Pilrig Pl. EH6 73 F5
Pilrig St. EH6 73 E4
Pilton Av. EH5 71 E3
Pilton Cres. EH5 71 F3
Pilton Dr. EH5 71 E3
Pilton Dr. N. EH5 71 E2
Pilton Gdns. EH5 71 E3
Pilton Ln. EH5 71 E3
Pilton Pk. EH5 71 E3
Pilton Pl. EH5 71 E3
Pinkhill EH12 80 A5
Pipe La. EH15 86 B2
Pipe St. EH15 86 B2
Pirniefield Bk. EH6 75 D4
Pirniefield Gdns. EH6 75 D4
Pirniefield Gro. EH6 75 D4
Pirniefield Pl. EH6 75 D4
Pirniefield Ter. EH6 75 D4
Pirrie St. EH6 73 F4

Pitlochry Pl. EH7 84 B1
Pitsligo Rd. EH10 92 C2
Pitt St. EH6 73 E3
Pittencrieff Ct. EH6 72 C3
  Craighall Ter.
Pittville St. EH15 86 C3
Pittville St. La. EH15 86 C3
Playfair Steps EH2 83 D3
  The Mound
Pleasance EH8 83 F4
Plewlands Av. EH10 92 A4
Plewlands Gdns. 92 A4
  EH10
Plewlands Ter. EH10 92 A4
Pleydell Pl. EH16 104 B1
Polwarth Cres. EH11 92 B1
Polwarth Gdns. 92 A1
  EH11
Polwarth Gro. EH11 92 A2
Polwarth Pk. EH11 92 A1
Polwarth Pl. EH11 92 A1
Polwarth Ter. EH11 92 A2
Ponton St. EH3 82 C5
Poplar La. EH6 74 B3
Port Hamilton EH3 82 C4
Porterfield Rd. EH4 71 E5
Portgower Pl. EH4 82 B1
Portland Pl. EH6 73 E2
  North Junct. St.
Portland St. EH6 73 E2
Portland Ter. EH6 73 E2
  North Junct. St.
Portobello High St. 86 B2
  EH15
Portobello Rd. EH8 85 E2
Portsburgh Sq. EH1 83 D4
  West Port
Potterrow EH8 83 E4
Pottery, The EH15 86 B2
  Pipe La.
Prestonfield Av. 94 B2
  EH16
Prestonfield Bk. 94 B2
  EH16
Prestonfield Cres. 94 B3
  EH16
Prestonfield Gdns. 94 B2
  EH16
Prestonfield Rd. 94 B2
  EH16
Prestonfield Ter. 94 B2
  EH16
Priestfield Av. EH16 94 C2
Priestfield Cres. 94 C2
  EH16
Priestfield Gdns. 94 C2
  EH16
Priestfield Gro. 94 B1
  EH16
Priestfield Rd. EH16 94 B1
Priestfield Rd. N. 94 B1
  EH16
Primrose Bk. Rd. 72 B2
  EH5
Primrose St. EH6 74 B4
Primrose Ter. EH11 91 F1
Prince Regent St. 73 E2
  EH6
Princes St. EH1 82 C3
Princes St. EH2 82 C3
Promenade EH15 86 A1
Promenade Ter. 86 B2
  EH15
Prospect Bk. Cres. 74 C4
  EH6
Prospect Bk. Gdns. 74 C5
  EH6
Prospect Bk. Gro. 75 D4
  EH6

Prospect Bk. Pl. EH6 75 D4
Prospect Bk. Rd. 74 C4
  EH6
Prospect Bk. Ter. 75 D4
  EH6

Q
Quality St. EH4 69 F5
Quality St. La. EH4 69 F5
Quarry Clo. EH8 83 F4
Quarry Cotts. EH15 96 C2
Quarrybank EH14 98 C1
Quarrybank Clo. 98 C1
  EH14
Quarrybank Ct. 98 C1
  EH14
Quarrybank End 98 C1
  EH14
Quarryview EH14 98 C1
Quayside St. EH6 73 F3
Queen Charlotte La. 74 B3
  EH6
  Queen Charlotte St.
Queen Charlotte St. 74 B3
  EH6
Queen Margaret Clo. 102 C4
  EH10
Queen St. EH2 82 C2
Queen St. Gdns. E. 83 D2
  EH3
Queen St. Gdns. W. 83 D2
  EH3
Queen's Av. EH4 80 C1
Queen's Av. S. EH4 81 D1
Queen's Bay Cres. 87 E4
  EH15
Queen's Cres. EH9 94 A2
Queen's Dr. EH8 84 A5
Queen's Gdns. EH4 81 D1
Queen's Pk. Av. EH8 84 C2
Queen's Pk. Ct. EH8 85 D3
Queen's Rd. EH4 81 D1
Queen's Wk. EH16 95 F2
Queensferry Rd. 81 D1
  EH4
Queensferry Rd. 68 A5
  (Cram.) EH4
Queensferry St. EH2 82 B3
Queensferry St. La. 82 B3
  EH2
Queensferry Ter. EH4 81 F2
Quilts, The EH6 73 F3
Quilts Wynd EH6 73 E3

R
Raeburn Ms. EH4 82 B1
Raeburn Pl. EH4 82 B1
Raeburn St. EH4 82 B1
Rae's Ct. EH16 104 A4
Ramsay Gdn. EH1 83 D3
Ramsay La. EH1 83 D3
Ramsay Pl. EH15 86 C2
Randolph Cliff EH3 82 B3
Randolph Cres. EH3 82 B3
Randolph La. EH3 82 C3
Randolph Pl. EH3 82 C3
Rankeillor St. EH8 83 F5
Rankin Av. EH9 94 A4
Rankin Dr. EH9 93 F4
Rankin Rd. EH9 94 A3
Rannoch Gro. EH4 79 E2
Rannoch Pl. EH4 79 E2
Rannoch Rd. EH4 79 E2
Rannoch Ter. EH4 79 E2
Ransome Gdns. EH4 79 E2
Ratcliffe Ter. EH9 93 F2
Rathbone Pl. EH15 86 C2

Ravelston Ct. EH12 81 E3
Ravelston Dykes 81 E3
  EH4
Ravelston Dykes 81 D3
  EH12
Ravelston Dykes 80 B3
  La. EH4
Ravelston Dykes 80 C2
  Rd. EH4
Ravelston Gdn. EH4 81 D3
Ravelston Hts. EH4 80 C2
Ravelston Ho. Gro. 81 D2
  EH4
Ravelston Ho. Ln. 81 D2
  EH4
Ravelston Ho. Pk. 81 D2
  EH4
Ravelston Ho. Rd. 81 D2
  EH4
Ravelston Pk. EH4 81 F3
Ravelston Pl. EH4 82 A3
  Belford Rd.
Ravelston Ri. EH4 81 D3
Ravelston Ter. EH4 82 A2
Ravenscroft Gdns. 105 E4
  EH17
Ravenscroft Pl. 105 E4
  EH17
Ravenscroft St. 105 E4
  EH17
Ravenswood Av. 94 C5
  EH16
Redbraes Gro. EH7 73 D4
Redbraes Pl. EH7 73 D4
Redford EH13 100 C3
Redford Av. EH13 100 C3
Redford Bk. EH13 100 C3
Redford Cres. EH13 100 C3
Redford Dr. EH13 100 B3
Redford Gdns. EH13 100 C3
Redford Gro. EH13 101 D2
Redford Ln. EH13 100 C3
Redford Neuk EH13 101 D3
Redford Pl. EH13 101 D2
Redford Rd. EH13 100 C3
Redford Ter. EH13 100 C3
Redford Wk. EH13 100 C3
Redgauntlet Ter. 95 D5
  EH16
Redhall Av. EH14 90 B4
Redhall Bk. Rd. 90 C5
  EH14
Redhall Cres. EH14 90 B4
Redhall Dr. EH14 90 B4
Redhall Gdns. EH14 90 B4
Redhall Gro. EH14 90 B4
Redhall Ho. Dr. 90 C5
  EH14
Redhall Pl. EH14 90 B4
Redhall Rd. EH14 90 B4
Redhall Vw. EH14 90 C5
Redheughs Av. 88 B2
  EH12
Redheughs Rigg 88 B1
  EH12
Reekie's Ct. EH8 83 F4
  Nicolson St.
Regent Bri. EH1 83 E2
  Waterloo Pl.
Regent Pl. EH7 84 B2
Regent Rd. EH1 83 F3
Regent Rd. EH7 83 F3
Regent St. EH15 86 C3
Regent St. La. EH15 86 C3
Regent Ter. EH7 84 A2
Regent Ter. Ms. EH7 84 A2
Regis Ct. EH4 68 B4
Register Pl. EH2 83 E2
Reid Ter. EH3 82 B1

Reid's Clo. EH8   84 A3
Reid's Ct. EH8   84 A3
  Canongate
Relugas Gdns. EH9   93 F3
Relugas Pl. EH9   93 F3
Relugas Rd. EH9   93 F3
Rennie's Isle EH6   74 B2
Restalrig Av. EH7   85 D2
Restalrig Circ. EH7   75 D5
Restalrig Cres. EH7   75 D5
Restalrig Dr. EH7   85 D1
Restalrig Gdns. EH7   85 D1
Restalrig Pk. EH7   74 C5
Restalrig Rd. EH6   74 C4
Restalrig Rd. EH7   74 C4
Restalrig Rd. S. EH7   85 D2
Restalrig Sq. EH7   75 D5
Restalrig Ter. EH6   74 B4
Riccarton Cres.,   98 A4
  Currie EH14
Riccarton Gro.,   98 A4
  Currie EH14
Riccarton Mains Rd.,   98 A3
  Currie EH14
Richmond La. EH8   83 F4
Richmond Pl. EH8   83 F4
Richmond Ter. EH11   82 B4
Riding Pk. EH4   68 B4
Riego St. EH3   82 C4
Rillbank Cres. EH9   93 E1
Rillbank Ter. EH9   93 E1
Ringwood Pl. EH16   104 B1
Rintoul Pl. EH3   82 C1
Riselaw Cres. EH10   102 A2
Riselaw Pl. EH10   102 A1
Riselaw Rd. EH10   102 A1
Riselaw Ter. EH10   102 A1
Ritchie Pl. EH11   92 A1
Riversdale Cres.   81 D5
  EH12
Riversdale Gro.   81 D4
  EH12
Riversdale Rd. EH12   81 D4
Riverside EH4   68 B1
Robb's Ln. EH14   91 D2
Robb's Ln. Gro.   91 D2
  EH14
Robert Burns Dr.   94 B5
  EH16
Robertson Av. EH11   91 E1
Robertson's Clo.   83 F4
  EH1
Robertson's Ct. EH8   84 A3
  Calton Rd.
Rocheid Pk. EH4   71 F4
Rocheid Path EH3   72 B5
Rochester Ter. EH10   92 B2
Rodney Pl. EH7   83 D1
Rodney St. EH7   83 D1
Romero Pl. EH16   94 A1
Ronaldson's Wf. EH6   73 F3
  Sandport Pl.
Rose Pk. EH5   72 B3
Rose St. EH2   82 C3
Rose St. N. La. EH2   82 C3
Rose St. S. La. EH2   82 C3
Rosebank Cotts.   82 B4
  EH3
Rosebank Gdns. EH5   72 A3
Rosebank Gro. EH5   72 A3
Rosebank Rd. EH5   72 A3
Rosebery Cres.   82 A4
  EH12
Rosebery Cres. La.   82 A4
  EH12
Roseburn Av. EH12   81 E4
Roseburn Cliff EH12   81 E4
Roseburn Cres.   81 E4
  EH12

Roseburn Dr. EH12   81 E4
Roseburn Gdns.   81 E4
  EH12
Roseburn Maltings   81 F4
  EH12
Roseburn Pl. EH12   81 E4
Roseburn St. EH12   81 E5
Roseburn Ter. EH12   81 E4
Rosefield Av. EH15   86 B3
Rosefield Av. La.   86 B3
  EH15
Rosefield La. EH15   86 B3
Rosefield Pl. EH15   86 B3
Rosefield St. EH15   86 B3
Rosemount Bldgs.   82 B4
  EH3
Roseneath Pl. EH9   93 E1
Roseneath St. EH9   93 E1
Roseneath Ter. EH9   93 E1
Rosevale Pl. EH6   74 C4
Rosevale Ter. EH6   74 C4
Roseville Gdns. EH5   72 C2
Ross Gdns. EH9   93 F3
Ross Pl. EH9   94 A3
Ross Rd. EH16   94 B4
Rossie Pl. EH7   84 B1
Rosslyn Cres. EH6   73 E5
Rosslyn Ter. EH6   73 E5
Rothesay Ms. EH3   82 A3
Rothesay Pl. EH3   82 B3
Rothesay Ter. EH3   82 B3
Roull Gro. EH12   89 E1
Roull Pl. EH12   89 F1
Roull Rd. EH12   89 E1
Rowallan Ct. EH12   78 B4
  Craigievar Wynd
Roxburgh Pl. EH8   83 F4
Roxburgh St. EH8   83 F4
Roxburgh Ter. EH8   83 F4
  Drummond St.
Royal Circ. EH3   82 C2
Royal Cres. EH3   83 D1
Royal Pk. Pl. EH8   84 C2
Royal Pk. Ter. EH8   84 C2
Royal Ter. EH7   83 F2
Royal Ter. Gdns. EH7   83 F2
Royal Ter. Ms. EH7   84 A2
Royston Mains Av.   71 D2
  EH5
Royston Mains Clo.   71 E2
  EH5
Royston Mains Cres.   71 D2
  EH5
Royston Mains Gdns.   71 E2
  EH5
Royston Mains Grn.   71 E2
  EH5
Royston Mains Pl.   71 D2
  EH5
Royston Mains Rd.   71 E2
  EH5
Royston Mains St.   71 D2
  EH5
Royston Ter. EH3   72 B4
Russell Gdns. EH12   81 F4
Russell Pl. EH5   72 B2
Russell Rd. EH11   81 F4
Russell Rd. EH12   81 F4
Rustic Cotts. EH14   91 E4
  Colinton Rd.
Rutherford Dr. EH16   94 C5
Rutland Ct. EH3   82 C4
Rutland Ct. La. EH3   82 C4
Rutland Pl. EH1   82 C3
  West End
Rutland Sq. EH1   82 C4
Rutland St. EH1   82 C3
Ryehill Av. EH6   74 C4
Ryehill Gdns. EH6   74 C4

Ryehill Gro. EH6   74 C5
Ryehill Pl. EH6   74 C4
Ryehill Ter. EH6   74 C4

S

Saddletree Ln. EH16   95 D4
St. Alban's Rd. EH9   93 E3
St. Andrew Pl. EH6   74 B4
St. Andrew Sq. EH1   83 E2
St. Andrew Sq. EH2   83 E2
St. Anthony Cn. EH6   73 F3
  St. Anthony St.
St. Anthony La. EH6   73 F3
  St. Anthony St.
St. Anthony Pl. EH6   73 F3
St. Anthony St. EH6   73 F3
St. Bernard's Cres.   82 B2
  EH4
St. Bernard's Pl. EH3   82 C2
  Saunders St.
St. Bernard's Row   82 C1
  EH4
St. Catherine's Gdns.   80 B5
  EH12
St. Catherine's Pl.   93 F1
  EH9
St. Clair Av. EH6   74 B5
St. Clair Pl. EH6   74 B5
St. Clair Rd. EH6   74 B5
St. Clair St. EH6   74 B5
St. Clair Ter. EH10   92 A4
St. Colme St. EH3   82 C3
St. David's Pl. EH3   82 B4
  Morrison St.
St. David's Ter. EH3   82 B4
  Morrison St.
St. Fillan's Ter. EH10   92 C4
St. Giles' St. EH1   83 E3
St. James Cen. EH1   83 E2
St. James Pl. EH1   83 E2
  Elder St. E.
St. James Sq. EH1   83 E2
  Leith St.
St. John St. EH8   83 F3
St. John's Av. EH12   79 F5
St. John's Cres.   80 A5
  EH12
St. John's Gdns.   79 F5
  EH12
St. John's Hill EH8   83 F4
St. John's Rd. EH12   79 D5
St. John's Ter. EH12   79 F5
St. Katharine's Brae   104 A3
  EH16
St. Katharine's Cres.   104 A3
  EH16
St. Katharine's Ln.   104 B4
  EH16
St. Leonard's Bk.   84 A5
  EH8
St. Leonard's Crag   84 A5
  EH8
  St. Leonard's La.
St. Leonard's Hill   83 F5
  EH8
St. Leonard's La. EH8   83 F5
St. Leonard's St. EH8   83 F5
St. Margaret's Pl.   93 D2
  EH9
St. Margaret's Rd.   92 C2
  EH9
St. Mark's La. EH15   86 C3
St. Mark's Pl. EH15   86 C3
St. Mary's Pl. EH15   87 D4
St. Mary's Pl. La.   87 D4
  EH15
St. Mary's St. EH1   83 F3
St. Ninian's Dr. EH12   79 E4

St. Ninian's Rd. 79 E4
EH12
St. Ninian's Ter. 92 A4
EH10
St. Patrick Sq. EH8 83 F3
St. Patrick St. EH8 83 F5
St. Peter's Bldgs. EH3 82 B5
Gilmore Pl.
St. Peter's Pl. EH3 82 B5
St. Ronan's Ter. 92 C4
EH10
St. Stephen Pl. EH3 82 C1
St. Stephen St. EH3 82 C1
St. Teresa Pl. EH10 92 A2
St. Thomas Rd. EH9 93 E3
St. Vincent St. EH3 82 C1
Salamander Pl. EH6 74 C3
Salamander St. EH6 74 C3
Salisbury EH9 93 F1
Salisbury Rd. EH16 94 A1
Salmond Pl. EH7 84 B2
Salvesen Cres. EH4 70 A2
Salvesen Gdns. EH4 70 B2
Salvesen Gro. EH4 70 B2
Salvesen Ter. EH4 70 B2
Sandford Gdns. 86 B3
EH15
Sandport EH6 74 B2
Sandport Pl. EH6 73 F2
Sandport St. EH6 73 F2
Sauchiebank EH11 81 F5
Saughton Av. EH11 91 D2
Saughton Cres. 80 C5
EH12
Saughton Gdns. 80 C5
EH12
Saughton Gro. EH12 80 C5
Saughton Ln. EH12 80 C5
Saughton Mains Av. 90 A2
EH11
Saughton Mains Bk. 90 B2
EH11
Saughton Mains 90 A3
Cotts. EH11
Saughton Mains Gdns.
Saughton Mains Dr. 90 A3
EH11
Saughton Mains Gdns. 90 A3
EH11
Saughton Mains Gro. 90 B3
EH11
Saughton Mains Ln. 90 A3
EH11
Saughton Mains Pk. 90 A2
EH11
Saughton Mains Pl. 90 A3
EH11
Saughton Mains St. 90 A2
EH11
Saughton Mains Ter. 90 A2
EH11
Saughton Pk. EH12 80 C5
Saughton Rd. EH11 90 A2
Saughton Rd. N. 79 F5
EH12
Saughtonhall Av. 80 C5
EH12
Saughtonhall Av. W. 80 C5
EH12
Saughtonhall Circ. 81 D5
EH12
Saughtonhall Cres. 80 C5
EH12
Saughtonhall Dr. 80 C5
EH12
Saughtonhall Gdns. 81 D5
EH12
Saughtonhall Gro. 81 D5
EH12

Saughtonhall Pl. 80 C5
EH12
Saughtonhall Ter. 81 D5
EH12
Saunders St. EH3 82 C2
Savile Pl. EH9 94 A3
Savile Ter. EH9 94 A3
Saxe Coburg St. 82 C1
EH3
Saxe-Coburg Pl. 82 C1
EH3
Saxe-Coburg Ter. 82 C1
EH3
Saxe Coburg St.
School Brae EH4 68 B2
Sciennes EH9 93 F1
Sciennes Gdns. EH9 93 F1
Sciennes Hill Pl. EH9 93 F1
Sciennes
Sciennes Ho. Dr. EH9 93 F1
Sciennes
Sciennes Ho. Pl. 93 F1
EH9
Sciennes Pl. EH9 93 F1
Sciennes Rd. EH9 93 E1
Scone Gdns. EH8 85 D2
Scotland St. EH3 83 D1
Seacot EH6 75 D4
Seafield Av. EH6 75 D4
Seafield Pl. EH6 75 D4
Seafield Rd. EH6 75 D4
Seafield Rd. E. EH15 86 A1
Seafield St. EH6 75 E4
Seafield Ter. EH6 75 D4
Seafield Av.
Seafield Way EH15 75 F5
Seaforth Dr. EH4 81 D1
Seaforth Ter. EH4 81 D1
Sealcarr St. EH5 71 E1
Seaport St. EH6 74 B3
Bernard St.
Seaview Cres. EH15 87 E4
Seaview Ter. EH15 87 F4
Semple St. EH3 82 C4
Seton Pl. EH9 93 F1
Shaftesbury Pk. EH11 91 F2
Shandon Cres. EH11 91 F2
Shandon Pl. EH11 91 F2
Shandon Rd. EH11 91 F2
Shandon St. EH11 91 F2
Shandon Ter. EH11 91 F2
Shandwick Pl. EH2 82 B3
Shanter Way EH16 94 B5
Cumnor Cres.
Sharpdale Ln. EH16 94 B4
Shaw's Pl. EH7 73 E5
Shaw's Sq. EH1 83 F1
Gayfield Sq.
Shaw's St. EH7 73 E5
Shaw's Ter. EH7 73 E5
Sheriff Bk. EH6 73 F3
Sheriff Brae EH6 73 F3
Sheriff Pk. EH6 73 F3
Shore EH6 74 B3
Shore Pl. EH6 74 B3
Shrub Mt. EH15 86 B2
Shrub Pl. EH7 73 E5
Shrub Pl. La. EH7 73 E5
Shrub Pl.
Sienna Gdns. EH9 93 F1
Sighthill Av. EH11 89 F4
Sighthill Bk. EH11 89 E4
Sighthill Ct. EH11 89 E4
Sighthill Cres. EH11 89 E5
Sighthill Dr. EH11 89 E5
Sighthill Gdns. EH11 89 E4
Sighthill Grn. EH11 89 E4
Sighthill Gro. EH11 89 F4
Sighthill Ln. EH11 89 E4

Sighthill Neuk EH11 89 E4
Sighthill Pk. EH11 89 E4
Sighthill Pl. EH11 89 E4
Sighthill Ri. EH11 89 E5
Sighthill Rd. EH11 89 E5
Sighthill St. EH11 89 E5
Sighthill Ter. EH11 89 E4
Sighthill Vw. EH11 89 E4
Sighthill Wynd EH11 89 E4
Silverknowes Av. 69 E4
EH4
Silverknowes Bk. 69 F4
EH4
Silverknowes Brae 69 F4
EH4
Silverknowes Ct. 69 F4
EH4
Silverknowes Cres. 69 F3
EH4
Silverknowes Dell 69 F4
EH4
Silverknowes Dr. 69 F4
EH4
Silverknowes 69 F4
Eastway EH4
Silverknowes Gdns. 69 F3
EH4
Silverknowes Grn. 70 A4
EH4
Silverknowes Gro. 69 F3
EH4
Silverknowes Hill 69 F4
EH4
Silverknowes Ln. 69 F4
EH4
Silverknowes 70 A4
Midway EH4
Silverknowes Neuk 70 A5
EH4
Silverknowes 69 F3
Parkway EH4
Silverknowes Pl. 69 F3
EH4
Silverknowes Rd. 69 E2
EH4
Silverknowes Rd. E. 69 F4
EH4
Silverknowes Rd. S. 69 F5
EH4
Silverknowes 70 A4
Southway EH4
Silverknowes Ter. 69 E4
EH4
Silverknowes Vw. 70 A4
EH4
Silvermills EH3 82 C1
Simon Sq. EH8 83 F4
Sinclair Ct. EH11 91 F1
Sinclair Gdns. EH11 91 F1
Sinclair Pl. EH11 91 E1
Sir Harry Lauder Rd. 86 B3
EH15
Slateford Rd. EH11 91 E2
Slateford Rd. EH14 91 D3
Slater's Steps EH8 84 A3
Holyrood Rd.
Sleigh Dr. EH7 84 C1
Sleigh Gdns. EH7 85 D1
Sloan St. EH6 73 F5
Smithfield St. EH11 91 E1
Smith's Pl. EH6 73 F4
Society EH1 83 E4
Chambers St.
Solicitor's Bldgs. EH1 83 E4
Cowgate
Somerset Pl. EH6 74 B4
Sour Howe EH13 101 F4
South Barnton Av. 69 E5
EH4

South Beechwood EH12 80 B5
South Bri. EH1 83 E3
South Bri. EH8 83 E3
South Charlotte St. EH2 82 C3
South Clerk St. EH8 83 F5
South Coll. St. EH8 83 E4
South E. Circ. Pl. EH3 82 C2
South Elixa Pl. EH8 85 E3
South Ettrick Rd. EH10 92 A2
South Fort St. EH6 73 E3
South Gayfield La. EH1 83 F1
Gayfield Sq.
South Gillsland Rd. EH10 92 A3
South Gray St. EH9 94 A2
South Gray's Clo. EH1 83 F3
South Groathill Av. EH4 81 D1
South Gyle Access EH12 89 D2
South Gyle Bdy. EH12 88 C1
South Gyle Cres. EH12 88 C2
South Gyle Cres. La. EH12 88 C2
South Gyle Gdns. EH12 88 C1
South Gyle Ln. EH12 88 C1
South Gyle Mains EH12 88 C1
South Gyle Pk. EH12 88 C1
South Gyle Rd. EH12 88 C1
South Gyle Wynd EH12 89 D2
South Lauder Rd. EH9 93 F2
South Laverockbank Av. EH5 72 C2
South Learmonth Av. EH4 82 A2
South Learmonth Gdns. EH4 82 A2
South Lorne Pl. EH6 73 F5
South Maybury EH12 78 B5
South Meadow Wk. EH9 93 E1
Roseneath Ter.
South Mellis Pk. EH8 85 F3
South Morton St. EH15 87 D4
South Oswald Rd. EH9 93 D3
South Oxford St. EH8 94 A1
South Pk. EH6 73 D2
South Parrotshot EH15 96 B1
South St. Andrew St. EH2 83 E2
South St. David St. EH2 83 E2
South Sloan St. EH6 73 F5
South Steil EH10 91 F5
South Trinity Rd. EH5 72 B3
Southfield Bk. EH15 86 A5
Southfield Fm. Gro. EH15 85 F4
Southfield Gdns. E. EH15 86 A4

Southfield Gdns. W. EH15 86 A4
Southfield Ln. EH15 86 A5
Southfield Pl. EH15 86 B4
Southfield Pl. N. EH15 86 A5
Southfield Sq.
Southfield Pl. S. EH15 86 A5
Southfield Sq.
Southfield Rd. E. EH15 86 A5
Southfield Rd. W. EH15 85 F5
Southfield Sq. EH15 86 A5
Southfield Ter. EH15 86 A5
Southfield Vills. EH15 86 B4
Stanley St.
Southhouse Av. EH17 104 B4
Southhouse Bdy. EH17 104 B5
Southhouse Cres. EH17 104 B5
Southhouse Gdns. EH17 104 B5
Southhouse Gro. EH17 104 B5
Southhouse Ln. EH17 104 B4
Southhouse Medway EH17 104 B4
Southhouse Path EH17 104 B4
Southhouse Rd. EH17 104 B4
Southhouse Sq. EH17 104 B5
Southhouse Ter. EH17 104 C4
Soutra Ct. EH16 104 B3
Spa Pl. EH15 86 B2
Spence St. EH16 94 A1
Spencer Pl. EH5 72 B2
Spey St. EH7 73 E5
Spey St. La. EH7 73 E5
Spey Ter. EH7 73 E5
Spiers Pl. EH6 73 F3
Spinney, The EH17 105 D3
Spittal St. EH3 82 C4
Spittal St. La. EH3 82 C4
Spittal St.
Spittalfield Cres. EH8 83 F5
St. Leonard's St.
Spottiswoode Rd. EH9 93 D1
Spottiswoode St. EH9 93 D1
Spring Gdns. EH8 84 B2
Springfield EH6 73 F4
Springfield Bldgs. EH6 73 F4
Springfield St.
Springfield La. EH6 73 F4
Springfield St. EH6 73 F4
Springvalley Gdns. EH10 92 B3
Springvalley Ter. EH10 92 B3
Springwell Pl. EH11 82 A5
Springwood Pk. EH16 104 B1
Spylaw Av. EH13 99 F2
Spylaw Bk. Rd. EH13 99 F2
Spylaw Ho. EH13 100 A3
Spylaw Pk. EH13 99 F2
Spylaw Rd. EH10 92 A2
Spylaw St. EH13 100 A3

Stable La. EH10 92 B3
Stafford St. EH3 82 B3
Stair Pk. EH12 81 D4
Stanedykehead EH16 103 F3
Stanhope Pl. EH12 81 F4
Stanhope St. EH12 81 F4
Stanley Pl. EH7 84 C2
Stanley Rd. EH6 72 C2
Stanley St. EH15 86 B4
Stanwell St. EH6 73 F4
Stapeley Av. EH7 85 F1
Starbank Rd. EH5 72 C2
Station Brae EH15 86 B3
Station Rd. EH12 79 F5
Stead's Pl. EH6 73 F4
Steel's Pl. EH10 92 C3
Steils, The EH10 101 E1
Stenhouse Av. EH11 90 B2
Stenhouse Av. W. EH11 90 B2
Stenhouse Cotts. EH11 90 B3
Stenhouse Cres. EH11 90 B2
Stenhouse Cross EH11 90 B2
Stenhouse Dr. EH11 90 A2
Stenhouse Gdns. EH11 90 B2
Stenhouse Gdns. N. EH11 90 B2
Stenhouse Gro. EH11 90 B2
Stenhouse Mill Cres. EH11 90 C3
Stenhouse Mill La. EH11 90 C3
Stenhouse Mill Wynd EH11 90 C3
Stenhouse Pl. E. EH11 90 B2
Stenhouse Pl. W. EH11 90 B2
Stenhouse Rd. EH11 90 B3
Stenhouse St. E. EH11 90 B2
Stenhouse St. W. EH11 90 A2
Stenhouse Ter. EH11 90 C2
Stennis Gdns. EH17 104 C2
Stevenlaw's Clo. EH1 83 E3
High St.
Stevenson Av. EH11 91 D1
Stevenson Dr. EH11 90 B2
Stevenson Gro. EH11 91 D1
Stevenson Rd. EH11 91 D1
Stevenson Ter. EH11 91 D1
Stewart Ter. EH11 91 E1
Stewartfield EH6 73 D4
Stirling Rd. EH5 72 B2
Storrie's All. EH6 73 F3
Giles St.
Strachan Gdns. EH4 80 B1
Strachan Rd. EH4 80 B1
Straiton Pl. EH15 86 C2
Strathalmond Pk. EH4 78 A1
Strathalmond Rd. EH4 78 A1
Strathearn Pl. EH9 92 C2
Strathearn Rd. EH9 93 D2
Strathfillan Rd. EH9 93 D2
Stuart Cres. EH12 78 C3
Stuart Grn. EH12 78 C3
Stuart Pk. EH12 78 C3
Stuart Sq. EH12 78 C3
Stuart Wynd EH12 78 C3

Succoth Av. EH12	81	E3
Succoth Ct. EH12	81	E3
Succoth Gdns. EH12	81	E3
Succoth Pk. EH12	81	E3
Succoth Pl. EH12	81	E3
Suffolk Rd. EH16	94	A3
Summer Pl. EH3	72	C5
Summerbank EH3	83	D1
Summerfield Gdns. EH6	74	C4
Summerfield Pl. EH6	74	C4
Summerhall EH9	83	F5
Summerhall Pl. EH9	93	F1
Causewayside		
Summerhall Sq. EH9	93	F1
Summerside Pl. EH6	73	D2
Summerside St. EH6	73	D3
Summertrees Ct. EH16	94	C5
Sunbury Ms. EH4	82	A3
Sunbury Pl. EH4	82	A3
Sunbury St. EH4	82	A3
Sunnybank Pl. EH7	84	B2
Sunnybank Ter. EH7	84	B2
Sunnyside EH7	84	B1
Surgeon Sq. EH1	83	F4
Infirmary St.		
Surrey Pl. EH12	81	F4
Borthwick Pl.		
Surrey Sq. EH12	81	F4
Sutherland St.		
Sutherland St. EH12	81	F4
Swan Spring Av. EH10	102	A2
Swanfield EH6	73	F3
Swanston Av. EH10	102	A4
Swanston Cres. EH10	102	A4
Swanston Dr. EH10	102	B5
Swanston Gdns. EH10	102	A4
Swanston Grn. EH10	102	A4
Swanston Gro. EH10	102	B5
Swanston Ln. EH10	102	A4
Swanston Muir EH10	101	E4
Swanston Pk. EH10	102	A4
Swanston Pl. EH10	102	A4
Swanston Rd. EH10	102	A4
Swanston Row EH10	102	A4
Swanston Ter. EH10	102	B4
Swanston Vw. EH10	102	A4
Swanston Village EH10	102	A5
Swanston Way EH10	102	A4
Sycamore Gdns. EH12	79	F5
Saughton Rd. N.		
Sycamore Ter. EH12	79	F5
Sydney Pk. EH7	85	F1
Sydney Pl. EH7	85	F1
Sydney Ter. EH7	85	F1
Sylvan Pl. EH9	93	E1
T		
Talisman Pl. EH16	94	C4
Tanfield EH3	72	C5
Tanfield La. EH3	72	C5
Tanfield		
Tantallon Pl. EH9	93	F1
Tarvit St. EH3	82	C5
Tay St. EH11	92	A1
Taylor Gdns. EH6	73	F3
Taylor Pl. EH7	84	B2

Telfer Subway EH11	82	A5
Telferton EH7	86	A2
Telford Dr. EH4	71	D5
Telford Gdns. EH4	71	D5
Telford Pl. EH4	71	D5
Telford Rd. EH4	81	D1
Temple Pk. Cres. EH11	92	A1
Templeland Gro. EH12	79	E4
Templeland Rd. EH12	79	D4
Tennant St. EH6	73	F4
Terrars Cft. EH8	84	A5
Teviot Pl. EH1	83	E4
Teviot Pl. EH8	83	E4
Teviotdale Pl. EH3	82	C1
Thirlestane La. EH9	93	D2
Thirlestane Rd. EH9	93	D1
Thistle Ct. EH2	83	D2
Thistle St.		
Thistle Pl. EH11	92	B1
Thistle St. EH2	83	D2
Thistle St. N. E. La. EH2	83	D2
Thistle St. N. W. La. EH2	83	D2
Thistle St. S. E. La. EH2	83	D2
Thistle St. S. W. La. EH2	83	D2
Thomson Cres., Currie EH14	98	B4
Thomson Dr., Currie EH14	98	B4
Thomson Gro., Currie EH14	98	B4
Thomson Rd., Currie EH14	98	B4
Thomson's Ct. EH1	83	D4
Grassmarket		
Thorburn Gro. EH13	100	C3
Thorburn Rd. EH13	100	B3
Thorntree St. EH6	74	B4
Thorntreeside EH6	74	B4
Thornville Ter. EH6	74	B5
Thornybauk EH3	82	B5
Timber Bush EH6	74	B2
Tinto Pl. EH6	73	E4
Tipperlinn Rd. EH10	92	B2
Tolbooth Wynd EH6	73	F3
Torduff Rd. EH13	100	A5
Torphichen Pl. EH3	82	B4
Torphichen St. EH3	82	B4
Torphin Bk. EH13	99	F4
Torphin Rd. EH13	99	F4
Torrance Pk. EH4	79	D2
Toward Ct. EH12	78	B4
Craigievar Wynd		
Tower Pl. EH6	74	B2
Tower St. EH6	74	B2
Tower St. La. EH6	74	B2
Townswomen's Guild Wk. EH1	83	E5
Trafalgar La. EH6	73	E3
Trafalgar St. EH6	73	E3
Traquair Pk. E. EH12	80	A5
Traquair Pk. W. EH12	79	F5
Trench Knowe EH10	102	A4
Tressilian Gdns. EH16	94	C5
Trinity Ct. EH5	72	A3
Trinity Cres. EH5	72	B2
Trinity Gro. EH5	72	B2
Trinity Mains EH5	72	B3
Trinity Rd. EH5	72	B2
Trinity Way EH5	72	B3

Tron Sq. EH1	83	E3
Trotter Haugh EH9	93	E3
Tryst Pk. EH10	101	F4
Turlies EH13	99	F2
Hailes Gdns.		
Turnbull's Entry EH8	83	E4
Potterrow		
Turnhouse Fm. Rd. EH12	77	D2
Turnhouse Rd. EH12	77	F4
Tyler's Acre Av. EH12	89	F1
Tyler's Acre Gdns. EH12	89	F1
Tyler's Acre Rd. EH12	89	F1
Tynecastle Bldgs. EH11	81	F5
McLeod St.		
Tynecastle La. EH11	91	F1
Tynecastle Pl. EH11	91	F1
Gorgie Rd.		
Tynecastle Ter. EH11	91	F1
Gorgie Rd.		
Tytler Gdns. EH8	84	B2
U		
Ulster Cres. EH8	85	D3
Ulster Dr. EH8	85	E3
Ulster Gdns. EH8	85	E4
Ulster Gro. EH8	85	E4
Ulster Ter. EH8	85	E4
Union Ct. EH8	83	F4
Richmond Pl.		
Union Pl. EH1	83	F2
Union St. EH1	83	F1
Upper Bow EH1	83	E3
Upper Coltbridge Ter. EH12	81	E3
Upper Craigour EH17	95	E5
Upper Craigour Way EH17	95	E5
Upper Cramond Ct. EH4	68	B4
Upper Damside EH4	82	A3
Upper Dean Ter. EH4	82	B2
Upper Gilmore Pl. EH3	82	C5
Upper Gilmore Ter. EH3	82	C5
Upper Gray St. EH9	93	F1
Upper Gro. Pl. EH3	82	B4
Upper Hermitage EH6	74	B4
V		
Valleyfield St. EH3	82	C5
Vanburgh Pl. EH6	74	B4
Vandeleur Av. EH7	85	F1
Vandeleur Gro. EH7	85	F2
Vandeleur Pl. EH7	85	F1
Veitch's Sq. EH4	82	C1
Vennel EH1	83	D4
Ventnor Pl. EH9	94	B2
Ventnor Ter. EH9	94	A2
Vernon Cotts. EH15	86	C3
Pittville St. La.		
Vexhim Pk. EH15	96	C1
Victor Pk. Ter. EH12	79	E4
Victoria St. EH1	83	E4
Victoria Ter. EH1	83	E4
Victoria St.		
Viewcraig Gdns. EH8	83	F4
Viewcraig St. EH8	83	F4

Viewfield Rd., Jun.Grn. EH14 99 E2
Viewforth EH10 92 B1
Viewforth EH11 82 B5
Viewforth Gdns. EH10 92 C1
Viewforth Sq. EH10 92 B1
Viewforth Ter. EH10 92 B1
Violet Bk. EH8 84 B2
Spring Gdns.
Violet Ter. EH11 91 F1
Vivian Ter. EH4 69 F5

W

Wakefield Av. EH7 86 A1
Walker St. EH3 82 B3
Walker Ter. EH11 82 B4
Walkers Ct. EH1 89 F5
Walkers Rigg EH14 89 F5
Walkers Wynd EH14 89 F5
Walter Scott Av. EH16 94 C5
Wardie Av. EH5 72 A3
Wardie Cres. EH5 71 F2
Wardie Dell EH5 71 F2
Wardie Gro. EH5 71 F2
Wardie Ho. La. EH5 72 A2
Boswall Rd.
Wardie Pk. EH5 72 A3
Wardie Rd. EH5 72 A3
Wardie Sq. EH5 72 A2
Wardie Steps EH5 72 A2
Wardieburn Dr. EH5 71 F2
Wardieburn Pl. E. EH5 71 F2
Wardieburn Pl. N. EH5 71 F2
Wardieburn Pl. S. EH5 71 F2
Wardieburn Pl. W. EH5 71 E2
Wardieburn Rd. EH5 71 F2
Wardieburn St. E. EH5 71 F2
Wardieburn St. W. EH5 71 E2
Wardieburn Ter. EH5 71 E2
Wardiefield EH5 71 F2
Wardlaw Pl. EH11 91 F1
Wardlaw St. EH11 91 F1
Wardlaw Ter. EH11 91 F1
Warrender Pk. Cres. EH9 92 C1
Warrender Pk. Rd. EH9 91 D3
Warrender Pk. Ter. EH9 91 D3
Warriston Av. EH3 72 C4
Warriston Clo. EH1 83 E3
High St.
Warriston Cres. EH3 72 C5
Warriston Dr. EH3 72 B4
Warriston Gdns. EH3 72 B4
Warriston Gro. EH3 72 B4
Warriston Pl. EH3 72 C5
Warriston Rd. EH3 72 C5
Warriston Rd. EH7 72 C3
Warriston Ter. EH3 72 B4
Washington La. EH11 82 A5
Washington St. EH11 82 A5
Water St. EH6 74 B3
Waterloo Pl. EH1 83 E2
Water's Clo. EH6 74 B3
Shore

Waterside Ct. EH12 81 E4
Coltbridge Av.
Watertoun Rd. EH9 93 F3
Watson Cres. EH11 92 A1
Watson's Bldgs. EH4 69 F5
Main St.
Wauchope Av. EH16 95 F2
Wauchope Cres. EH16 95 F2
Wauchope Ho. EH16 96 A3
Wauchope Pl. EH16 95 F2
Wauchope Rd. EH16 96 A2
Wauchope Sq. EH16 96 A2
Wauchope Ter. EH16 95 F2
Waverley Bri. EH1 83 E3
Waverley Pk. EH8 84 B2
Waverley Pk. Ter. EH8 84 B2
Waverley Pl. EH7 84 B2
Waverley Steps EH2 83 E3
Websters Land EH1 83 D4
West Port
Weir Ct. EH11 89 E4
Well Ct. EH4 82 B3
Wellington Pl. EH6 74 B3
Wellington St. EH7 84 A1
Wemyss Pl. EH3 82 C2
Wemyss Pl. Ms. EH3 82 C2
Werberside Ms. EH4 71 E4
West Adam St. EH8 83 F4
West Annandale St. EH7 73 D5
West App. Rd. EH3 82 B5
West App. Rd. EH11 82 A5
West Bow EH1 83 D4
West Bowling Grn. St. EH6 73 E3
West Brighton Cres. EH15 86 B3
West Bryson Rd. EH11 92 A1
West Caiystane Rd. EH10 102 A3
West Camus Rd. EH10 102 A3
West Carnethy Av. EH13 100 A4
West Castle Rd. EH10 92 B1
West Catherine Pl. EH12 81 F4
West Cherrybank EH6 72 C2
West Coates EH12 81 F4
West Coll. St. EH8 83 E4
West Ct. EH4 81 D2
West Ct. EH16 95 F3
West Craigs Av. EH12 78 A5
West Craigs Cres. EH12 78 A5
West Craigs Ind. Est. EH12 78 A4
West Cromwell St. EH6 73 F2
Cromwell Pl.
West Crosscauseway EH8 83 F5
West End EH2 82 C3
West End Pl. EH11 82 A5
West Ferryfield EH5 71 F4
West Fountain Pl. EH11 82 A5
West Gorgie Parks EH14 91 D3
West Gra. Gdns. EH9 93 E2
Grange Ln.
West Granton Gro. EH4 71 D3

West Granton Rd. EH5 70 C2
West Harbour Rd. EH5 71 E1
West Mains Rd. EH9 93 F4
West Maitland St. EH12 82 B4
West Mayfield EH9 94 A2
West Mill La. EH4 82 B3
Dean Path
West Mill Rd. EH13 99 F3
West Montgomery Pl. EH7 84 A1
West Newington Pl. EH9 93 F1
West Nicolson St. EH8 83 F4
West Norton Pl. EH7 84 A2
West Pk. Pl. EH11 82 A5
West Pier EH5 71 E1
West Pilton Av. EH4 70 C4
West Pilton Bk. EH4 70 B3
West Pilton Cres. EH4 70 B3
West Pilton Crossway EH4 70 C3
West Pilton Dr. EH4 70 C3
West Pilton Gdns. EH4 70 C3
West Pilton Grn. EH4 70 C3
West Pilton Gro. EH4 70 C3
West Pilton Lea EH4 70 C3
West Pilton Ln. EH4 70 C3
West Pilton March EH4 71 D3
West Pilton Pk. EH4 70 C3
West Pilton Pl. EH4 71 D3
West Pilton Ri. EH4 70 C3
West Pilton Rd. EH4 71 D3
West Pilton St. EH4 70 C3
West Pilton Ter. EH4 70 C3
West Pilton Vw. EH4 70 C4
West Port EH1 83 D4
West Port EH3 83 D4
West Powburn EH9 93 F3
West Preston St. EH8 93 F1
West Register St. EH2 83 E2
West Relugas Rd. EH9 93 E3
West Richmond St. EH8 83 F4
West Savile Rd. EH16 94 A3
West Savile Ter. EH9 93 F3
West Scotland St. La. EH3 83 D1
West Shore Rd. EH5 70 B2
West Silvermills La. EH3 82 C1
West Stanhope Pl. EH12 81 F4
Stanhope Pl.
West Telferton EH7 86 A2
West Tollcross EH3 82 C5
West Werberside EH4 71 E4
West Winnelstrae EH5 71 F4
West Wds. EH4 71 E5
Westbank Ln. EH15 86 B2
Westbank Pl. EH15 86 B2
Westbank St. EH15 86 B2
Westburn Av. EH14 98 C1
Westburn Gro. EH14 98 C1

Westburn Middlefield 98 C1
EH14
Westburn Pk. EH14 99 D1
Wester Broom Av. 89 D1
EH12
Wester Broom Dr. 89 D1
EH12
Wester Broom Gdns. 89 D1
EH12
Wester Broom Gro. 89 D1
EH12
Wester Broom Pl. 89 D1
EH12
Wester Broom Ter. 89 D1
EH12
Wester Clo. EH6 73 D1
Newhaven Main St.
Wester Coates Av. 81 F4
EH12
Wester Coates Gdns. 81 F4
EH12
Wester Coates Pl. 81 F3
EH12
Wester Coates Rd. 81 F4
EH12
Wester Coates Ter. 81 F4
EH12
Wester Drylaw Av. 70 B5
EH4
Wester Drylaw Dr. 70 B5
EH4
Wester Drylaw Pk. 70 C5
EH4
Wester Drylaw Pl. 70 B5
EH4
Wester Drylaw Row 81 D1
EH4
Wester Hailes Pk. 99 E1
EH14
Wester Hailes Rd. 89 D5
EH11
Wester Hailes Rd. 99 D1
EH14
Wester Hailes Rd., 99 D1
Jun.Grn. EH14
Wester Hill EH10 101 E1
Wester Steil EH10 91 F5
Western Cor. EH12 80 C4
Saughtonhall Dr.
Western Gdns. EH12 81 D4
Western Pl. EH12 81 D4
Western Ter. EH12 81 D4
Westfield Av. EH11 91 D1
Westfield Ct. EH11 91 D1
Westfield Rd. EH11 91 E1
Westfield St. EH11 91 E1
Westgarth Av. EH13 100 B3
Westhall Gdns. 92 C1
EH10
Westland Cotts. 105 E4
EH17
Ravenscroft Pl.
Westland Hos. EH17 105 E4
Ravenscroft Pl.
Westmost Clo. EH6 72 C1
Newhaven Main St.
Westside Plaza 99 D1
EH14
Wheatfield Pl. EH11 91 E1
Wheatfield Rd. EH11 91 E1
Wheatfield St. EH11 91 F1
Wheatfield Ter. EH11 91 E1
Whins Pl. EH15 86 B2
Figgate St.
White Dales EH10 102 C4
White Horse Clo. 84 A3
EH8
Abbeyhill
White Pk. EH11 91 F1

Whitehall Ct. EH4 80 C1
Whitehill Rd. EH15 97 D2
Whitehill Rd. (Newcr.), 97 E3
Muss. EH21
Whitehill St. (Newcr.), 97 D3
EH22
Whitehill Rd., Dalk. 97 D3
EH21
Whitehill St. (Newcr.), 97 E2
Muss. EH21
Whitehouse Ln. EH9 92 C1
Whitehouse Rd. EH4 68 A4
Whitehouse Ter. 93 D2
EH9
Whitingford EH6 73 D3
Whitson Cres. EH11 90 C1
Whitson Gro. EH11 90 C1
Whitson Pl. E. EH11 90 C1
Whitson Pl. W. EH11 90 C1
Whitson Rd. EH11 90 B1
Whitson Ter. EH11 90 C1
Whitson Wk. EH11 90 B1
Whitson Way EH11 90 B1
Whyte Pl. EH7 84 B2
Wilfrid Ter. EH8 85 D2
William Jameson Pl. 86 B2
EH15
Pipe St.
William Jameson St. 86 B2
EH15
Pipe St.
William St. EH3 82 B3
William St. La. N. E. 82 B3
EH3
William St. La. N. W. 82 B3
EH3
William St. La. S. E. 82 B3
EH3
William St. La. S. W. 82 B3
EH3
Williamfield EH15 86 B3
Rosefield Av.
Williamfield Sq. 86 B3
EH15
Rosefield Av.
Willowbank Row 73 D2
EH6
Willowbrae Av. EH8 85 D3
Willowbrae Gdns. 85 E3
EH8
Willowbrae Rd. EH8 85 E3
Wilson's Ct. EH8 84 A3
Canongate
Wilson's Pk. EH15 86 C2
Wilton Rd. EH16 94 A4
Windmill Clo. EH8 83 E4
Potterrow
Windmill La. EH8 83 E5
Buccleuch Pl.
Windmill Pl. EH8 83 F5
Chapel St.
Windmill St. EH8 83 F5
Chapel St.
Windsor Pl. EH15 86 C3
Windsor St. EH7 83 F1
Windsor St. La. EH7 83 F1
Winton Dr. EH10 102 C5
Winton Gdns. EH10 102 C5
Winton Gro. EH10 102 B4
Winton Ln. EH10 102 C5
Winton Pk. EH10 102 B5
Winton Ter. EH10 102 B5
Wishaw Ter. EH7 84 C2
Wisp, The EH16 96 C2
Wisp Grn. EH15 96 C2
Wolrige Rd. EH16 104 A1
Wolseley Cres. EH8 85 D2
Wolseley Gdns. EH8 85 D2
Wolseley Cres.
Wolseley Pl. EH8 85 D2
Wolseley Cres.

Wolseley Ter. EH8 85 D2
Woodbine Ter. EH6 74 B5
Woodburn Pl. EH10 92 C3
Woodburn Ter. 92 C3
EH10
Woodfield Av. EH13 99 F3
Woodfield Pk. EH13 99 F3
Woodhall Av., 99 D3
Jun.Grn. EH14
Woodhall Bk. EH13 99 F4
Woodhall Dr., 99 D3
Jun.Grn. EH14
Woodhall Gro. EH13 99 F4
Woodhall Millbrae, 99 E3
Jun.Grn. EH14
Woodhall Rd. EH13 99 F3
Woodhall Ter., 99 D3
Jun.Grn. EH14
Woodlands Gro. 85 F5
EH15
Woodside Ter. EH15 87 E4
Woodstock Pl. EH16 94 C5
Woodville Ter. EH6 74 B5
Wright's Hos. EH10 92 C1
Wyvern Pk. EH9 93 E2

Y

Yardheads EH6 73 F3
Yeaman La. EH11 82 A5
Yeaman Pl. EH11 92 A1
Yewlands Cres. 104 B2
EH16
Yewlands Gdns. 104 B2
EH16
Yoole Pl. EH15 86 B2
Pipe St.
York Bldgs. EH2 83 E2
Queen St.
York La. EH1 83 E2
York Pl. EH1 83 E2
York Rd. EH5 72 C2
Young St. EH2 82 C3
Young St. La. N. 82 C3
EH2
Young St. La. S. 82 C3
EH2

Z

Zetland Pl. EH5 72 B2

Edinburgh Directory

TRANSPORT

Air

Edinburgh Airport
Tel: 0131 333 1000. 13km (8 miles) west of the city centre, with good road access and a useful airlink bus service from Waverley Bridge. A first-rate internal service, with shuttle flights to London Heathrow and regular flights to Gatwick and Manchester. International services operate from here with direct flights to Paris, Amsterdam, Brussels and Dublin. An extension in 1999 has improved the terminal facilities. Gift shop, restaurant, buffet and bars. Facilities for the disabled.

Bicycles

There are specially marked cycle lanes in the city and cyclists are allowed to use bus lanes. Cycles are available for hire.
Central Cycle Hire: 13 Lochrin Place, Tollcross. Tel: 0131 228 6333.
Rent a Bike: Blackfriars Street (off Royal Mile). Tel: 0131 556 5560.

Buses

Edinburgh is well served with buses, including evening and night services. Various companies operate routes but the most comprehensive services are from Lothian Regional Transport, 1/4 Shrub Place, Leith Walk. Bus enquiries tel: 0131 555 6363. A timetable may be obtained from the Ticket Centre, 31 Waverley Bridge. General details of routes are displayed on the front of each bus, and bus numbers are displayed at each stop. Tickets are issued by the driver, but exact change is needed for the ticket machines. Or you can buy a day or week pass, which allows you unlimited travel on LRT buses in the period for which it is valid.

Cars

Car Hire

A car can easily be hired by anyone who has held a full
driving licence for at least one year, is between the ages of 25
and 65, and has a clean driving licence or minor offences only.
Expect difficulties, restrictions or extra expense if you fall
outside any of these requirements. Telephone several
companies for prices. Rates will be presented differently by
each company, and comparisons can sometimes be difficult.
Major international companies such as Avis, Europcar and
Hertz have offices in the city and there are many other local
firms. They are all listed in the Yellow Pages telephone
directory, which can be found at main post offices and
libraries.

Driving

Visitors can drive on a valid foreign licence for a maximum
period of 12 months, or on an International Driving
Licence. In Scotland, as in the rest of the UK, you drive on
the left. Road signs are similar to those used in the rest of
Europe. Refer to the Highway Code for further
information. This can be purchased in many bookshops.
Road and weather information for the whole of Scotland is
available through AA Roadwatch and Weatherwatch tel:
0336 401117.

Coaches

St Andrews Square Coach Station

Coaches to all major destinations in England and Scotland,
with National Express and Scottish City Link both
operating from here. Telephone bookings not accepted.
National Express Enquiries tel: 0990 80 80 80.
Scottish City Link Coaches tel: 0990 50 50 50.
Traveline also provides information (see below).
LRT operates daily coach tours.

Taxis

Edinburgh has plenty of taxi ranks, particularly in the
vicinity of Waverley Bridge.
Central Taxis tel: 0131 229 2468.
City Cabs tel: 0131 228 1211.
Radiocabs tel: 0131 225 9000.

Trains

Waverley Station

National Rail Enquiries for train information tel: 0345 484950, or Traveline (see below). The main station, Waverley, nestles beneath the Castle amidst Princes Street gardens and is overlooked by the Scott monument. Get off at Haymarket Station for the west of Edinburgh.

Traveline

2 Cockburn Street. Tel: 0131 225 3858 or Freephone 0800 232323 if calling from within the Edinburgh and Lothians area. Open Mon–Fri 08.30–17.00. Freephone number is available until 20.00. Provides comprehensive public transport information for Edinburgh and the Lothians – train, bus and coach services – including timetables. Traveline also has details of accessible transport for people with disabilities.

USEFUL INFORMATION

Emergency

If you are involved in an emergency and require the services of the Police, Fire Brigade, Ambulance Service or Coastguard, dial 999. The call is free from any telephone. The procedure is: ask for the service you require – when connected give them the number shown on the telephone you are using, the address where help is needed and any other useful information.

Banks

City banks are usually open Mon–Fri 09.00–17.00 and some are also open Sat mornings 09.00–12.00. Closed Sun and public holidays. There are many cash dispensing machines outside major banks.

Bureau de Change

Foreign Exchange company at the Edinburgh and Scotland Information Centre, Waverley Market, 3 Princes Street tel: 0131 557 3953. Open Mon–Sat 08.15–20.00; also Sun 11.00–21.00.

City banks and many travel agents offer exchange facilities. St James Centre, Frederick Street, and South Gyle Post Offices have Bureau de Change. For opening hours, see Post Offices.

Many of the large hotels also offer exchange facilities, but the exchange rate may not be so good.

Chemist

Boots
46 Shandwick Place. Tel: 0131 225 6757. Open Mon–Fri 08.00–21.00, Sat 08.00–19.00, Sun 11.00–17.00.

Consulates

Australia: 37 George Street. Tel: 0131 624 3333. (AUS)
Austria: 49 Craig Crook Road. Tel: 0131 332 3344. (A)
Canada: 30 Lothian Road. Tel: 0131 220 4333. (CDN)
China: 43 Station Road. Tel: 0131 316 4789. (RC)
Denmark: 4 Royal Terrace. Tel: 0131 556 4263. (DK)
Finland: 22 Hanover Street. Tel: 0131 225 1295. (FIN)
France: 11 Randolph Crescent. Tel: 0131 225 7954. (F)
Germany: 16 Eglinton Crescent. Tel: 0131 337 2323. (D)
Iceland: 24 Jane Street. Tel: 0131 555 3532. (IS)
Ireland: 16 Randolph Crescent. Tel: 0131 226 7711. (IRL)
Italy: 32 Melville Street. Tel: 0131 226 3631. (I)
Japan: 2 Melville Crescent. Tel: 0131 225 4777. (J)
Monaco: 39 Castle Street. Tel: 0131 225 1200. (MC)
Netherlands: 53 George Street. Tel: 0131 220 3226. (NL)
Norway: 86 George Street. Tel: 0131 226 5701. (N)
Philippines: 22 Hill Street. Tel: 0131 225 1136. (RP)
Poland: 2 Kinnear Road. Tel: 0131 552 0301. (PL)
Portugal: 25 Bernard Street. Tel: 0131 555 2080. (P)
Russia: 58 Melville Street. Tel: 0131 225 7098. (RUS)
Spain: 63 North Castle Street. Tel: 0131 220 1843. (E)
Sweden: 22 Hanover Street. Tel: 0131 220 6050. (S)
Switzerland: 66 Hanover Place. Tel: 0131 226 5660. (CH)
USA: 3 Regent Terrace. Tel: 0131 556 8315. (USA)

Dental Treatment

A full list of dental surgeons will be found in the Yellow Pages telephone directory.

For emergency dental treatment contact:

Edinburgh Dental Institute, Level 3 Lauriston Buildings,
1 Lauriston Place. Tel: 0131 536 4900. Open Mon–Fri
09.00–15.00, but may close early if not busy.

Disabled Information

The Scottish Tourist Board produces a booklet, Practical
Information for Visitors with Disabilities, which covers
travel, accommodation and relevant organisations. Useful
advice and information can also be obtained from:

Holiday Care Service
2nd Floor
Imperial Buildings
Victoria Road, Horely
Surrey
RH6 7PZ

Telephone: 01293 774535

Artlink is an escort and transport service enabling anyone
with a disability to visit arts events and venues in
Edinburgh. The service is popular, so register in advance.
Tel: 0131 229 3555.

Doctors

Visitors to the UK can usually arrange free treatment at a
local Health Centre or General Practitioner (GP) surgery
nearest to their temporary address. Lists of these can be
obtained from police stations or the telephone directory, and
hotels usually have this information. Prescriptions for
medicines should be taken to a dispensing chemist/pharmacy
to be prepared. A standard charge is payable.

Anyone staying longer than three months can register with
the National Health Service which will generally, though
not always, give entitlement to free treatment.

Enquiries to Lothian Health Board, Primary Care
Department, Stevenson House, Gorgie Road. Tel: 0131 536
9000.

Drinking

Alcoholic drinks are sold for consumption in bars, pubs, clubs, licensed restaurants and hotels. Licensing hours vary but most places serve throughout the day until 23.00, with many places having extended hours at weekends, public holidays, and during Festivals.

Hospital Accident and Emergency Departments

In case of a serious accident or sudden life-threatening illness, dial 999 and ask for an ambulance. In other cases of injury or acute illness, make your own way to the nearest hospital Accident and Emergency (A&E) Department. All are open 24 hours. The A&E Hospital for the City of Edinburgh is:

Royal Infirmary of Edinburgh
1 Lauriston Place. Tel: 0131 536 1000.

Libraries

Edinburgh Central Library

George IV Bridge. Tel: 0131 225 5584. Open Mon–Thur 10.00–20.00, Fri 10.00–17.00, Sun 09.00–13.00. Children's library open Mon & Wed 13.00–20.00, Tue, Thu, Fri 10.00–17.00, Sat 09.00–13.00.

National Library of Scotland

George IV Bridge. Tel: 0131 225 4531. Research library only. Exhibition Hall open Mon–Sat 10.00–17.00, Sun 14.00–17.00.

Lost Property

Enquire at the nearest Police Station or:

Police Lost Property Office, Fettes Avenue. Tel: 0131 311 3141. Open Mon–Fri 08.00–17.00

Bus Lost Property Office, 1/4 Shrub Place, Leith Walk. Tel: 0131 554 4494. Open Mon–Fri 10.00–13.30.

Waverley Station. Tel: 0131 550 2333. Open Mon–Fri 08.00–18.00.

Money

Visitors may bring in as much currency and travellers' cheques as they wish. All Scottish and English notes are interchangeable.

Police

Lothians and Borders Police. Tel: 0131 311 3131.

Post Offices

These are usually open Mon–Fri 09.00–17.30, Sat 09.00–12.30, closed Sun. Smaller post offices will close for lunch 13.00–14.00, and may be closed for one mid-week afternoon.

Edinburgh city centre post offices:

St James Centre PO, 8/10 St James Centre, tel: 0131 556 0478. Open Mon 09.00–17.30, Tues–Fri 08.30–17.30, Sat 08.30–18.00.

Hope Street PO, 7 Hope Street, tel: 0131 226 6823. Open Mon–Fri 09.00–17.30, Sat 09.00–12.30.

Frederick Street PO, 40 Frederick Street, tel: 0131 226 6937. Open Mon–Fri 09.00–17.30, closed weekends.

South Gyle PO, 47 South Gyle Avenue, tel: 0131 317 1191. Open Mon–Fri 08.00–22.00, Sat 08.00–20.00, Sun 09.00–19.00.

Post Office Counters Helpline tel: 0345 223344.

Public Holidays

These do not coincide with public holidays in the rest of the UK, and can vary from city to city in Scotland.

Telephones

Full operating instructions are given in each telephone directory. Virtually all calls are dialled direct, including those overseas. However, your usual point of contact, should you need to enquire, is the operator – dial 100. For directory enquiries dial 192. The minimum coin needed for payphones is 10p. For calls within the Edinburgh area omit 0131 at the beginning of a number. Cards for phones are obtainable at newsagents and post offices. Calls are cheaper Mon–Fri 18.00–06.00, and cheapest from midnight Friday to midnight Sunday.

ENTERTAINMENT

Cinemas

ABC 8 Screen Multiplex
Westside Plaza, 120 Wester Hailes Road. Tel: 0131 453 1569. Twenty-four hour booking on 0541 453 3332 if dialling from Edinburgh. Popular new releases.

ABC
120 Lothian Road. Tel: 0131 229 3030 (recorded information) or 0131 228 1638 (to book tickets Mon–Sat 12.00–19.00, Sun 13.00–19.00). Three screens showing popular new releases. Bar.

Cameo Cinema
38 Home Street, Tollcross. Tel: 0131 228 4141. Three screens showing new releases and cult movies, screens 1 and 2 with disabled access. Late shows Thu, Fri and Sat. Bar.

Dominion Cinema
18 Newbattle Terrace, Morningside. Tel: 0131 447 4771. Popular new releases on four screens. Restaurant and bar.

Filmhouse
88 Lothian Road. Tel: 0131 228 2688. Box office open daily 12.00–21.00. Independent cinema with a constantly changing array of interesting British, American and Continental films. Wheelchair access. Café bar.

Odeon Cinema
7 Clerk Street. Tel: 0870 505 0007 or 0131 667 0971. Box office open daily 12.00–21.00. Five screens showing popular new releases, screens 2 and 3 with disabled access. Bar.

UCI Kinnaird Park
UCI 12 Cinemas, Kinnaird Park, Newcraighall Road. Tel: 0131 669 0777. Popular new releases. Disabled facilities.

Concert Halls

Queen's Hall
87 Clerk Street. Tel: 0131 668 2019. Originally the Hope Park Chapel of Ease, it was converted into a concert hall in 1979. Hosts a lively and varied programme of concerts from chamber music to rock, from jazz to opera. Home of the Scottish Chamber Orchestra.

Reid Concert Hall
Bristo Square (SW corner). Tel: 0131 650 4367. Built in 1858 as the Reid School of Music, and now providing a home for the University Collection of Historic Musical Instruments, which numbers 2000. Free lunchtime recitals during term-time between October and May, and evening concerts of classical and chamber music.

St Cecilia's Hall
Niddry Street, Cowgate. Built in 1763 for the Musical Society of Edinburgh and now owned by the University, which keeps the Russell Collection of Harpsichords and Clavichords here. The beautiful oval concert hall was restored in 1968 and provides an ideal setting for early music and Baroque concerts.

Usher Hall
Lothian Road (at junction with Grindlay Street). Tel: 0131 228 8616. Built in 1914 and paid for by the brewer Andrew Usher, a bust of whom may be seen in the lower crush hall. An imposing domed building of Darney stone, its handsome interior, with high vertiginous galleries, seats 2780. The venue for concerts by the Scottish National Orchestra, the Scottish Chamber Orchestra and other visiting orchestras, musicians and singers, particularly during the Edinburgh International Festival.

Theatres

Assembly Rooms
54 George Street. Tel: 0131 220 4349. The first assembly

rooms to be built in the New Town, designed by John Henderson and opened in 1784. The portico was added by William Burn in 1817. It contains several halls, large and small, which are used extensively during the Fringe Festival.

Edinburgh Festival Theatre

13–29 Nicolson Street. Tel: 0131 529 6000. Recently merged with the King's Theatre; both theatres now run by the Festival City Theatres Trust. At the heart of the Edinburgh International Festival, and the stage for Scottish Opera and the Scottish Ballet, the Festival Theatre also presents a wide programme throughout the year, including productions by international companies. Café bar.

Edinburgh Playhouse

18–22 Greenside Place. Tel: 0131 557 2590. Opened in 1929 as a cinema seating more than 3000. West End musicals, comedy and rock concerts are staged here. Restaurant and bars. Facilities for the disabled.

King's Theatre

2 Leven Street. Tel: 0131 529 6000. A traditionally decorated Edwardian theatre dating from 1906. Drama, dance, ballet, pantomime, opera, musicals and comedy.

Royal Lyceum Theatre

Grindlay Street. Tel: 0131 248 4848. Edinburgh's premier playhouse, built in 1883 and continuously lit by electricity ever since that date. Fine, richly decorated Victorian interior. Resident Royal Lyceum Theatre Company directs classic and contemporary plays, plus the occasional opera. Licensed restaurant and bar.

Traverse Theatre

10 Cambridge Street. Tel: 0131 228 1404. Exciting, original and innovative new works by contemporary Scottish and international playwrights. Modern purpose-built theatre adjacent to the Usher Hall. Licensed restaurant and bar.

Ticket Agencies and Information

For tickets for the Edinburgh Festival, Military Tattoo and other festivals see Edinburgh Festival (page 60).

Ticket Centre
33/34 Market Street. Tel: 0131 225 8616. Bookings for
shows out of Edinburgh in London, Paris and elsewhere.

Ticketline
Tel: 0131 220 4349. For a wide variety of concerts, dances,
and festival events. Based at the Assembly Rooms,
54 St George Street. Open Mon–Sat 10.00–17.00 (open
until 20.00 when there is a performance). General enquiries
tel: 0131 220 4348.

Tourist Information
Edinburgh and Lothians Tourist Board, Rooftop Plaza on
Waverley Shopping Centre, 3 Princes Street, tel: 0131 473
3800. An excellent centre giving all sorts of information
regarding what is on in the city and details of visitor
attractions, with free literature and a bookshop. It also acts
as a ticket and accommodation bureau. Open all year, seven
days a week.
Website: www.edinburgh.org

Bureau de change tel: 0131 557 3953.

Advanced reservations for accommodation, tel: 0131 473
3855 or email centres@elth.org

The local Tourist Information Centres spread throughout
Scotland are invaluable sources of local information –
always call in when you are travelling.

Weather
Edinburgh's annual rainfall is the same as that of southern
England, as is the average July temperature. In common
with most of the eastern side of the UK, there is plenty of
sunshine. However, during the winter, the east wind can
chill you to the bone as it comes from north-eastern Europe
and funnels through Edinburgh's wide streets. Weather
information for the whole of Scotland is available from
Weatherwatch tel: 0336 401117. See also Driving.